THE HEALING POWER
OF YOUR SUBCONSCIOUS
MIND

THE GPS GUIDES TO LIFE

Think and Grow Rich

As a Man Thinketh

The Power of Your Subconscious Mind

The Science of Getting Rich

The Richest Man in Babylon

The Science of Mind

The Master Key System

The Magic of Believing

THE HEALING POWER
OF YOUR SUBCONSCIOUS
MIND

A Powerful Guide to Heal Your Life

JOSEPH MURPHY

ST. MARTIN'S
ESSENTIALS
NEW YORK

Published in the United States by St. Martin's Essentials, an imprint of St. Martin's Publishing Group

INTRODUCTION. Copyright © 2024 by Joel Fotinos. All rights reserved. Printed in the United States of America. For information, address St. Martin's Publishing Group, 120 Broadway, New York, NY 10271.

www.stmartins.com

The Library of Congress Cataloging-in-Publication Data is available upon request.

ISBN 978-1-250-34966-8 (trade paperback)
ISBN 978-1-250-34967-5 (ebook)

Our books may be purchased in bulk for promotional, educational, or business use. Please contact your local bookseller or the Macmillan Corporate and Premium Sales Department at 1-800-221-7945, extension 5442, or by email at MacmillanSpecialMarkets@macmillan.com.

The Power of Your Subconscious Mind was originally published in 1963
Magic of Faith was originally published in 1954
How to Use Your Healing Power was originally published in 1957
The Healing Power of Love was originally published in 1958

First St. Martin's Essentials Edition: 2024

10 9 8 7 6 5 4 3 2 1

This edition seeks to faithfully reproduce the original publications of the authors' works and so has maintained the original spelling and grammar throughout, with only minor alterations for clarity or content.

CONTENTS

INTRODUCTION

Welcome to a book that can potentially transform your life. Before you begin, here is a little information that might be helpful as you read.

Joseph Murphy is most known for his bestselling book *The Power of Your Subconscious Mind*, which has sold millions of copies since its original publication in 1963. It's been translated around the world, and continues to sell tens of thousands of copies every year. And it is so important that we've included portions of it in this volume as well.

THE LIFE OF JOSEPH MURPHY

As I wrote in the introduction to an edition of *The Power of Your Subconscious Mind*, Joseph Murphy himself was a "floor sample" for these principles. He was born in County Cork, Ireland, in 1898, into a largely Catholic family and culture. He left for the United States, became a pharmacist, and opened his own drugstore. He later joined the US Army as a pharmacist, and after his service he decided to study religion and philosophy. His interest also included New Thought principles, especially those from Judge Thomas Troward, a pillar teacher of New Thought philosophy.

By then, Murphy had moved to Los Angeles, California, had become an independent minister, and started a church. His Sunday services became so popular he eventually moved them to the famous Wilshire Ebell Theater, and even then it was standing room only. He also began a weekly radio show, which eventually would reach more than a million listeners each week. Murphy also wrote over thirty books that were translated around the world.

THE HEALING POWER WITHIN YOU

The book you are holding is a collection of two of his most well-known specifically about healing: *The Healing Power of Love* and *How to Use Your Healing Power* as well as the most practical techniques from his magnus opus *The Power of Your Subconscious Mind*. What kind of healing? The body, the mind, the spirit, as well as creating more favorable circumstances in life.

Both of these short volumes use stories and ideas inspired by the Bible and Jesus as touchstones for healing principles that we can use in our lives today. Please note that Murphy is not using the stories in a religious context, but rather in psychological and spiritual ones. He believed that all readers, regardless of their background or religious heritage, can learn from and benefit from the teachings of the Bible and specifically of Jesus. He believed Jesus taught the power of the mind to heal all aspects of our lives.

In *How to Use Your Healing Power*, Murphy writes, "The Bible is a psychological textbook which teaches us how to overcome all problems. It explains how we get into trouble; then teaches us how to get out of trouble. It teaches a science of life."

Later he writes: "The same Healing Presence which Moses, Elihaj, Paul, and Jesus used is available to you now." For Murphy, the Bible, and specifically Jesus's teachings, are guidebooks to living in the here and now, with practices that we can use in our lives to heal whatever ails us. This compendium, *The Healing Power of Your Subconscious Mind*, will further explain Murphy's ideas.

Murphy has the gift of taking biblical ideas and stories and showing the psychological and spiritual lessons we can glean from them today. He demystifies the mystery so that we can grasp the simple-yet-powerful teachings that, as he says, are all there if we only read them scientifically, rather than dogmatically. He shows the keys they hold to unlock the healing power of our mind, and to create the life we desire.

HOW TO READ THIS BOOK

First of all, this is a book of ideas—not a series of prescriptions. Use this book to gain inspiration. However, as with all books dealing with the mind and body, it is best to consult with healing professionals before stopping or starting any healing process you currently practice. This book is not a substitute for medical or psychological care that you are receiving, or need to receive. Please consult your healing professionals before making any changes. This might sound like common sense, but it is important to emphasize that the healing stories of Murphy and others are meant to be *examples* of the principles in the book, rather than specific directions. Your own journey may look different than theirs.

This book is meant to inspire you in your *own* healing journey. Allow the ideas to challenge you, motivate you, and inform you of the power that is deep inside each of us, and can be accessed through our minds and thoughts. In this way, this book and others like it are like mental vitamins, which can strengthen us and bring mental and emotional nourishment, which of course then helps our bodies, our life circumstances, and our relationships. True healing, Murphy writes, often begins with our mind. This book is where you can learn some effective ways to do that.

In this vein, you can read this book either front to back, or by dipping into it based on chapter titles that interest you. I've found that with inspirational books, I tend to get the most out of them if I read them with a highlighter, a pen, and a journal next to me. As I read the text, I highlight words and sentences that jump out at me. I underline those that I want to remember further, and I write all of these in the journal. Later, I reflect on what I've written and then write about how they might relate to my life. In this way, the ideas go deep into my subconscious mind, where they can reappear in my life through thoughts, words, actions, and experiences. That's how I like to read books like this, but I know you'll find the way that works best for you.

Enjoy these two short books written *decades* ago, both of which use the inspiration from a book written *a couple of thousand years* ago—all of which can help you *today*, wherever you are. That is amazing, and *you* are amazing. I wish for you to have a beautiful experience with *The Healing Power of Your Subconscious Mind*.

To these wonderful texts we've added key sections of *The Power of Your Subconscious Mind*. These give you more straightforward instruction in how your mind works, and how to use it to create conditions of health and healing in every area of your life. These are the selections that can aid you the most in your healing journey.

Immerse yourself in this book, study it, and be inspired by it. You, like each of us, are responsible for your own life. Your own happiness, joy, peace, and healing can be accessed *within* you, and *only by* you. Allow this book to complement your life, and bring positive principles to consider using so you can create positivity into every area of your life. Who knows? Maybe just one idea you get from these pages herein might inspire a thought or action, which in turn inspires another thought or action, all of which lead to people and experiences that might change your life. One thought can create incredible change.

—Joel Fotinos

TECHNIQUES FROM

THE POWER
OF YOUR
SUBCONSCIOUS
MIND

(1963)

CONTENTS

THE TREASURE HOUSE WITHIN YOU

Infinite riches are all around you if you will open your mental eyes and behold the treasure house of infinity within you. There as a gold mine within you from which you can extract everything you need to live life gloriously, joyously, and abundantly.

Many are sound asleep because they do not know about this gold mine of infinite intelligence and boundless love within themselves. Whatever you want, you can draw forth. A magnetized piece of steel will lift about twelve times its own weight, and if you demagnetize this same piece of steel, it will not even lift a feather. Similarly, there are two types of men. There is the magnetized man who is full of confidence and faith. He knows that he is born to win and to succeed. Then, there is the type of man who is demagnetized. He is full of fears and doubts. Opportunities come, and he says, "I might fail; I might lose my money; people will laugh at me." This type of man will not get very far in life because, if he is afraid to go forward, he will simply stay where he is. Become a magnetized man and discover the master secret of the ages.

THE MASTER SECRET OF THE AGES

What, in your opinion, is the master secret of the ages? The secret of atomic energy? Thermonuclear energy? The neutron bomb? Interplanetary travel? No—not any of these. Then, what is this master secret? Where can one find it, and how can it be contacted and brought into action? The answer is extraordinarily simple. This secret is the marvelous, miracle-working power found in your own subconscious mind, the last place that most people would seek it.

THE MARVELOUS POWER OF YOUR SUBCONSCIOUS

You can bring into your life more power, more wealth, more health, more happiness, and more joy by learning to contact and release the hidden power of your subconscious mind.

You need not acquire this power; you already possess it. But, you want to learn how to use it; you want to understand it so that you can apply it in all departments of your life.

As you follow the simple techniques and processes set forth in this book, you can gain the necessary knowledge and understanding. You can be inspired by a new light, and you can generate a new force enabling you to realize your hopes and make all your dreams come true. Decide now to make your life grander, greater, richer, and nobler than ever before.

Within your subconscious depths lie infinite wisdom, infinite power, and infinite supply of all that is necessary, which is waiting for development and expression. Begin now to recognize these potentialities of your deeper mind, and they will take form in the world without.

The infinite intelligence within your subconscious mind can reveal to you everything you need to know at every moment of time and point of space provided you are open-minded and receptive. You can receive new thoughts and ideas enabling you to bring forth new inventions, make new discoveries, or write books and plays. Moreover, the infinite intelligence in your subconscious can impart to you wonderful kinds of knowledge of an original nature. It can reveal to you and open the way for perfect expression and true place in your life.

Through the wisdom of your subconscious mind you can attract the ideal companion, as well as the right business associate or partner. It can find the right buyer for your home, and provide you with all the money you need, and the financial freedom to be, to do, and to go as your heart desires.

It is your right to discover this inner world of thought, feeling, and power, of light, love, and beauty. Though invisible, its forces are mighty. Within your subconscious mind you will find the solution for every problem, and the cause for every effect. Because you can draw out the hidden powers, you come into actual possession of the power and wisdom necessary to move forward in abundance, security, joy, and dominion.

I have seen the power of the subconscious lift people up out of crippled states, making them whole, vital, and strong once more, and free to go out into the world to experience happiness, health, and joyous expression. There is a miraculous healing power in your subconscious that can heal the troubled mind and the broken heart. It can open the prison door of the mind and liberate you. It can free you from all kinds of material and physical bondage.

NECESSITY OF A WORKING BASIS

Substantial progress in any field of endeavor is impossible in the absence of a working basis which is universal in its application. You can become skilled in the operation of your subconscious mind. You can practice its powers with a certainty of results in exact proportion to your knowledge of its principles and to your application of them for definite specific purposes and goals you wish to achieve.

Being a former chemist, I would like to point out that if you combine hydrogen and oxygen in the proportions of two atoms of the former to one of the latter, water will be the result. You are very familiar with the fact that one atom of oxygen and one atom of carbon will produce carbon monoxide, a poisonous gas. But, if you add another atom of oxygen, you will get carbon dioxide, a harmless gas, and so on throughout the vast realm of chemical compounds.

You must not think that the principles of chemistry, physics, and mathematics differ from the principles of your subconscious mind. Let us consider a generally accepted principle: "Water seeks its own level." This is a universal principle which is applicable to water everywhere.

Consider another principle: "Matter expands when heated." This is true anywhere, at any time, and under all circumstances. You can heat a piece of steel, and it will expand regardless whether the steel is found in China, England, or India. It is a universal truth that matter expands when heated. It is also a universal truth that whatever you impress on your subconscious mind is expressed on the screen of space as condition, experience, and event.

Your prayer is answered because your subconscious mind is principle, and by principle I mean the way a thing works. For example, the principle of electricity is that it works from a higher to a lower potential. You do not change the principle of electricity when you use it, but by cooperating with nature, you can bring forth marvelous inventions and discoveries which bless humanity in countless ways.

Your subconscious mind is principle and works according to the law of belief. You must know what belief is, why it works, and how it works. Your Bible says in a simple, clear, and beautiful way: *Whosoever shall say unto this mountain, Be thou removed, and be thou cast into the sea; and shall not doubt in his heart, but shall believe that those things which he saith shall come to pass; he shall have whatsoever he saith.* MARK 11:23.

The law of your mind is the law of belief. This means to believe in the way your mind works, to believe in belief itself. The belief of your mind is the thought of your mind—that is simple—just that and nothing else.

All your experiences, events, conditions, and acts are the reactions of your subconscious mind to your thoughts. Remember, it is not the thing believed in, but the belief in your own mind which brings about the result. Cease believing in the false beliefs, opinions, superstitions, and fears of mankind. Begin to believe in the eternal verities and truths of life which never change. Then, you will move onward, upward, and Godward.

Whoever reads this book and applies the principles of the subconscious mind herein set forth, will be able to pray scientifically and effectively for himself and for others. Your prayer is answered according to the universal law of action and reaction. Thought is incipient action. The reaction is the response from your subconscious mind which corresponds with the nature of your thought. Busy your mind with the concepts of harmony, health, peace, and good will, and wonders will happen in your life.

THE DUALITY OF MIND

You have only one mind, but your mind possesses two distinctive characteristics. The line of demarcation between the two is well known to all thinking men and women today. The two functions of your mind are essentially unlike. Each is endowed with separate and distinct attributes and powers. The nomenclature generally used to distinguish the two functions of your mind is as follows: The objective and subjective mind, the conscious and subconscious mind, the waking and sleeping mind, the surface self and the deep self, the voluntary mind and the involuntary mind, the male and the female, and many other terms. You will find the terms "conscious" and "subconscious" used to represent the dual nature of your mind throughout this book.

THE CONSCIOUS AND SUBCONSCIOUS MINDS

An excellent way to get acquainted with the two functions of your mind is to look upon your own mind as a garden. You are a gardener, and you are planting seeds (thoughts) in your subconscious mind all day long, based on your habitual thinking. As you sow in your subconscious mind, so shall you reap in your body and environment.

Begin now to sow thoughts of peace, happiness, right action, good will, and prosperity. Think quietly and with interest on these qualities and accept them fully in your conscious reasoning mind. Continue to plant these wonderful seeds (thoughts) in the garden of your mind, and you will reap a glorious harvest. Your subconscious mind may be likened to the soil which will grow all kinds of seeds, good or bad. *Do men gather grapes of thorns, or figs of thistles?* Every thought is, therefore, a cause, and every condition is an effect. For this reason, it is essential that you take charge of your thoughts so as to bring forth only desirable conditions.

When your mind thinks correctly, when you understand the truth, when the thoughts deposited in your subconscious mind are constructive, harmonious, and peaceful, the magic working power of your subconscious will respond and bring about harmonious conditions, agreeable surroundings, and the best of everything. When you begin to control your thought processes, you can apply the powers of your subconscious to any problem or difficulty. In other words, you will actually be consciously cooperating with the infinite power and omnipotent law which governs all things.

Look around you wherever you live and you will notice that the vast majority of mankind lives in the world without; the more enlightened men are intensely interested in the world within. Remember, it is the world within, namely, your thoughts, feelings, and imagery that makes your world without. It is, therefore, the only creative power, and everything which you find in your world of expression has been created by you in the inner world of your mind consciously or unconsciously.

A knowledge of the interaction of your conscious and subconscious minds will enable you to transform your whole life. In order to change external conditions, you must change the cause. Most men try to change conditions and circumstances by working with conditions and circumstances. To remove discord, confusion, lack, and limitation, you must remove the cause, and the cause is the way you are using your conscious mind. In other words, the way you are thinking and picturing in your mind.

You are living in a fathomless sea of infinite riches. Your subconscious is very sensitive to your thoughts. Your thoughts form the mold or matrix through which the infinite intelligence, wisdom, vital forces, and energies of your subconscious flow. The practical application of the laws of your mind as illustrated in each chapter of this book will cause you to experience abundance for poverty, wisdom for superstition and ignorance, peace for pain, joy for sadness, light for darkness, harmony for discord, faith and confidence for fear, success for failure, and freedom from the law of averages. Certainly, there can be no more wonderful blessing than these from a mental, emotional, and material standpoint.

Most of the great scientists, artists, poets, singers, writers, and inventors have a deep understanding of the workings of the conscious and subconscious minds.

One time Caruso, the great operatic tenor, was struck with stage fright. He said his throat was paralyzed due to spasms caused by intense fear which constricted the muscles of his throat. Perspiration poured copiously down his face. He was ashamed because in a few minutes he had to go out on the stage, yet he was shaking with fear and trepidation. He said, "They will laugh at me. I can't sing." Then he shouted in the presence of those behind the stage, "The Little Me wants to strangle the Big Me within."

He said to the Little Me, "Get out of here, the Big Me wants to sing through me."

By the Big Me, he meant the limitless power and wisdom of his subconscious mind, and he began to shout, "Get out, get out, the Big Me is going to sing!"

His subconscious mind responded, releasing the vital forces within him. When the call came, he walked out on the stage and sang gloriously and majestically, enthralling the audience.

It is obvious to you now that Caruso must have understood the two levels of mind—the conscious or rational, and the subconscious or irrational level. Your subconscious mind is reactive and responds to the nature of your thoughts. When your conscious mind (the Little Me) is full of fear, worry, and anxiety, the negative emotions engendered in your subconscious mind (the Big Me) are released and flood the conscious mind with a sense of panic, foreboding, and despair. When this happens, you can, like Caruso, speak affirmatively and with a deep sense of authority to the irrational emotions generated in your deeper mind as follows: "Be still, be quiet, I am in control, you must obey me, you are subject to my command, you cannot intrude where you do not belong."

It is fascinating and intensely interesting to observe how you can speak authoritatively and with conviction to the irrational movement of your deeper self bringing silence, harmony, and peace to your mind. The subconscious is subject to the conscious mind, and that is why it is called subconscious or subjective.

OUTSTANDING DIFFERENCES AND MODES OF OPERATION

You will perceive the main differences by the following illustrations: The conscious mind is like the navigator or captain at the bridge of a ship. He directs the ship and signals orders to men in the engine room, who in turn control all the boilers, instruments, gauges, etc. The men in the engine room do not know where they are going; they follow orders. They would go on the rocks if the man on the bridge issued faulty or wrong instructions based on his findings with the compass, sextant, or other instruments. The men in the engine room obey him because he is in charge and issues orders which are automatically obeyed. Members of the crew do not talk back to the captain; they simply carry out orders.

The captain is the master of his ship, and his decrees are carried out. Likewise, your conscious mind is the captain and the master of your ship, which represents your body, environment, and all your affairs. Your subconscious mind takes the orders you give it based upon what your conscious mind believes and accepts as true.

When you repeatedly say to people, "I can't afford it," then your subconscious mind takes you at your word and sees to it that you will not be in a position to purchase what you want. As long as you persist in saying, "I can't afford that car, that trip to Europe, that home, that fur coat or ermine wrap," you can rest assured that your subconscious mind will follow your orders, and you will go through life experiencing the lack of all these things.

Last Christmas Eve a beautiful young university student looked at an attractive and rather expensive traveling bag in a store window. She was going home to Buffalo, New York, for the holidays. She was about to say, "I can't afford that bag," when she recalled something she had heard at one of my lectures which was, "Never finish a negative statement; reverse it immediately, and wonders will happen in your life."

She said, "That bag is mine. It is for sale. I accept it mentally, and my subconscious sees to it that I receive it."

At eight o'clock Christmas Eve her fiancé presented her with a bag exactly the same as the one she had looked at and mentally identified herself with at ten o'clock the same morning. She had filled her mind with the thought of expectancy and released the whole thing to her deeper mind which has the "know-how" of accomplishment.

This young girl, a student at the University of Southern California, said to me, "I didn't have the money to buy that bag, but now I know where to find money and all the things I need, and that is in the treasure house of eternity within me."

Another simple illustration is this: When you say, "I do not like mushrooms," and the occasion subsequently comes that you are served mushrooms in sauces or salads, you will get indigestion because your subconscious mind says to you, "The boss (your conscious mind) does not like mushrooms." This is an amusing example of the outstanding differences and modes of operation of your conscious and subconscious minds.

A woman may say, "I wake up at three o'clock, if I drink coffee at night." Whenever she drinks coffee, her subconscious mind nudges her, as if to say, "The boss wants you to stay awake tonight."

Your subconscious mind works twenty-four hours a day and makes provisions for your benefit, pouring all the fruit of your habitual thinking into your lap.

HOW HER SUBCONSCIOUS RESPONDED

A woman wrote me a few months ago as follows: "I am seventy-five years old, a widow with a grown family. I was living alone and on a pension. I heard your lectures on the powers of the subconscious mind wherein you said that ideas could be conveyed to the subconscious mind by repetition, faith, and expectancy.

"I began to repeat frequently with feeling, 'I am wanted. I am happily married to a kind, loving, and spiritual-minded man. I am secure!'

"I kept on doing this many times a day for about two weeks, and one day at the corner drugstore I was introduced to a retired pharmacist. I found him to be kind, understanding, and very religious. He was a perfect answer to my prayer. Within a week he proposed to me, and now we are on our honeymoon in Europe. I know that the intelligence within my subconscious mind brought both of us together in divine order."

This woman discovered that the treasure house was within her. Her prayer was felt as true in her heart, and her affirmation sank down by osmosis into her subconscious mind, which is the creative medium. The moment she succeeded in bringing about a subjective embodiment, her subconscious mind brought about the answer through the law of attraction. Her deeper mind, full of wisdom and intelligence, brought both of them together in divine order.

Be sure that you think on *whatsoever things are true, whatsoever things are honest, whatsoever things are just, whatsoever things are pure, whatsoever things are lovely, whatsoever things are of good report; if there be any virtue, and if there be any praise, think on these things.* PHILIPPIANS 4:8.

BRIEF SUMMARY OF IDEAS WORTH REMEMBERING

1. The treasure house is within you. Look within for the answer to your heart's desire.

2. The great secret possessed by the great men of all ages was their ability to contact and release the powers of their subconscious mind. You can do the same.

3. Your subconscious has the answer to all problems. If you suggest to your subconscious prior to sleep, "I want to get up at 6 A.M.," it will awaken you at that exact time.

4. Your subconscious mind is the builder of your body and can heal you. Lull yourself to sleep every night with the idea of perfect health, and your subconscious, being your faithful servant, will obey you.

5. Every thought is a cause, and every condition is an effect.

6. If you want to write a book, write a wonderful play, give a better talk to your audience, convey the idea lovingly and feelingly to your subconscious mind, and it will respond accordingly.

7. You are like a captain navigating a ship. He must give the right orders, and likewise, you must give the right orders

(thoughts and images) to your subconscious mind which controls and governs all your experiences.

8. Never use the terms "I can't afford it" or "I can't do this." Your subconscious mind takes you at your word and sees to it that you do not have the money or the ability to do what you want to do. Affirm, "I can do all things through the power of my subconscious mind."

9. The law of life is the law of belief. A belief is a thought in your mind. Do not believe in things to harm or hurt you. Believe in the power of your subconscious to heal, inspire, strengthen, and prosper you. According to your belief is it done unto you.

10. Change your thoughts, and you change your destiny.

HOW YOUR OWN
MIND WORKS

You have a mind, and you should learn how to use it. There are two levels of your mind—the conscious or rational level, and the subconscious or irrational level. You think with your conscious mind, and whatever you habitually think sinks down into your subconscious mind, which creates according to the nature of your thoughts. Your subconscious mind is the seat of your emotions and is the creative mind. If you think good, good will follow; if you think evil, evil will follow. This is the way your mind works.

The main point to remember is once the subconscious mind accepts an idea, it begins to execute it. It is an interesting and subtle truth that the law of the subconscious mind works for good and bad ideas alike. This law, when applied in a negative way, is the cause of failure, frustration, and unhappiness. However, when your habitual thinking is harmonious and constructive, you experience perfect health, success, and prosperity.

Peace of mind and a healthy body are inevitable when you begin to think and feel in the right way. Whatever you claim mentally and feel as true, your subconscious mind will accept and bring forth into your experience. The only thing necessary for you to do is to get your subconscious mind to accept your idea, and the law of your own subconscious mind will bring forth the health, peace, or the position you desire.

You give the command or decree, and your subconscious will faithfully reproduce the idea impressed upon it. The law of your mind is this: You will get a reaction or response from your subconscious mind according to the nature of the thought or idea you hold in your conscious mind.

Psychologists and psychiatrists point out that when thoughts are conveyed to your subconscious mind, impressions are made in the brain cells. As soon as your subconscious accepts any idea, it proceeds to put it into effect immediately. It works by association of ideas and uses every bit of knowledge that you have gathered in your lifetime to bring about its purpose. It draws on the infinite power, energy, and wisdom within you. It lines up all the laws of nature to get its way. Sometimes it seems to bring about an immediate solution to your difficulties, but at other times it may take days, weeks, or longer. . . . *Its ways are past finding out.*

CONSCIOUS AND SUBCONSCIOUS
TERMS DIFFERENTIATED

You must remember that these are not two minds. They are merely two spheres of activity within one mind. Your conscious mind is the reasoning mind. It is that phase of mind which chooses. For example, you choose your books, your home, and your partner in life. You make all your decisions with your conscious mind. On the other hand, without any conscious choice on your part, your heart is kept functioning automatically, and the process of digestion, circulation, and breathing are carried on by your subconscious mind through processes independent of your conscious control.

Your subconscious mind accepts what is impressed upon it or what you consciously believe. It does not reason things out like your conscious mind, and it does not argue with you controversially. Your subconscious mind is like the soil which accepts any kind of seed, good or bad. Your thoughts are active and might be likened unto seeds. Negative, destructive thoughts continue to work negatively in your subconscious mind, and in due time will come forth into outer experience which corresponds with them.

Remember, your subconscious mind does not engage in proving whether your thoughts are good or bad, true or false, but it responds according to the nature of your thoughts or suggestions. For example, if you consciously assume something as true, even though it may be false, your subconscious mind will accept it as true and proceed to bring about results which must necessarily follow, because you consciously assumed it to be true.

EXPERIMENTS BY PSYCHOLOGISTS

Innumerable experiments by psychologists and others on persons in the hypnotic state have shown that the subconscious mind is incapable of making selections and comparisons which are necessary for a reasoning process. They have shown repeatedly that your subconscious mind will accept any suggestions, however false. Having once accepted any suggestion, it responds according to the nature of the suggestion given.

To illustrate the amenability of your subconscious mind to suggestion, if a practiced hypnotist suggests to one of his subjects that he is Napoleon Bonaparte, or even a cat or a dog, he will act out the part with inimitable accuracy. His personality becomes changed for the time being. He believes himself to be whatever the operator tells him he is.

A skilled hypnotist may suggest to one of his students in the hypnotic state that his back itches, to another that his nose is bleeding, to another that he is a marble statue, to another that he is freezing and the temperature is below zero. Each one will follow out the line of his particular suggestion, totally oblivious to all his surroundings which do not pertain to his idea.

These simple illustrations portray clearly the difference between your conscious reasoning mind and your subconscious mind which is impersonal, nonselective, and accepts as true whatever your conscious mind believes to be true. Hence, the importance of selecting thoughts, ideas, and premises which bless, heal, inspire, and fill your soul with joy.

THE TERMS OBJECTIVE AND SUBJECTIVE MIND CLARIFIED

Your conscious mind is sometimes referred to as your objective mind because it deals with outward objects. The objective mind takes cognizance of the objective world. Its media of observation are your five physical senses. Your objective mind is your guide and director in your contact with your environment. You gain knowledge through your five senses. Your objective mind learns through observation, experience, and education. As previously pointed out, the greatest function of the objective mind is that of reasoning.

Suppose you are one of the thousands of tourists who come to Los Angeles annually. You would come to the conclusion that it is a beautiful city based upon your observation of the parks, pretty gardens, majestic buildings, and lovely homes. This is the working of your objective mind.

Your subconscious mind is oftentimes referred to as your subjective mind. Your subjective mind takes cognizance of its environment by means independent of the five senses. Your subjective mind perceives by intuition. It is the seat of your emotion and the storehouse of memory. Your subjective mind performs its highest functions when your objective senses are in abeyance. In a word, it is that intelligence which makes itself manifest when the objective mind is suspended or in a sleepy, drowsy state.

Your subjective mind sees without the use of the natural organs of vision. It has the capacity of clairvoyance and clairaudience. Your subjective mind can leave your body, travel to distant lands, and bring back information oftentimes of the most exact and truthful character. Through your subjective mind you can read the thoughts of others, read the contents of sealed envelopes and closed safes. Your subjective mind has the ability to apprehend the thoughts of others without the use of the ordinary objective means of communication. It is of the greatest importance that we understand the interaction of the objective and subjective mind in order to learn the true art of prayer.

THE SUBCONSCIOUS CANNOT REASON LIKE YOUR CONSCIOUS MIND

Your subconscious mind cannot argue controversially. Hence, if you give it wrong suggestions, it will accept them as true and will proceed to bring them to pass as conditions, experiences, and events. All things that have happened to you are based on thoughts impressed on your subconscious mind through belief. If you have conveyed erroneous concepts to your subconscious mind, the sure method of overcoming them is by the repetition of constructive, harmonious thoughts frequently repeated which your subconscious mind accepts, thus forming new and healthy habits of thought and life, for your subconscious mind is the seat of habit.

The habitual thinking of your conscious mind establishes deep grooves in your subconscious mind. This is very favorable for you if your habitual thoughts are harmonious, peaceful, and constructive.

If you have indulged in fear, worry, and other obstructive forms of thinking, the remedy is to recognize the omnipotence of your subconscious mind and decree freedom, happiness, and perfect health. Your subconscious mind, being creative and one with your divine source, will proceed to create the freedom and happiness which you have earnestly decreed.

THE TREMENDOUS POWER OF SUGGESTION

You must realize by now that your conscious mind is the "watchman at the gate," and its chief function is to protect your subconscious mind from false impressions. You are now aware of one of the basic laws of mind: Your subconscious mind is amenable to suggestion. As you know, your subconscious mind does not make comparisons, or contrasts, neither does it reason and think things out for itself. This latter function belongs to your conscious mind. It simply reacts to the impressions given to it by your conscious mind. It does not show a preference for one course of action over another.

The following is a classic example of the tremendous power of suggestion. Suppose you approach a timid-looking passenger on board ship and say to him something like this: "You look very ill. How pale you are! I feel certain you are going to be seasick. Let me help you to your cabin." The passenger turns pale. Your suggestion of seasickness associates itself with his own fears and forebodings. He accepts your aid down to the berth, and there your negative suggestion, which was accepted by him, is realized.

DIFFERENT REACTIONS TO
THE SAME SUGGESTION

It is true that different people will react in different ways to the same suggestion because of their subconscious conditioning or belief. For example, if you go to a sailor on the ship and say to him sympathetically, "My dear fellow, you're looking very ill. Aren't you feeling sick? You look to me as if you were going to be seasick."

According to his temperament he either laughs at your "joke," or expresses a mild irritation. Your suggestion fell on deaf ears in this instance because your suggestion of seasickness was associated in his mind with his own immunity from it. Therefore, it called up not fear or worry, but self-confidence.

The dictionary says that a suggestion is the act or instance of putting something into one's mind, the mental process by which the thought or idea suggested is entertained, accepted, or put into effect. You must remember that a suggestion cannot impose something on the subconscious mind against the will of the conscious mind. In other words, your conscious mind has the power to reject the suggestion given. In the case of the sailor, he had no fear of seasickness. He had convinced himself of his immunity, and the negative suggestion had absolutely no power to evoke fear.

The suggestion of seasickness to the other passenger called forth his indwelling fear of seasickness. Each of us has his own inner fears, beliefs, opinions, and these inner assumptions rule and govern our lives. A suggestion has no power in and of itself except it is accepted mentally by you. This causes your subconscious powers to flow in a limited and restricted way according to the nature of the suggestion.

HOW HE LOST HIS ARM

Every two or three years I give a series of lectures at the London Truth Forum in Caxton Hall. This is a Forum I founded a number of years ago. Dr. Evelyn Fleet, the director, told me about an article which appeared in the English newspapers dealing with the power of suggestion. This is the suggestion a man gave to his subconscious mind over a period of about two years: "I would give my right arm to see my daughter cured." It appeared that his daughter had a crippling form of arthritis together with a so-called incurable form of skin disease. Medical treatment had failed to alleviate the condition, and the father had an intense longing for his daughter's healing, and expressed his desire in the words just quoted.

Dr. Evelyn Fleet said that the newspaper article pointed out that one day the family was out riding when their car collided with another. The father's right arm was torn off at the shoulder, and immediately the daughter's arthritis and skin condition vanished.

You must make certain to give your subconscious only suggestions which heal, bless, elevate, and inspire you in all your ways. Remember that your subconscious mind cannot take a joke. It takes you at your word.

HOW AUTOSUGGESTION BANISHES FEAR

Illustrations of autosuggestion: Autosuggestion means suggesting something definite and specific to oneself. Herbert Parkyn, in his excellent manual of autosuggestion,* records the following incident. It has its amusing side, so that one remembers it. "A New York visitor in Chicago looks at his watch, which is set an hour ahead of Chicago time, and tells a Chicago friend that it is

---

* Herbert Parkyn, *Autosuggestion* (London: Fowler, 1916).

twelve o'clock. The Chicago friend, not considering the difference in time between Chicago and New York, tells the New
Yorker that he is hungry and that he must go to lunch."

Autosuggestion may be used to banish various fears and
other negative conditions. A young singer was invited to give an
audition. She had been looking forward to the interview, but on
three previous occasions she had failed miserably due to fear of
failure. This young lady had a very good voice, but she had been
saying to herself, "When the time comes for me to sing, maybe
they won't like me. I will try, but I'm full of fear and anxiety."

Her subconscious mind accepted these negative autosuggestions as a request and proceeded to manifest them and
bring them into her experience. The cause was an involuntary
autosuggestion, i.e., silent fear thoughts emotionalized and
subjectified.

She overcame it by the following technique: Three times
a day she isolated herself in a room. She sat down comfortably
in an armchair, relaxed her body, and closed her eyes. She
stilled her mind and body as best she could. Physical inertia
favors mental passivity and renders the mind more receptive
to suggestion. She counteracted the fear suggestion by saying
to herself, "I sing beautifully. I am poised, serene, confident,
and calm." She repeated this statement slowly, quietly, and
with feeling from five to ten times at each sitting. She had
three such "sittings" every day and one immediately prior to
sleep. At the end of a week she was completely poised and
confident. When the invitation to audition came, she gave a
remarkable, wonderful audition.

HOW SHE RESTORED HER MEMORY

A woman, aged seventy-five, was in the habit of saying to
herself, "I am losing my memory." She reversed the procedure

and practiced induced autosuggestion several times a day as follows: "My memory from today on is improving in every department. I shall always remember whatever I need to know at every moment of time and point of space. The impressions received will be clearer and more definite. I shall retain them automatically and with ease. Whatever I wish to recall will immediately present itself in the correct form in my mind. I am improving rapidly every day, and very soon my memory will be better than it has ever been before." At the end of three weeks, her memory was back to normal, and she was delighted.

HOW HE OVERCAME A NASTY TEMPER

Many men who complained of irritability and bad temper proved to be very susceptible to autosuggestion and obtained marvelous results by using the following statements three or four times a day—morning, noon, and at night prior to sleep for about a month. "Henceforth, I shall grow more good-humored. Joy, happiness, and cheerfulness are now becoming my normal states of mind. Every day I am becoming more and more lovable and understanding. I am now becoming the center of cheer and good will to all those about me, infecting them with good humor. This happy, joyous, and cheerful mood is now becoming my normal, natural state of mind. I am grateful."

THE CONSTRUCTIVE AND DESTRUCTIVE
POWER OF SUGGESTION

Some illustrations and comments on heterosuggestion: Heterosuggestion means suggestions from another person. In all ages the power of suggestion has played a part in the life and thought of man in every period of time and in each country of the earth. In many parts of the world it is the controlling power in religion.

Suggestion may be used to discipline and control ourselves, but it can also be used to take control and command over
others who do not know the laws of mind. In its constructive
form it is wonderful and magnificent. In its negative aspects it is
one of the most destructive of all the response patterns of the
mind, resulting in patterns of misery, failure, suffering, sickness, and disaster.

HAVE YOU ACCEPTED ANY OF THESE?

From infancy on the majority of us have been given many negative suggestions. Not knowing how to thwart them, we unconsciously accepted them. Here are some of the negative
suggestions: "You can't." "You'll never amount to anything."
"You mustn't." "You'll fail." "You haven't got a chance." "You're
all wrong." "It's no use." "It's not what you know, but who you
know." "The world is going to the dogs." "What's the use, nobody cares." "It's no use trying so hard." "You're too old now."
"Things are getting worse and worse." "Life is an endless
grind." "Love is for the birds." "You just can't win." "Pretty
soon you'll be bankrupt." "Watch out, you'll get the virus."
"You can't trust a soul," etc.

Unless, as an adult, you use constructive autosuggestion, which is a reconditioning therapy, the impressions
made on you in the past can cause behavior patterns that
cause failure in your personal and social life. Autosuggestion
is a means releasing you from the mass of negative verbal
conditioning that might otherwise distort your life pattern,
making the development of good habits difficult.

YOU CAN COUNTERACT NEGATIVE SUGGESTIONS

Pick up the paper any day, and you can read dozens of items
that could sow the seeds of futility, fear, worry, anxiety, and

impending doom. If accepted by you, these thoughts of fear could cause you to lose the will for life. Knowing that you can reject all these negative suggestions by giving your subconscious mind constructive autosuggestions, you counteract all these destructive ideas.

Check regularly on the negative suggestions that people make to you. You do not have to be influenced by destructive heterosuggestion. All of us have suffered from it in our childhood and in our teens. If you look back, you can easily recall how parents, friends, relatives, teachers, and associates contributed in a campaign of negative suggestions. Study the things said to you, and you will discover much of it was in the form of propaganda. The purpose of much of what was said was to control you or instill fear into you.

This heterosuggestion process goes on in every home, office, factory, and club. You will find that many of these suggestions are for the purpose of making you think, feel, and act as others want you to and in ways that are to their advantage.

HOW SUGGESTION KILLED A MAN

Here is an illustration of heterosuggestion: A relative of mine went to a crystal gazer in India who told him that he had a bad heart and predicted that he would die at the next new moon. He began to tell all members of his family about this prediction, and he arranged his will.

This powerful suggestion entered into his subconscious mind because he accepted it completely. My relative also told me that this crystal gazer was believed to have some strange occult powers, and he could do harm or good to a person. He died as predicted not knowing that he was the cause of his own death. I suppose many of us have heard similar stupid, ridiculous, superstitious stories.

Let us look at what happened in the light of our knowledge of the way the subconscious mind works. Whatever the conscious, reasoning mind of man believes, the subconscious mind will accept and act upon. My relative was happy, healthy, vigorous, and robust when he went to see the fortune-teller. She gave him a very negative suggestion which he accepted. He became terrified, and constantly dwelt upon the fact that he was going to die at the next new moon. He proceeded to tell everyone about it, and he prepared for the end. The activity took place in his own mind, and his own thought was the cause. He brought about his own so-called death, or rather destruction of the physical body, by his fear and expectation of the end.

The woman who predicted his death had no more power than the stones and sticks in the field. Her suggestion had no power to create or bring about the end she suggested. If he had known the laws of his mind, he would have completely rejected the negative suggestion and refused to give her words any attention, knowing in his heart that he was governed and controlled by his own thought and feeling. Like tin arrows aimed at a battleship, her prophecy could have been completely neutralized and dissipated without hurting him.

The suggestions of others in themselves have absolutely no power whatever over you except the power that you give them through your own thoughts. You have to give your mental consent; you have to entertain the thought. Then, it becomes your thought, and you do the thinking. Remember, you have the capacity to choose. Choose life! Choose love! Choose health!

THE POWER OF AN ASSUMED MAJOR PREMISE

Your mind works like a syllogism. This means that whatever major premise your conscious mind assumes to be true determines the conclusion your subconscious mind comes to in regard to any particular question or problem in your mind. If your premise is true, the conclusion must be true as in the following example:

> *Every virtue is laudable;*
> *Kindness is a virtue;*
> *Therefore, kindness is laudable.*

Another example is as follows:

> *All formed things change and pass away;*
> *The Pyramids of Egypt are formed things;*
> *Therefore, some day the Pyramids will pass away.*

The first statement is referred to as the major premise, and the right conclusion must necessarily follow the right premise.

A college professor, who attended some of my science of mind lectures in May 1962, at Town Hall, New York, said to me, "Everything in my life is topsy-turvy, and I have lost health, wealth, and friends. Everything I touch turns out wrong."

I explained to him that he should establish a major premise in his thinking, that the infinite intelligence of his subconscious mind was guiding, directing, and prospering him spiritually, mentally, and materially. Then, his subconscious mind would automatically direct him wisely in his investments, decisions, and also heal his body and restore his mind to peace and tranquility.

This professor formulated an overall picture of the way he wanted his life to be, and this was his major premise:

"Infinite intelligence leads and guides me in all my ways. Perfect health is mine, and the Law of Harmony operates in my mind and body. Beauty, love, peace, and abundance are mine. The principle of right action and divine order govern my entire life. I know my major premise is based on the eternal truths of life, and I know, feel, and believe that my subconscious mind responds according to the nature of my conscious mind thinking."

He wrote me as follows: "I repeated the above statements slowly, quietly, and lovingly several times a day knowing that they were sinking deep down into my subconscious mind, and that results must follow. I am deeply grateful for the interview you gave me, and I would like to add that all departments of my life are changing for the better. It works!"

THE SUBCONSCIOUS DOES NOT ARGUE CONTROVERSIALLY

Your subconscious mind is all-wise and knows the answers to all questions. It does not argue with you or talk back to you. It does not say, "You must not impress me with that." For example, when you say, "I can't do this," "I am too old now," "I can't meet this obligation," "I was born on the wrong side of the tracks," "I don't know the right politician," you are impregnating your subconscious with these negative thoughts, and it responds accordingly. You are actually blocking your own good, thereby bringing lack, limitation, and frustration into your life.

When you set up obstacles, impediments, and delays in your conscious mind, you are denying the wisdom and intelligence resident in your subconscious mind. You are actually saying in effect that your subconscious mind cannot solve your problem. This leads to mental and emotional congestion, followed by sickness and neurotic tendencies.

To realize your desire and overcome your frustration, affirm boldly several times a day: "The infinite intelligence which gave me this desire leads, guides, and reveals to me the perfect plan for the unfolding of my desire. I know the deeper wisdom of my subconscious is now responding, and what I feel and claim within is expressed in the without. There is a balance, equilibrium, and equanimity."

If you say, "There is no way out; I am lost; there is no way out of this dilemma; I am stymied and blocked," you will get no answer or response from your subconscious mind. If you want the subconscious to work for you, give it the right request, and attain its cooperation. It is always working for you. It is controlling your heartbeat this minute and also your breathing. It heals a cut on your finger, and its tendency is lifeward, forever seeking to take care of you and preserve you. Your subconscious has a mind of its own, but it accepts your patterns of thought and imagery.

When you are seeking an answer to a problem, your subconscious will respond, but it expects you to come to a decision and to a true judgment in your conscious mind. You must acknowledge the answer is in your subconscious mind. However, if you say, "I don't think there is any way out; I am all mixed up and confused; why don't I get an answer?" you are neutralizing your prayer. Like the soldier marking time, you do not get anywhere.

Still the wheels of your mind, relax, let go, and quietly affirm: "My subconscious knows the answer. It is responding to me now. I give thanks because I know the infinite intelligence of my subconscious knows all things and is revealing the perfect answer to me now. My real conviction is now setting free the majesty and glory of my subconscious mind. I rejoice that it is so."

REVIEW OF HIGHLIGHTS

1. Think good, and good follows. Think evil, and evil follows. You are what you think all day long.

2. Your subconscious mind does not argue with you. It accepts what your conscious mind decrees. If you say, "I can't afford it," it may be true, but do not say it. Select a better thought, decree, *"I'll buy it. I accept it in my mind."*

3. You have the power to choose. Choose health and happiness. You can choose to be friendly, or you can choose to be unfriendly. Choose to be cooperative, joyous, friendly, lovable, and the whole world will respond. This is the best way to develop a wonderful personality.

4. Your conscious mind is the "watchman at the gate." Its chief function is to protect your subconscious mind from false impressions. Choose to believe that something good can happen and is happening now. Your greatest power is your capacity to choose. *Choose happiness and abundance.*

5. The suggestions and statements of others have no power to hurt you. The only power is the movement of your own thought. You can choose to reject the thoughts or statements of others and affirm the good. You have the power to choose how you will react.

6. Watch what you say. You have to account for every idle word. Never say, "I will fail; I will lose my job; I can't pay the rent." *Your subconscious cannot take a joke.* It brings all these things to pass.

7. Your mind is not evil. No force of nature is evil. It depends how you use the powers of nature. Use your mind to bless, heal, and inspire all people everywhere.

8. Never say, "I can't." Overcome that fear by substituting the following: "I can do all things through the power of my own subconscious mind."

9. Begin to think from the standpoint of the eternal truths and principles of life and not from the standpoint of fear, ignorance, and superstition. *Do not let others do your thinking for you.* Choose your own thoughts and make your own decisions.

10. You are the captain of your soul (subconscious mind) and the master of your fate. Remember, you have the capacity to choose. Choose life! Choose love! Choose health! Choose happiness!

11. Whatever your conscious mind assumes and believes to be true, your subconscious mind will accept and bring to pass. Believe in good fortune, divine guidance, right action, and all the *blessings* of life.

THE MIRACLE-WORKING POWER OF YOUR SUBCONSCIOUS

The power of your subconscious is enormous. It inspires you, it guides you, and it reveals to you names, facts, and scenes from the storehouse of memory. Your subconscious started your heartbeat, controls the circulation of your blood, regulates your digestion, assimilation, and elimination. When you eat a piece of bread, your subconscious mind transmutes it into tissue, muscle, bone, and blood. This process is beyond the ken of the wisest man who walks the earth. Your subconscious mind controls all the vital processes and functions of your body and knows the answer to all problems.

Your subconscious mind never sleeps, never rests. It is always on the job. You can discover the miracle-working power of your subconscious by plainly stating to your subconscious prior to sleep that you wish a certain specific thing accomplished. You will be delighted to discover that forces within you will be released, leading to the desired result. Here, then, is a source of power and wisdom which places you in touch with omnipotence or the power that moves the world, guides the planets in their course, and causes the sun to shine.

Your subconscious mind is the source of your ideals, aspirations, and altruistic urges. It was through the subconscious mind that Shakespeare perceived great truths hidden from the average man of his day. Undoubtedly, it was the response of his subconscious mind that caused the Greek sculptor, Phidias, to portray beauty, order, symmetry, and proportion in marble and bronze. It enabled the Italian artist, Raphael, to paint Madonnas, and Ludwig van Beethoven to compose symphonies.

In 1955 I lectured at the Yoga Forest University, Rishikesh, India, and there I chatted with a visiting surgeon from Bombay. He told me about Dr. James Esdaille, a Scotch surgeon, who worked in Bengal before ether or other modern methods of anesthesia were discovered. Between 1843 and 1846, Dr. Esdaille performed about four hundred major operations of all kinds, such as amputations, removal of tumors and cancerous growths, as well as operations on the eye, ear, and throat. All operations were conducted under mental anesthesia only. This Indian doctor at Rishikesh informed me that the postoperative mortality rate of patients operated on by Dr. Esdaille was extremely low, probably two or three percent. Patients felt no pain, and there were no deaths during the operations.

Dr. Esdaille suggested to the subconscious minds of all his patients, who were in a hypnotic state, that no infection or septic condition would develop. You must remember that this was before Louis Pasteur, Joseph Lister, and others who pointed out the bacterial origin of disease and causes of infection due to unsterilized instruments and virulent organisms.

This Indian surgeon said that the reason for the low mortality rate and the general absence of infection, which was reduced to a minimum, was undoubtedly due to the suggestions of Dr. Esdaille to the subconscious minds of his patients. They responded according to the nature of his suggestion.

It is simply wonderful, when you conceive how a surgeon, over one hundred twenty years ago, discovered the miraculous wonder-working powers of the subconscious mind. Doesn't it cause you to be seized with a sort of mystic awe when you stop and think of the transcendental powers of your subconscious mind? Consider its extrasensory perceptions, such as its capacity for clairvoyance and clairaudience, its independence of time and space, its capacity to render you free from all pain and suffering, and its capacity to get the answer to all problems, be they what they may. All these and many more reveal to you that there is a power and an intelligence within you that far transcends your intellect, causing you to marvel at the wonders of it all. All these experiences cause you to rejoice and believe in the miracle-working powers of your own subconscious mind.

YOUR SUBCONSCIOUS IS YOUR BOOK OF LIFE

Whatever thoughts, beliefs, opinions, theories, or dogmas you write, engrave, or impress on your subconscious mind, you shall experience them as the objective manifestation of circumstances, conditions, and events. What you write on the inside, you will experience on the outside. You have two sides to your life, objective and subjective, visible and invisible, thought and its manifestation.

Your thought is received by your brain, which is the organ of your conscious reasoning mind. When your conscious or objective mind accepts the thought completely, it is sent to the solar plexus, called the brain of your abdomen, where it becomes flesh and is made manifest in your experience.

As previously outlined, your subconscious cannot argue. It acts only from what you write on it. It accepts your verdict or the conclusions of your conscious mind as final. This is why you are always writing on the book of life, because your thoughts become your experiences. The American essayist Ralph Waldo Emerson said, "Man is what he thinks all day long."

WHAT IS IMPRESSED IN THE SUBCONSCIOUS
IS EXPRESSED

William James, the father of American psychology, said that the power to move the world is in your subconscious mind. Your subconscious mind is one with infinite intelligence and boundless wisdom. It is fed by hidden springs, and is called the law of life. Whatever you impress upon your subconscious mind, the latter will move heaven and earth to bring it to pass. You must, therefore, impress it with right ideas and constructive thoughts.

The reason there is so much chaos and misery in the world is because people do not understand the interaction of their conscious and subconscious minds. When these two principles work in accord, in concord, in peace, and synchronously together, you will have health, happiness, peace, and joy. There is no sickness or discord when the conscious and subconscious work together harmoniously and peacefully.

The tomb of Hermes was opened with great expectancy and a sense of wonder because people believed that the greatest secret of the ages was contained therein. The secret was *as within, so without; as above, so below.*

In other words, whatever is impressed in your subconscious mind is expressed on the screen of space. This same truth was proclaimed by Moses, Isaiah, Jesus, Buddha, Zoroaster, Laotze, and the illumined seers of the ages. Whatever you feel as true subjectively is expressed as conditions, experiences, and events. Motion and emotion must balance. *As in heaven* [your own mind], *so on earth* [in your body and environment]. This is the great law of life.

You will find throughout all nature the law of action and reaction, of rest and motion. These two must balance, then there will be harmony and equilibrium. You are here to let the life principle flow through you rhythmically and harmoniously. The intake and the outgo must be equal. The impression and the expression must be equal. All your frustration is due to unfulfilled desire.

If you think negatively, destructively, and viciously, these thoughts generate destructive emotions which must be expressed and find an outlet. These emotions, being of a negative nature, are frequently expressed as ulcers, heart trouble, tension, and anxieties.

What is your idea or feeling about yourself now? Every part of your being expresses that idea. Your vitality, body, financial status, friends, and social status represent a perfect reflection of the idea you have of yourself. This is the real meaning of what is impressed in your subconscious mind, and which is expressed in all phases of your life.

We injure ourselves by the negative ideas which we entertain. How often have you wounded yourself by getting angry, fearful, jealous, or vengeful? These are the poisons that enter your subconscious mind. You were not born with these negative attitudes. Feed your subconscious mind life-giving thoughts, and you will wipe out all the negative patterns lodged therein. As you continue to do this, all the past will be wiped out and remembered no more.

THE SUBCONSCIOUS HEALS A MALIGNANCY
OF THE SKIN

A personal healing will ever be the most convincing evidence of the healing power of the subconscious mind. Over forty years ago I resolved a malignancy of the skin through prayer. Medical therapy had failed to check the growth, and it was getting progressively worse.

A clergyman, with a deep psychological knowledge, explained to me the inner meaning of the 139th Psalm wherein it says, *In thy book all my members were written, which in continuance were fashioned, when as yet there was none of them.* He explained that the term *book* meant my subconscious mind which fashioned and molded all my organs from an invisible cell. He also pointed out that inasmuch as my subconscious mind made my body, it could also recreate it and heal it according to the perfect pattern within it.

This clergyman showed me his watch and said, "This had a maker, and the watchmaker had to have the idea first in mind before the watch became an objective reality, and if the watch was out of order, the watchmaker could fix it." My friend reminded me that the subconscious intelligence which created my body was like a watchmaker, and it also knew exactly how to heal, restore, and direct all the vital functions and processes of my body, but that I had to give it the perfect idea of health. This would act as cause, and the effect would be a healing.

I prayed in a very simple way as follows: "My body and all its organs were created by the infinite intelligence in my subconscious mind. It knows how to heal me. Its wisdom fashioned all my organs, tissues, muscles, and bones. This infinite healing presence within me is now transforming every atom of my being making me whole and perfect now. I give thanks for the healing I know is taking place now. Wonderful are the works of the creative intelligence within me."

I prayed aloud for about five minutes two or three times a day repeating the above simple prayer. In about three months my skin was whole and perfect.

As you can see, all I did was give life-giving patterns of wholeness, beauty, and perfection to my subconscious mind, thereby obliterating the negative images and patterns of thought lodged in my subconscious mind which were the cause of all my trouble. Nothing appears on your body except when the mental equivalent is first in your mind, and as you change your mind by drenching it with incessant affirmatives, you change your body. This is the basis of all healing. . . . *Marvelous are thy works; and that my soul* [subconscious mind] *knoweth right well.* PSALMS 139:14.

HOW THE SUBCONSCIOUS CONTROLS ALL FUNCTIONS OF THE BODY

While you are awake or sound asleep upon your bed, the ceaseless, tireless action of your subconscious mind controls all the vital functions of your body without the help of your conscious mind. For example, while you are asleep your heart continues to beat rhythmically, your lungs do not rest, and the process of inhalation and exhalation, whereby your blood absorbs fresh air, goes on just the same as when you are awake. Your subconscious controls your digestive processes and glandular secretions, as well as all the other mysterious operations of your body. The hair on your face continues to grow whether you are asleep or awake. Scientists tell us that the skin secretes much more perspiration during sleep than during the waking hours. Your eyes, ears, and other senses are active during sleep. For instance, many of our great scientists have received answers to perplexing problems while they were asleep. They saw the answers in a dream.

Oftentimes your conscious mind interferes with the normal rhythm of the heart, lungs, and functioning of the stomach and intestines by worry, anxiety, fear, and depression. These patterns of thought interfere with the harmonious functioning of your subconscious mind. When mentally disturbed, the best procedure is to let go, relax, and still the wheels of your thought processes. Speak to your subconscious mind, telling it to take over in peace, harmony, and divine order. You will find that all the functions of your body will become normal again. Be sure to speak to your subconscious mind with authority and conviction, and it will conform to your command.

Your subconscious seeks to preserve your life and restore you to health at all costs. It causes you to love your children which also illustrates an instinctive desire to preserve all life. Let us suppose you accidentally ate some bad food. Your subconscious mind would cause you to regurgitate it. If you inadvertently took some poison, your subconscious powers would proceed to neutralize it. If you completely entrusted yourself to its wonder-working power, you would be entirely restored to health.

HOW TO GET THE SUBCONSCIOUS TO WORK FOR YOU

The first thing to realize is that your subconscious mind is always working. It is active night and day, whether you act upon it or not. Your subconscious is the builder of your body, but you cannot consciously perceive or hear that inner silent process. Your business is with your conscious mind and not your subconscious mind. Just keep your conscious mind busy with the expectation of the best, and make sure the thoughts you habitually think are based on whatsoever things are lovely, true, just, and of good report. Begin now to take care of your conscious mind, knowing in your heart and soul that your subconscious mind is always expressing, reproducing, and manifesting according to your habitual thinking.

Remember, just as water takes the shape of the pipe it flows through, the life principle in you flows through you according to the nature of your thoughts. Claim that the healing presence in your subconscious is flowing through you as harmony, health, peace, joy, and abundance. Think of it as a living intelligence, a lovely companion on the way. Firmly believe it is continually flowing through you vivifying, inspiring, and prospering you. It will respond exactly this way. It is done unto you as you believe.

HEALING PRINCIPLE OF THE SUBCONSCIOUS RESTORES ATROPHIED OPTIC NERVES

There is the well-known, duly authenticated case of Madame Bire of France, recorded in the archives of the medical department of Lourdes, France. She was blind, the optic nerves were atrophied and useless. She visited Lourdes and had what she termed a miraculous healing. Ruth Cranston, a Protestant young lady who investigated and wrote about healings at Lourdes in *McCall's* magazine, November, 1955, writes about Madame Bire as follows: "At Lourdes she regained her sight incredibly, with the optic nerves still lifeless and useless, as several doctors could testify after repeated examinations. A month later, upon reexamination, it was found that the seeing mechanism had been restored to normal. But at first, so far as medical examination could tell, she was seeing with 'dead eyes.'"

I have visited Lourdes several times where I, too, witnessed some healings, and of course, as we shall explain in the next chapter, there is no doubt that healings take place at many shrines throughout the world, Christian and non-Christian.

Madame Bire, to whom we just referred, was not healed by the waters of the shrine, but by her own subconscious mind which responded to her belief. The healing principle within her subconscious mind responded to the nature of her thought. Belief is a thought in the subconscious mind. It means to accept something as true. The thought accepted executes itself automatically. Undoubtedly, Madame Bire went to the shrine with expectancy and great faith, knowing in her heart she would receive a healing. Her subconscious mind responded accordingly, releasing the ever present healing forces. The subconscious mind which created the eye can certainly bring a dead nerve back to life. What the creative principle created, it can recreate. *According to your belief is it done unto you.*

HOW TO CONVEY THE IDEA OF PERFECT HEALTH TO YOUR SUBCONSCIOUS MIND

A Protestant minister I knew in Johannesburg, South Africa, told me the method he used to convey the idea of perfect health to his subconscious mind. He had cancer of the lung. His technique, as given to me in his own handwriting, is exactly as follows: "Several times a day I would make certain that I was completely relaxed mentally and physically. I relaxed my body by speaking to it as follows, 'My feet are relaxed, my ankles are relaxed, my legs are relaxed, my abdominal muscles are relaxed, my heart and lungs are relaxed, my head is relaxed, my whole being is completely relaxed.' After about five minutes I would be in a sleepy drowsy state, and then I affirmed the following truth: 'The perfection of God is now being expressed through me. The idea of perfect health is now filling my subconscious mind. The image God has of me is a perfect image, and my subconscious mind recreates my body in perfect accordance with the perfect image held in the mind of God.'" This minister had a remarkable healing. This is a simple easy way of conveying the idea of perfect health to your subconscious mind.

Another wonderful way to convey the idea of health to your subconscious is through disciplined or scientific imagination. I told a man who was suffering from functional paralysis to make a vivid picture of himself walking around in his office, touching the desk, answering the telephone, and doing all the things he ordinarily would do if he were healed. I explained to him that this idea and mental picture of perfect health would be accepted by his subconscious mind.

He lived the role and actually felt himself back in the office. He knew that he was giving his subconscious mind something definite to work upon. His subconscious mind was the film upon which the picture was impressed. One day, after several weeks of frequent conditioning of the mind with this mental picture, the telephone rang by prearrangement and kept ringing while his wife and nurse were out. The telephone was about twelve feet away, but nevertheless he managed to answer it. He was healed at that hour. The healing power of his subconscious mind responded to his mental imagery, and a healing followed.

This man had a mental block, which prevented impulses from the brain reaching his legs; therefore, he said he could not walk. When he shifted his attention to the healing power within him, the power flowed through his focused attention, enabling him to walk.

Whatsoever ye shall ask in prayer, believing, ye shall receive. MATTHEW 21:22.

IDEAS WORTH REMEMBERING

1. Your subconscious mind controls all the vital processes of your body and knows the answer to all problems.
2. Prior to sleep, turn over a specific request to your subconscious mind and prove its miracle-working power to yourself.
3. Whatever you impress on your subconscious mind is

expressed on the screen of space as conditions, experiences, and events. Therefore, you should carefully watch all ideas and thoughts entertained in your conscious mind.

4. The law of action and reaction is universal. Your thought is action, and the reaction is the automatic response of your subconscious mind to your thought. Watch your thoughts!

5. All frustration is due to unfulfilled desires. If you dwell on obstacles, delays, and difficulties, your subconscious mind responds accordingly, and you are blocking your own good.

6. The Life Principle will flow through you rhythmically and harmoniously if you consciously affirm: "I believe that the subconscious power which gave me this desire is now fulfilling it through me." This dissolves all conflicts.

7. You can interfere with the normal rhythm of your heart, lungs, and other organs by worry, anxiety, and fear. Feed your subconscious with thoughts of harmony, health, and peace, and all the functions of your body will become normal again.

8. Keep your conscious mind busy with the expectation of the best, and your subconscious will faithfully reproduce your habitual thinking.

9. Imagine the happy ending or solution to your problem, feel the thrill of accomplishment, and what you imagine and feel will be accepted by your subconscious mind and bring it to pass.

MENTAL HEALINGS
IN ANCIENT TIMES

Down through the ages men of all nations have somehow instinctively believed that somewhere there resided a healing power which could restore to normal the functions and sensations of man's body. They believed that this strange power could be invoked under certain conditions, and that the alleviation of human suffering would follow. The history of all nations presents testimony in support of this belief.

In the early history of the world the power of secretly influencing men for good or evil, including the healing of the sick, was said to be possessed by the priests and holy men of all nations. Healing of the sick was supposed to be a power derived directly by them from God, and the procedures and processes of healing varied throughout the world. The healing processes took the form of supplications to God attended by various ceremonies, such as the laying on of hands, incantations, and the application of amulets, talismans, rings, relics, and images.

For example, in the religions of antiquity priests in the ancient temples gave drugs to the patient and practiced hypnotic suggestions prior to the patient's sleep, telling him that the gods would visit him in his sleep and heal him. Many healings followed. Obviously, all this was the work of potent suggestions to the subconscious mind.

After the performance of certain mysterious rites, the devotees of Hecate would see the goddess during sleep, provided that before going to sleep they had prayed to her according to weird and fantastic instructions. They were told to mix lizards with resin, frankincense, and myrrh, and pound all this together in the open air under the crescent moon. Healings were reported in many cases following this grotesque procedure.

It is obvious that these strange procedures, as mentioned in the illustrations given, favored suggestion and acceptance by the subconscious mind of these people by making a powerful appeal to their imagination. Actually, in all these healings, the subconscious mind of the subject was the healer.

In all ages unofficial healers have obtained remarkable results in cases where authorized medical skill has failed. This gives cause for thought. How do these healers in all parts of the world effect their cures? The answer to all these healings is due to the blind belief of the sick person which released the healing power resident in his subconscious mind. Many of the remedies and methods employed were rather strange and fantastic which fired the imagination of the patients, causing an aroused emotional state. This state of mind facilitated the suggestion of health, and was accepted both by the conscious and subconscious mind of the sick. This will be elaborated on further in the next chapter.

BIBLICAL ACCOUNTS ON THE USE
OF THE SUBCONSCIOUS POWERS

What things soever ye desire, when ye pray, believe that ye receive them, and ye shall have them. MARK 11:24.

Note the difference in tenses. The inspired writer tells us to believe and accept as true the fact that our desire has already been accomplished and fulfilled, that it is already completed, and that its realization will follow as a thing in the future.

The success of this technique depends on the confident conviction that the thought, the idea, the picture is already a fact in mind. In order for anything to have substance in the realm of mind, it must be thought of as actually existing there.

Here in a few cryptic words is a concise and specific direction for making use of the creative power of thought by impressing upon the subconscious the particular thing which you desire. Your thought, idea, plan, or purpose is as real on its own plane as your hand or your heart. In following the Biblical technique, you completely eliminate from your mind all consideration of conditions, circumstances, or anything which might imply adverse contingencies. You are planting a seed (concept) in the mind which, if you leave it undisturbed, will infallibly germinate into external fruition.

The prime condition which Jesus insisted upon was faith. Over and over again you read in the Bible, *According to your faith is it done unto you.* If you plant certain types of seeds in the ground, you have faith they will grow after their kind. This is the way of seeds, and trusting the laws of growth and agriculture, you know that the seeds will come forth after their kind. Faith as mentioned in the Bible is a way of thinking, an attitude of mind, an inner certitude, knowing that the idea you fully accept in your conscious mind will be embodied in your subconscious mind and made manifest. Faith is, in a sense, accepting as true what your reason and senses deny, i.e., a shutting out of the little, rational, analytical, conscious mind and embracing an attitude of complete reliance on the inner power of your subconscious mind.

A classical instance of Bible technique is recorded in MATTHEW 9:28–30. *And when he was come into the house, the blind men came to him: and Jesus saith unto them, Believe ye that I am able to do this? They said unto him, Yea, Lord. Then touched he their eyes, saying, according to your faith be it unto you. And their eyes were opened; and Jesus straitly charged them, saying, See that no man know it.*

In the words *according to your faith be it unto you,* you can see that Jesus was actually appealing to the cooperation of the subconscious mind of the blind men. Their faith was their great expectancy, their inner feeling, their inner conviction that something miraculous would happen, and that their prayer would be answered, and it was. This is the time-honored technique of healing, utilized alike by all healing groups throughout the world regardless of religious affiliation.

In the words *see that no man know it,* Jesus enjoins the newly healed patients not to discuss their healing because they might be subjected to the skeptical and derogatory criticisms of the unbelieving. This might tend to undo the benefits they had received at the hand of Jesus by depositing thoughts of fear, doubt, and anxiety in the subconscious mind.

. . . for with authority and power he commandeth the unclean spirits, and they come out. LUKE 4:36.

When the sick came to Jesus to be healed, they were healed by their faith together with his faith and understanding of the healing power of the subconscious mind. Whatever he decreed, he felt inwardly to be true. He and the people needing help were in the one universal subjective mind, and his silent inner knowing and conviction of the healing power changed the negative destructive patterns in the patients' subconscious. The resultant healings were the automatic response to the internal mental change. His command was his appeal to the subconscious mind of the patients plus his awareness, feeling, and absolute trust in the response of the subconscious mind to the words which he spoke with authority.

MIRACLES AT VARIOUS SHRINES
THROUGHOUT THE WORLD

It is an established fact that cures have taken place at various shrines throughout the world, such as in Japan, India, Europe, and America. I have visited several of the famous shrines in Japan. At the world famous shrine called Diabutsu is a gigantic divinity of bronze where Buddha is seated with folded hands, and the head is inclined in an attitude of profound contemplative ecstasy. It is 42 feet in height and is called the great Buddha. Here I saw young and old making offerings at its feet. Money, fruit, rice, and oranges were offered. Candles were lit, incense was burned, and prayers of petition recited.

The guide explained the chant of a young girl as she murmured a prayer, bowed low, and placed two oranges as an offering. She also lit a candle. He said she had lost her voice, and it was restored at the shrine. She was thanking Buddha for restoring her voice. She had the simple faith that Buddha would give her back her singing voice if she followed a certain ritual, fasted, and made certain offerings. All this helped to kindle faith and expectancy, resulting in a conditioning of her mind to the point of belief. Her subconscious mind responded to her belief.

To illustrate further the power of imagination and blind belief I will relate the case of a relative of mine who had tuberculosis. His lungs were badly diseased. His son decided to heal his father. He came home to Perth, Western Australia, where his father lived, and said to him that he had met a monk who had returned from one of the healing shrines in Europe. This monk sold him a piece of the true cross. He said that he gave the monk the equivalent of $500 for it.

This young man had actually picked up a splinter of wood from the sidewalk, went to the jeweler's, and had it set in a ring so that it looked real. He told his father that many were healed just by touching the ring or the cross. He inflamed and fired his father's imagination to the point that the old gentleman snatched the ring from him, placed it over his chest, prayed silently, and went to sleep. In the morning he was healed. All the clinic's tests proved negative.

You know, of course, it was not the splinter of wood from the sidewalk that healed him. It was his imagination aroused to an intense degree, plus the confident expectancy of a perfect healing. Imagination was joined to faith or subjective feeling, and the union of the two brought about a healing. The father never learned of the trick that had been played upon him. If he had, he probably would have had a relapse. He remained completely cured and passed away fifteen years later at the age of 89.

ONE UNIVERSAL HEALING PRINCIPLE

It is a well-known fact that all of the various schools of healing effect cures of the most wonderful character. The most obvious conclusion, which strikes your mind is that there must be some underlying principle which is common to them all, namely, the subconscious mind, and the one process of healing is faith.

It will now be in order to recall to your mind once more the following fundamental truths:

First that you possess mental functions which have been distinguished by designating one the conscious mind and the other the subconscious mind.

Secondly, your subconscious mind is constantly amenable to the power of suggestion. Furthermore, your subconscious mind has complete control of the functions, conditions, and sensations of your body.

I venture to believe that all the readers of this book are familiar with the fact that symptoms of almost any disease can be induced in hypnotic subjects by suggestion. For example, a subject in the hypnotic state can develop a high temperature, flushed face, or chills according to the nature of the suggestion given. By experiment, you can suggest to the person that he is paralyzed and cannot walk: it will be so. By illustration, you can hold a cup of cold water under the nose of the hypnotic subject and tell him, "This is full of pepper; smell it!" He will proceed to sneeze. What do you think caused him to sneeze, the water or the suggestion?

If a man says he is allergic to Timothy grass, you can place a synthetic flower or an empty glass in front of his nose, when he is in a hypnotic state, and tell him it is Timothy grass. He will portray the usual allergic symptoms. This indicates that the cause of the disease is in the mind. The healing of the disease can also take place mentally.

You realize that remarkable healings take place through osteopathy, chiropractic medicine, and naturopathy, as well as through all the various religious bodies throughout the world, but it is obvious that all of these healings are brought about through the subconscious mind—the only healer there is.

Notice how it heals a cut on your face caused by shaving. It knows exactly how to do it. The doctor dresses the wound and says, "Nature heals it!" Nature refers to natural law, the law of the subconscious mind, or self-preservation which is the function of the subconscious mind. The instinct of self-preservation is the first law of nature. Your strongest instinct is the most potent of all autosuggestions.

WIDELY DIFFERENT THEORIES

It would be tedious and unprofitable to discuss to any great extent the numerous theories advanced by different religious sects and prayer therapy groups. There are a great number who claim that because their theory produces results it is, therefore, the correct one. This, as explained in this chapter, cannot be true.

You are aware that there are all types of healing. Franz Anton Mesmer, a German physician (1734–1815) who practiced in Paris, discovered that by applying magnets to the diseased body, he could cure that disease miraculously. He also performed cures with various other pieces of glass and metals. He discontinued this form of healing and claimed that his cures were due to "animal magnetism," theorizing that this substance was projected from the healer to the patient.

His method of treating disease from then on was by hypnotism, which was called mesmerism in his day. Other physicians said that all his healings were due to suggestion and nothing else.

All of these groups, such as psychiatrists, psychologists, osteopaths, chiropractors, physicians, and all the churches are using the one universal power resident in the subconscious mind. Each may proclaim the healings are due to their theory. The process of all healing is a definite, positive, mental attitude, an inner attitude, or a way of thinking, called faith. Healing is due to a confident expectancy, which acts as a powerful suggestion to the subconscious mind releasing its healing potency.

One man does not heal by a different power than another. It is true he may have his own theory or method. There is only one process of healing and that is faith. There is only one healing power, namely, your subconscious mind. Select the theory and method you prefer. You can rest assured, if you have faith, you shall get results.

VIEWS OF PARACELSUS

Philippus Paracelsus, a famous Swiss alchemist and physician, who lived from 1493 to 1541, was a great healer in his day. He stated what is now an obvious scientific fact when he uttered these words, "Whether the object of your faith be real or false, you will nevertheless obtain the same effects. Thus, if I believed in Saint Peter's statue as I should have believed in Saint Peter himself, I shall obtain the same effects that I should have obtained from Saint Peter. But that is superstition. Faith, however, produces miracles; and whether it is true or false faith, it will always produce the same wonders."

The views of Paracelsus were also entertained in the sixteenth century by Pietro Pomponazzi, an Italian philosopher and contemporary of Paracelsus, who said, "We can easily conceive the marvelous effects which confidence and imagination can produce, particularly when both qualities are reciprocated between the subjects and the person who influences them. The cures attributed to the influence of certain relics are the effect of their imagination and confidence. Quacks and philosophers know that if the bones of any skeleton were put in place of the saint's bones, the sick would nonetheless experience beneficial effects, if they believed that they were veritable relics."

Then, if you believe in the bones of saints to heal, or if you believe in the healing power of certain waters, you will get results because of the powerful suggestion given to your subconscious mind. It is the latter that does the healing.

BERNHEIM'S EXPERIMENTS

Hippolyte Bernheim, professor of medicine at Nancy, France, 1910–1919, was the expounder of the fact that the suggestion of the physician to the patient was exerted through the subconscious mind.

Bernheim, in his *Suggestive Therapeutics,* page 197, tells a story of a man with paralysis of the tongue which had yielded to no form of treatment. His doctor told the patient that he had a new instrument with which he promised to heal him. He introduced a pocket thermometer into the patient's mouth. The patient imagined it to be the instrument, which was to save him. In a few moments he cried out joyfully that he could once more move his tongue freely.

"Among our cases," continues Bernheim, "facts of the same sort will be found. A young girl came into my office, having suffered from complete loss of speech for nearly four weeks. After making sure of the diagnosis, I told my students that loss of speech sometimes yielded instantly to electricity, which might act simply by its suggestive influence. I sent for the induction apparatus. I applied my hand over the larynx and moved a little, and said, 'Now you can speak aloud.' In an instant I made her say 'a,' then 'b,' then 'Maria.' She continued to speak distinctly; the loss of voice had disappeared."

Here Bernheim is showing the power of faith and expectancy on the part of the patient which acts as a powerful suggestion to the subconscious mind.

PRODUCING A BLISTER BY SUGGESTION

Bernheim states that he produced a blister on the back of a patient's neck by applying a postage stamp and suggesting to the patient that it was a fly-plaster. This has been confirmed by the experiments and experiences of many doctors in many parts of the world, which leave no doubt that structural changes are a possible result of oral suggestion to patients.

THE CAUSE OF BLOODY STIGMATA

In Hudson's *Law of Psychic Phenomena*, page 153, he states, "Hemorrhages and bloody stigmata may be induced in certain subjects by means of suggestion.

"Dr. M. Bourru put a subject into the somnambulistic condition, and gave him the following suggestion: 'At four o'clock this afternoon, after the hypnosis, you will come into my office, sit down in the armchair, cross your arms upon your breast, and your nose will begin to bleed.' At the hour appointed the young man did as directed. Several drops of blood came from the left nostril.

"On another occasion the same investigator traced the patient's name on both his forearms with the dull point of an instrument. Then when the patient was in the somnambulistic condition, he said, 'At four o'clock this afternoon you will go to sleep, and your arms will bleed along the lines which I have traced, and your name will appear written on your arms in letters of blood.' He was watched at four o'clock and seen to fall asleep. On the left arm the letters stood out in bright relief, and in several places there were drops of blood. The letters were still visible three months afterward, although they had gradually grown faint."

These facts demonstrate at once the correctness of the two fundamental propositions previously stated, namely, the constant amenability of the subconscious mind to the power of suggestion and the perfect control, which the subconscious mind exercises over the functions, sensations, and conditions of the body.

All the foregoing phenomena dramatize vividly abnormal conditions induced by suggestion, and are conclusive proof that *as a man thinketh in his heart* [subconscious mind] *so is he.*

HEALING POINTS IN REVIEW

1. Remind yourself frequently that the healing power is in your own subconscious mind.

2. Know that faith is like a seed planted in the ground; it grows after its kind. Plant the idea (seed) in your mind, water and fertilize it with expectancy, and it will manifest.

3. The idea you have for a book, new invention, or play is real in your mind. This is why you can believe you have it now. Believe in the reality of your idea, plan, or invention, and as you do, it will become manifest.

4. In praying for another, know that your silent inner knowing of wholeness, beauty, and perfection can change the negative patterns of the other's subconscious mind and bring about wonderful results.

5. The miraculous healings you hear about at various shrines are due to imagination and blind faith which act on the subconscious mind, releasing the healing power.

6. All disease originates in the mind. Nothing appears on the body unless there is a mental pattern corresponding to it.

7. The symptoms of almost any disease can be induced in you by hypnotic suggestion. This shows you the power of your thought.

8. There is only one process of healing and that is faith. There is only one healing power, namely, your subconscious mind.

9. Whether the object of your faith is real or false, you will get results. Your subconscious mind responds to the thought in your mind. Look upon faith as a thought in your mind, and that will suffice.

MENTAL HEALINGS
IN MODERN TIMES

Everyone is definitely concerned with the healing of bodily conditions and human affairs. What is it that heals? Where is this healing power? These are questions asked by everyone. The answer is that this healing power is in the subconscious mind of each person, and a changed mental attitude on the part of the sick person releases this healing power.

No mental or religious science practitioner, psychologist, psychiatrist, or medical doctor ever healed a patient. There is an old saying, "The doctor dresses the wound, but God heals it." The psychologist or psychiatrist proceeds to remove the mental blocks in the patient so that the healing principle may be released, restoring the patient to health. Likewise, the surgeon removes the physical block enabling the healing currents to function normally. No physician, surgeon, or mental science practitioner claims that "he healed the patient." The one healing power is called by many names—Nature, Life, God, Creative Intelligence, and Subconscious Power.

As previously outlined, there are many different methods used to remove the mental, emotional, and physical blocks which inhibit the flow of the healing life principle animating all of us. The healing principle resident in your subconscious mind can and will, if properly directed by you or some other person, heal your mind and body of all disease. This healing principle is operative in all men regardless of creed, color, or race. You do not have to belong to some particular church in order to use and participate in this healing process. Your subconscious will heal the burn or cut on your hand even though you profess to be an atheist or agnostic.

The modern mental therapeutic procedure is based on the truth that the infinite intelligence and power of your subconscious mind responds according to your faith. The mental science practitioner or minister follows the injunction of the Bible, i.e., he goes into his closet and shuts the door, which means he stills his mind, relaxes, lets go, and thinks of the infinite healing presence within him. He closes the door of his mind to all outside distractions as well as appearances, and then he quietly and knowingly turns over his request or desire to his subconscious mind, realizing that the intelligence of his mind will answer him according to his specific needs.

The most wonderful thing to know is this: Imagine the end desired and feel its reality; then the infinite life principle will respond to your conscious choice and your conscious request. This is the meaning of *believe you have received, and you shall receive.* This is what the modern mental scientist does when he practices prayer therapy.

ONE PROCESS OF HEALING

There is only one universal healing principle operating through everything—the cat, the dog, the tree, the grass, the wind, the earth—for everything is alive. This life principle operates through the animal, vegetable, and mineral kingdoms as instinct and the law of growth. Man is consciously aware of this life principle, and he can consciously direct it to bless himself in countless ways.

There are many different approaches, techniques, and methods in using the universal power, but there is only one process of healing, which is faith, for *according to your faith is it done unto you*.

THE LAW OF BELIEF

All religions of the world represent forms of belief, and these beliefs are explained in many ways. The law of life is belief. What do you believe about yourself, life, and the universe? *It is done unto you as you believe.*

Belief is a thought in your mind, which causes the power of your subconscious to be distributed into all phases of your life according to your thinking habits. You must realize the Bible is not talking about your belief in some ritual, ceremony, form, institution, man, or formula. It is talking about belief itself. The belief of your mind is simply the thought of your mind. *If thou canst believe, all things are possible to him that believeth.* MARK 9:23.

It is foolish to believe in something to hurt or harm you. Remember, it is not the thing believed in that hurts or harms you, but the belief or thought in your mind, which creates the result. All your experiences, all your actions, and all the events and circumstances of your life are but the reflections and reactions to your own thought.

PRAYER THERAPY IS THE COMBINED FUNCTION OF THE CONSCIOUS AND SUBCONSCIOUS MIND SCIENTIFICALLY DIRECTED

Prayer therapy is the synchronized, harmonious, and intelligent function of the conscious and subconscious levels of mind specifically directed for a definite purpose. In scientific prayer or prayer therapy, you must know what you are doing and why you are doing it. You trust the law of healing. Prayer therapy is sometimes referred to as mental treatment, and another term is scientific prayer.

In prayer therapy you consciously choose a certain idea, mental picture, or plan which you desire to experience. You realize your capacity to convey this idea or mental image to your subconscious by feeling the reality of the state assumed. As you remain faithful in your mental attitude, your prayer will be answered. Prayer therapy is a definite mental action for a definite specific purpose.

Let us suppose that you decide to heal a certain difficulty by prayer therapy. You are aware that your problem or sickness, whatever it may be, must be caused by negative thoughts charged with fear and lodged in your subconscious mind, and that if you can succeed in cleansing your mind of these thoughts, you will get a healing.

You, therefore, turn to the healing power within your own subconscious mind and remind yourself of its infinite power and intelligence and its capacity to heal all conditions. As you dwell on these truths, your fear will begin to dissolve, and the recollection of these truths also corrects the erroneous beliefs.

You give thanks for the healing that you know will come, and then you keep your mind off the difficulty until you feel guided, after an interval, to pray again. While you are praying, you absolutely refuse to give any power to the negative conditions or to admit for a second that the healing will not come. This attitude of mind brings about the harmonious union of the conscious and subconscious mind, which releases the healing power.

FAITH HEALING, WHAT IT MEANS,
AND HOW BLIND FAITH WORKS

What is popularly termed faith healing is not the faith mentioned in the Bible, which means knowledge of the interaction of the conscious and subconscious mind. A faith healer is one who heals without any real scientific understanding of the powers and forces involved. He may claim that he has a special gift of healing, and the sick person's blind belief in him or his powers may bring results.

The voodoo doctor in South Africa and other parts of the world may heal by incantations, or a person may be healed by touching the so-called bones of saints, or anything else which cause the patients to honestly believe in the method or process.

Any method which causes you to move from fear and worry to faith and expectancy will heal. There are many persons, each of whom claims that because his personal theory produces results, it is, therefore, the correct one. This, as already explained in this chapter, cannot be true.

To illustrate how blind faith works: You will recall our discussion of the German physician Franz Anton Mesmer. In 1776 he claimed many cures when he stroked diseased bodies with artificial magnets. Later on he threw away his magnets and evolved the theory of animal magnetism. This he held to be a fluid, which pervades the universe, but is most active in the human organism.

He claimed that this magnetic fluid, which was going forth from him to his patients healed them. People flocked to him, and many wonderful cures were effected.

Mesmer moved to Paris, and while there the Government appointed a commission composed of physicians and members of the Academy of Science, of which Benjamin

Franklin was a member, to investigate his cures. The report admitted the leading facts claimed by Mesmer, but held that there was no evidence to prove the correctness of his magnetic fluid theory, and said the effects were due to the imagination of the patients.

Soon after this, Mesmer was driven into exile, and died in 1815. Shortly afterward, Dr. Braid of Manchester undertook to show that magnetic fluid had nothing to do with the production of the healings of Dr. Mesmer. Dr. Braid discovered that patients could be thrown into hypnotic sleep by suggestion, during which many of the well-known phenomena ascribed to magnetism by Mesmer could be produced.

You can readily see that all these cures were undoubtedly brought about by the active imagination of the patients together with a powerful suggestion of health to their subconscious minds. All this could be termed blind faith as there was no understanding in those days as to how the cures were brought about.

SUBJECTIVE FAITH AND WHAT IT MEANS

You will recall the proposition, which need not be repeated at length, that the subjective or subconscious mind of an individual is as amenable to the control of his own conscious objective mind as it is by the suggestions of another. It follows that whatever may be your objective belief, if you will assume to have faith actively or passively, your subconscious mind will be controlled by the suggestion, and your desire will be fulfilled.

The faith required in mental healings is a purely subjective faith, and it is attainable upon the cessation of active opposition on the part of the objective or conscious mind.

In the healing of the body it is, of course, desirable to

secure the concurrent faith of both the conscious and subconscious mind. However, it is not always essential if you will enter into a state of passivity and receptivity by relaxing the mind and the body and getting into a sleepy state. In this drowsy state your passivity becomes receptive to subjective impression.

Recently, I was asked by a man, "How is it that I got a healing through a minister? I did not believe what he said when he told me that there is no such thing as disease and that matter does not exist."

This man at first thought his intelligence was being insulted, and he protested against such a palpable absurdity. The explanation is simple. He was quieted by soothing words and told to get into a perfectly passive condition, to say nothing, and think of nothing for the time being. His minister also became passive, and affirmed quietly, peacefully, and constantly for about one half hour that this man would have perfect health, peace, harmony, and wholeness. He felt immense relief and was restored to health.

It is easy to see that his subjective faith had been made manifest by his passivity under treatment, and the suggestions of perfect healthfulness by the minister were conveyed to his subconscious mind. The two subjective minds were men *en rapport*.

The minister was not handicapped by antagonistic autosuggestions of the patient arising from objective doubt of the power of the healer or the correctness of the theory. In this sleepy, drowsy state the conscious mind resistance is reduced to a minimum, and results followed. The subconscious mind of the patient being necessarily controlled by such suggestion exercised its functions in accordance therewith, and a healing followed.

THE MEANING OF ABSENT TREATMENT

Suppose you learned that your mother was sick in New York City and you lived in Los Angeles. Your mother would not be physically present where you are, but you could pray for her. *It is the Father within which doeth the work.*

The creative law of mind (subconscious mind) serves you and will do the work. Its response to you is automatic. Your treatment is for the purpose of inducing an inner realization of health and harmony in your mentality. This inner realization, acting through the subconscious mind, operates through your mother's subconscious mind as there is but one creative mind. Your thoughts of health, vitality, and perfection operate through the one universal subjective mind, and set a law in motion on the subjective side of life, which manifests through her body as a healing.

In the mind principle there is no time or space. It is the same mind that operates through your mother no matter where she may be. In reality there is no absent treatment as opposed to present treatment for the universal mind is omnipresent. You do not try to send out thoughts or hold a thought. Your treatment is a conscious movement of thought, and as you become conscious of the qualities of health, well-being, and relaxation, these qualities will be resurrected in the experience of your mother, and results will follow.

The following is a perfect example of what is called absent treatment. Recently, a listener of our radio program in Los Angeles prayed as follows for her mother in New York who had a coronary thrombosis: "The healing presence is right where my mother is. Her bodily condition is but a reflection of her thought-life like shadows cast on the screen. I know that in order to change the images on the screen I must change the projection reel. My mind is the projection reel, and I now project in my own mind the image of wholeness, harmony, and perfect health for my mother. The infinite healing presence, which created my mother's body and all her organs is now saturating every atom of her being, and a river of peace flows through every cell of her body. The doctors are divinely guided and directed, and whoever touches my mother is guided to do the right thing. I know that disease has no ultimate reality; if it had, no one could be healed. I now align myself with the infinite principle of love and life, and I know and decree that harmony, health, and peace are now being expressed in my mother's body."

She prayed in the above manner several times daily, and her mother had a most remarkable recovery after a few days, much to the amazement of her specialist. He complimented her on her great faith in the power of God.

The conclusion arrived at in the daughter's mind set the creative law of mind in motion on the subjective side of life, which manifested itself through her mother's body as perfect health and harmony. What the daughter felt as true about her mother was simultaneously resurrected in the experience of her mother.

RELEASING THE KINETIC ACTION OF THE SUBCONSCIOUS MIND

A psychologist friend of mine told me that one of his lungs was infected. X rays and analysis showed the presence of tuberculosis. At night before going to sleep he would quietly affirm, "Every cell, nerve, tissue, and muscle of my lungs is now being made whole, pure, and perfect. My whole body is being restored to health and harmony."

These are not his exact words, but they represent the essence of what he affirmed. A complete healing followed in about a month's time. Subsequent X rays showed a perfect healing.

I wanted to know his method, so I asked him why he repeated the words prior to sleep. Here is his reply: "The kinetic action of the subconscious mind continues throughout your sleep-time period. Hence, give the subconscious mind something good to work on as you drop off into slumber." This was a very wise answer. In thinking of harmony and perfect health, he never mentioned his trouble by name.

I strongly suggest that you cease talking about your ailments or giving them a name. The only sap from which they draw life is your attention and fear of them. Like the above-mentioned psychologist, become a mental surgeon. Then your troubles will be cut off like dead branches are pruned from a tree.

If you are constantly naming your aches and symptoms, you inhibit the kinetic action, which means the release of the healing power and energy of your subconscious mind. Furthermore, by the law of your own mind, these imaginings tend to take shape, *As the thing I greatly feared*. Fill your mind with the great truths of life and walk forward in the light of love.

SUMMARY OF YOUR AIDS TO HEALTH

1. Find out what it is that heals you. Realize that correct directions given to your subconscious mind will heal your mind and body.

2. Develop a definite plan for turning over your requests or desires to your subconscious mind.

3. Imagine the end desired and feel its reality. Follow it through, and you will get definite results.

4. Decide what belief is. Know that belief is a thought in your mind, and what you think you create.

5. It is foolish to believe in sickness as something to hurt or to harm you. Believe in perfect health, prosperity, peace, wealth, and divine guidance.

6. Great and noble thoughts upon which you habitually dwell become great acts.

7. Apply the power of prayer therapy in your life. Choose a certain plan, idea, or mental picture. Mentally and emotionally unite with that idea, and as you remain faithful to your mental attitude, your prayer will be answered.

8. Always remember, if you really want the power to heal, you can have it through faith, which means knowledge of the working of your conscious and subconscious mind. Faith comes with understanding.

9. Blind faith means that a person may get results in healing without any scientific understanding of the powers and forces involved.

10. Learn to pray for your loved ones who may be ill. Quiet your mind, and your thoughts of health, vitality, and perfection operating through the one universal subjective mind will be felt and resurrected in the mind of your loved one.

PRACTICAL TECHNIQUES IN MENTAL HEALINGS

An engineer has a technique and a process for building a bridge or an engine. Like the engineer, your mind also has a technique for governing, controlling, and directing your life. You must realize that methods and techniques are primary.

In building the Golden Gate bridge, the chief engineer understood mathematical principles, stresses, and strains. Secondly, he had a picture of the ideal bridge across the bay. The third step was his application of tried and proven methods by which the principles were implemented until the bridge took form and we drive on it. There also are techniques and methods by which your prayers are answered. If your prayer is answered, there is a way in which it is answered, and this is a scientific way. Nothing happens by chance. This is a world of law and order. In this chapter you will find practical techniques for the unfolding and nurture of your spiritual life. Your prayers must not remain up in the air like a balloon. They must go somewhere and accomplish something in your life.

When we come to analyze prayer we discover there are many different approaches and methods. We will not consider in this book the formal, ritual prayers used in religious services. These have an important place in group worship. We are immediately concerned with the methods of personal prayer as it is applied in your daily life and as it is used to help others.

Prayer is the formulation of an idea concerning something we wish to accomplish. Prayer is the soul's sincere desire. Your desire is your prayer. It comes out of your deepest needs and it reveals the things you want in life. *Blessed are they that hunger and thirst after righteousness: for they shall be filled.* That is really prayer, life's hunger and thirst for peace, harmony, health, joy, and all the other blessings of life.

THE PASSING-OVER TECHNIQUE FOR IMPREGNATING THE SUBCONSCIOUS

This consists essentially in inducing the subconscious mind to take over your request as handed it by the conscious mind. This passing-over is best accomplished in the reverie-like state. Know that in your deeper mind are Infinite Intelligence and Infinite Power. Just calmly think over what you want; see it coming into fuller fruition from this moment forward. Be like the little girl who had a very bad cough and a sore throat. She declared firmly and repeatedly, "It is passing away now. It is passing away now." It passed away in about an hour. Use this technique with complete simplicity and naïveté.

YOUR SUBCONSCIOUS WILL ACCEPT YOUR BLUEPRINT

If you were building a new home for yourself and family, you know that you would be intensely interested in regard to the blueprint for your home; you would see to it that the builders conformed to the blueprint. You would watch the material and select only the best wood, steel, in fact, the best of everything. What about your mental home and your mental blueprint for happiness and abundance? All your experiences and everything that enters into your life depend upon the nature of the mental building blocks which you use in the construction of your mental home.

If your blueprint is full of mental patterns of fear, worry, anxiety, or lack, and if you are despondent, doubtful, and cynical, then the texture of the mental material you are weaving into your mind will come forth as more toil, care, tension, anxiety, and limitation of all kinds.

The most fundamental and the most far-reaching activity in life is that which you build into your mentality every waking hour. Your word is silent and invisible; nevertheless, it is real.

You are building your mental home all the time, and your thought and mental imagery represent your blueprint. Hour by hour, moment by moment, you can build radiant health, success, and happiness by the thoughts you think, the ideas which you harbor, the beliefs that you accept, and the scenes that you rehearse in the hidden studio of your mind. This stately mansion, upon the construction of which you are perpetually engaged, is your personality, your identity in this plane, your whole life story on this earth.

Get a new blueprint; build silently by realizing peace, harmony, joy, and good will in the present moment. By dwelling upon these things and claiming them, your subconscious will accept your blueprint and bring all these things to pass. *By their fruits ye shall know them.*

THE SCIENCE AND ART OF TRUE PRAYER

The term "science" means knowledge which is coordinated, arranged, and systematized. Let us think of the science and art of true prayer as it deals with the fundamental principles of life and the techniques and processes by which they can be demonstrated in your life, as well as in the life of every human being when he applies them faithfully. The art is your technique or process, and the science behind it is the definite response of creative mind to your mental picture or thought.

Ask, and it shall be given you; seek, and ye shall find; knock, and it shall be opened unto you. MATTHEW 7:7.

Here you are told you shall receive that for which you ask. It shall be opened to you when you knock, and you shall find that for which you are searching. This teaching implies the definiteness of mental and spiritual laws. There is always a direct response from the Infinite Intelligence of your subconscious mind to your conscious thinking. If you ask for bread, you will not receive a stone. You must ask *believing,* if you are to receive. Your mind moves from the thought to the thing. Unless there is first an image in the mind, it cannot move, for there would be nothing for it to move toward. Your prayer, which is your mental act, must be accepted as an image in your mind before the power from your subconscious will play upon it and make it productive. You must reach a point of acceptance in your mind, an unqualified and undisputed state of agreement.

This contemplation should be accompanied by a feeling of joy and restfulness in foreseeing the certain accomplishment of your desire. The sound basis for the art and science of true prayer is your knowledge and complete confidence that the movement of your conscious mind will gain a definite response from your subconscious mind, which is one with boundless wisdom and infinite power. By following this procedure, your prayers will be answered.

THE VISUALIZATION TECHNIQUE

The easiest and most obvious way to formulate an idea is to visualize it, to see it in your mind's eye as vividly as if it were alive. You can see with the naked eye only what already exists in the external world; in a similar way, that which you can visualize in your mind's eye already exists in the invisible realms of your mind. Any picture, which you have in your mind, is *the substance of things hoped for and the evidence of things not seen*. What you form in your imagination is as real as any part of your body. The idea and the thought are real and will one day appear in your objective world if you are faithful to your mental image.

This process of thinking forms impressions in your mind; these impressions in turn become manifested as facts and experiences in your life. The builder visualizes the type of building he wants; he sees it as he desires it to be completed. His imagery and thought processes become a plastic mold from which the building will emerge—a beautiful or an ugly one, a skyscraper or a very low one. His mental imagery is projected as it is drawn on paper. Eventually, the contractor and his workers gather the essential materials, and the building progresses until it stands finished, conforming perfectly to the mental patterns of the architect.

I use the visualization technique prior to speaking from the platform. I quiet the wheels of my mind in order that I may present to the subconscious mind my images of thought. Then, I picture the entire auditorium and the seats filled with men and women, and each one of them illumined and inspired by the infinite healing presence within each one. I see them as radiant, happy, and free.

Having first built up the idea in my imagination, I quietly sustain it there as a mental picture while I imagine I hear men and women saying, "I am healed," "I feel wonderful," "I've had an instantaneous healing," "I'm transformed." I keep this up for about ten minutes or more, knowing and feeling that each person's mind and body are saturated with love, wholeness, beauty, and perfection. My awareness grows to the point where in my mind I can actually hear the voices of the multitude proclaiming their health and happiness; then I release the whole picture and go onto the platform. Almost every Sunday some people stop and say that their prayers were answered.

MENTAL MOVIE METHOD

The Chinese say, "A picture is worth a thousand words." William James, the father of American psychology, stressed the fact that the subconscious mind will bring to pass any picture held in the mind and backed by faith. *Act as though I am, and I will be.*

A number of years ago I was in the Middle West lecturing in several states, and I desired to have a permanent location in the general area from which I could serve those who desired help. I traveled far, but the desire did not leave my mind. One evening, while in a hotel in Spokane, Washington, I relaxed completely on a couch, immobilized my attention, and in a quiet, passive manner imagined that I was talking to a large audience, saying in effect, "I am glad to be here; I have prayed for the ideal opportunity." I saw in my mind's eye the imaginary audience, and I felt the reality of it all. I played the role of the actor, dramatized this mental movie, and felt satisfied that this picture was being conveyed to my subconscious mind, which would bring it to pass in its own way. The next morning, on awakening, I felt a great sense of peace and satisfaction, and in a few days' time I received a telegram asking me to take over an organization in the Midwest, which I did, and I enjoyed it immensely for several years.

The method outlined here appeals to many who have described it as "the mental movie method." I have received numerous letters from people who listen to my radio talks and weekly public lectures, telling me of the wonderful results they get using this technique in the sale of their property. I suggest to those who have homes or property for sale that they satisfy themselves in their own mind that their price is right. Then, I claim that the Infinite Intelligence is attracting to them the buyer who really wants to have the property and who will love it and prosper in it. After having done this I suggest that they quiet their mind, relax, let go, and get into a drowsy, sleepy state, which reduces all mental effort to a minimum. Then, they are to picture the check in their hands, rejoice in the check, give thanks for the check, and go off to sleep feeling the naturalness of the whole mental movie created in their own mind. They must act as though it were an objective reality, and the subconscious mind will take it as an impression, and through the deeper currents of the mind the buyer and the seller are brought together. A mental picture held in the mind, backed by faith, will come to pass.

THE BAUDOIN TECHNIQUE

Charles Baudoin was a professor at the Rousseau Institute in France. He was a brilliant psychotherapist and a research director of the New Nancy School of Healing, who in 1910 taught that the best way to impress the subconscious mind was to enter into a drowsy, sleepy state, or a state akin to sleep in which all effort was reduced to a minimum. Then in a quiet, passive, receptive way, by reflection, he would convey the idea to the subconscious. The following is his formula: "A very simple way of securing this (impregnation of the subconscious mind) is to condense the idea which is to be the object of suggestion, to sum it up in a brief phrase which can be readily graven on the memory, and to repeat it over and over again as a lullaby."

Some years ago, a young lady in Los Angeles was engaged in a prolonged bitter family lawsuit over a will. Her husband had bequeathed his entire estate to her, and his sons and daughters by a previous marriage were bitterly fighting to break the will. The Baudoin technique was outlined to her, and this is what she did: She relaxed her body in an armchair, entered into the sleepy state and, as suggested, condensed the idea of her need into a phrase consisting of six words easily graven on the memory. "It is finished in Divine Order." The significance to her of these words meant that Infinite Intelligence operating through the laws of her subconscious mind would bring about a harmonious adjustment through the principle of harmony. She continued this procedure every night for about ten nights. After she got into a sleepy state, she would affirm slowly, quietly, and feelingly the statement: "It is finished in Divine Order," over and over again, feeling a sense of inner peace and an all-pervading tranquility; then she went off into her deep, normal sleep.

On the morning of the eleventh day, following the use of the above technique, she awakened with a sense of well-being, a conviction that *it was finished*. Her attorney called her the same day, saying that the opposing attorney and his clients were willing to settle. A harmonious agreement was reached, and litigation was discontinued.

THE SLEEPING TECHNIQUE

By entering into a sleepy, drowsy state, effort is reduced to a minimum. The conscious mind is submerged to a great extent when in a sleepy state. The reason for this is that the highest degree of outcropping of the subconscious occurs prior to sleep and just after we awaken. In this state the negative thoughts, which tend to neutralize your desire and so prevent acceptance by your subconscious mind, are no longer present.

Suppose you want to get rid of a destructive habit. Assume a comfortable posture, relax your body, and be still. Get into a sleepy state, and in that sleepy state, say quietly, over and over again as a lullaby, "I am completely free from this habit; harmony and peace of mind reign supreme." Repeat the above slowly, quietly, and lovingly for five or ten minutes night and morning. Each time you repeat the words the emotional value becomes greater. When the urge comes to repeat the negative habit, repeat the above formula out loud by yourself. By this means you induce the subconscious to accept the idea, and a healing follows.

THE "THANK YOU" TECHNIQUE

In the Bible, Paul recommends that we make known our requests with praise and thanksgiving. Some extraordinary results follow this simple method of prayer. The thankful heart is always close to the creative forces of the universe, causing countless blessings to flow toward it by the law of reciprocal relationship, based on a cosmic law of action and reaction.

For instance, a father promises his son a car for graduation; the boy has not yet received the car, but he is very thankful and happy, and is as joyous as though he had actually received the car. He knows his father will fulfill his promise, and he is full of gratitude and joy even though he has not yet received the car, objectively speaking. He has, however, received it with joy and thankfulness in his mind.

I shall illustrate how Mr. Broke applied this technique with excellent results. He said, "Bills are piling up, I am out of work, I have three children and no money. What shall I do?" Regularly every night and morning, for a period of about three weeks, he repeated the words, "Thank you, Father, for my wealth," in a relaxed, peaceful manner until the feeling or mood of thankfulness dominated his mind. He imagined he was addressing the infinite power and intelligence within him knowing, of course, that he could not see the creative intelligence or infinite mind. He was seeing with the inner eye of spiritual perception, realizing that his thought-image of wealth was the *first cause,* relative to the money, position, and food he needed. His thought-feeling was the substance of wealth untrammeled by antecedent conditions of any kind. By repeating, "Thank you, Father," over and over again, his mind and heart were lifted up to the point of acceptance, and when fear, thoughts of lack, poverty, and distress came into his mind, he would say, "Thank you, Father," as often as necessary. He knew that as he kept up the thankful attitude he would recondition his mind to the idea of wealth, which is what happened.

The sequel to his prayer is very interesting. After praying in the above-mentioned manner, he met a former employer of his on the street whom he had not seen for twenty years. The man offered him a very lucrative position and advanced him $500 on a temporary loan. Today, Mr. Broke is vice president of the company for which he works. His recent remark to me was, "I shall never forget the wonders of 'Thank you, Father.' It has worked wonders for me."

THE AFFIRMATIVE METHOD

The effectiveness of an affirmation is determined largely by your understanding of the truth and the meaning back of the words, *"In praying use not vain repetition."* Therefore, the power of your affirmation lies in the intelligent application of definite and specific positives. For example, a boy adds three and three and puts down seven on the blackboard. The teacher affirms with mathematical certainty that three and three are six; therefore, the boy changes his figures accordingly. The teacher's statement did not make three and three equal six because the latter was already a mathematical truth. The mathematical truth caused the boy to rearrange the figures on the blackboard. It is abnormal to be sick; it is normal to be healthy. Health is the truth of your being. When you affirm health, harmony, and peace for yourself or another, and when you realize these are universal principles of your own being, you will rearrange the negative patterns of your subconscious mind based on your faith and understanding of that which you affirm.

The result of the affirmative process of prayer depends on your conforming to the principles of life, regardless of appearances. Consider for a moment that there is a principle of mathematics and none of error; there is a principle of truth but none of dishonesty. There is a principle of intelligence but none of ignorance; there is a principle of harmony and none of discord. There is a principle of health but none of disease, and there is a principle of abundance but none of poverty.

The affirmative method was chosen by the author for use on his sister who was to be operated on for the removal of gallstones in a hospital in England. The condition described was based on the diagnosis of hospital tests and the usual X-ray procedures. She asked me to pray for her. We were separated geographically about 6,500 miles, but there is no time or space in the mind principle. Infinite mind or intelligence is present in its entirety at every point simultaneously. I withdrew all thought from the contemplation of symptoms and from the corporeal personality altogether. I affirmed as follows: "This prayer is for my sister Catherine. She is relaxed and at peace, poised, balanced, serene, and calm. The healing intelligence of her subconscious mind, which created her body is now transforming every cell, nerve, tissue, muscle, and bone of her being according to the perfect pattern of all organs lodged in her subconscious mind. Silently, quietly, all distorted thought patterns in her subconscious mind are removed and dissolved, and the vitality, wholeness, and beauty of the life principle are made manifest in every atom of her being. She is now open and receptive to the healing currents, which are flowing through her like a river, restoring her to perfect health, harmony, and peace. All distortions and ugly images are now washed away by the infinite ocean of love and peace flowing through her, and it is so."

I affirmed the above several times a day, and at the end of two weeks my sister had an examination, which showed a remarkable healing, and the X ray proved negative.

To affirm is to state that it is so, and as you maintain this attitude of mind as true, regardless of all evidence to the contrary, you will receive an answer to your prayer. Your thought can only affirm, for even if you deny something, you are actually affirming the presence of what you deny. Repeating an affirmation, knowing what you are saying and why you are saying it, leads the mind to that state of consciousness where it accepts that which you state as true. Keep on affirming the truths of life until you get the subconscious reaction, which satisfies.

THE ARGUMENTATIVE METHOD

This method is just what the word implies. It stems from the procedure of Dr. Phineas Parkhurst Quimby of Maine. Dr. Quimby, a pioneer in mental and spiritual healing, lived and practiced in Belfast, Maine, about one hundred years ago.

A book called *The Quimby Manuscripts*, published in 1921 by Thomas Y. Crowell Company, New York City, and edited by Horatio Dresser, is available in your library. This book gives newspaper accounts of this man's remarkable results in prayer treatment of the sick. Quimby duplicated many of the healing miracles recorded in the Bible. In brief, the argumentative method employed according to Quimby consists of spiritual reasoning where you convince the patient and yourself that his sickness is due to his false belief, groundless fears, and negative patterns lodged in his subconscious mind. You reason it out clearly in your mind and convince your patient that the disease or ailment is due only to a distorted, twisted pattern of thought, which has taken form in his body. This wrong belief in some external power and external causes has now externalized itself as sickness, and can be changed by changing the thought patterns.

You explain to the sick person that the basis of all healing is a change of belief. You also point out that the subconscious mind created the body and all its organs; therefore, it knows how to heal it, can heal it, and is doing so now as you speak. You argue in the courtroom of your mind that the disease is a shadow of the mind based on disease-soaked, morbid thought imagery. You continue to build up all the evidence you can muster on behalf of the healing power within, which created all the organs in the first place, and which has a perfect pattern of every cell, nerve, and tissue within it. Then, you render a verdict in the courthouse of your mind in favor of yourself or your patient. You liberate the sick one by faith and spiritual understanding. Your mental and spiritual evidence is overwhelming; there being but one mind, what you feel as true will be resurrected in the experience of the patient. This procedure is essentially the argumentative method used by Dr. Quimby of Maine from 1849 to 1869.

THE ABSOLUTE METHOD IS LIKE
MODERN SOUND WAVE THERAPY

Many people throughout the world practice this form of prayer treatment with wonderful results. The person using the absolute method mentions the name of the patient, such as John Jones, then quietly and silently thinks of God and His qualities and attributes, such as, God is all bliss, boundless love, infinite intelligence, all-powerful, boundless wisdom, absolute harmony, indescribable beauty, and perfection. As he quietly thinks along these lines he is lifted up in consciousness into a new spiritual wave length, at which times he feels the infinite ocean of God's love is now dissolving everything unlike itself in the mind and body of John Jones for whom he is praying. He feels all the power and love of God are now focused on John Jones, and whatever is bothering or vexing him is now completely neutralized in the presence of the infinite ocean of life and love.

The absolute method of prayer might be likened to the sound wave or sonic therapy recently shown me by a distinguished physician in Los Angeles. He has an ultra sound wave machine, which oscillates at a tremendous speed and sends sound waves to any area of the body to which it is directed. These sound waves can be controlled, and he told me of achieving remarkable results in dissolving arthritic calcareous deposits, as well as the healing and removal of other disturbing conditions.

To the degree that we rise in consciousness by contemplating qualities and attributes of God, do we generate spiritual electronic waves of harmony, health, and peace. Many remarkable heal-ings follow this technique of prayer.

A CRIPPLE WALKS

Dr. Phineas Parkhurst Quimby, of whom we spoke previously in this chapter, used the absolute method in the latter years of his healing career. He was really the father of psychosomatic medicine and the first psychoanalyst. He had the capacity to diagnose clairvoyantly the cause of the patient's trouble, pains, and aches.

The following is a condensed account of the healing of a cripple as recorded in Quimby's Manuscripts:

Quimby was called on to visit a woman who was lame, aged, and bedridden. He states that her ailment was due to the fact that she was imprisoned by a creed so small and contracted that she could not stand upright and move about. She was living in the tomb of fear and ignorance; further-more, she was taking the Bible literally, and it frightened her. "In this tomb," Quimby said, "was the presence and power of God trying to burst the bands, break through the bonds, and rise from the dead." When she would ask others for an explanation of some passage of the Bible, the answer would be a stone; then she would hunger for the bread of life. Dr. Quimby diagnosed her case as a mind cloudy and stagnated, due to excitation and fear, caused by the inability to see clearly the meaning of the passage of the Bible which she had been reading. This showed itself in the body by her heavy and sluggish feeling, which would terminate as pa-ralysis.

At this point Quimby asked her what was meant in the Bible verses: *Yet a little while am I with you, and then I go unto Him that sent me. Ye shall seek me, and shall not find me: and where I am, thither ye cannot come.* JOHN 7:33–34. She replied that it meant Jesus went to heaven. Quimby explained what it really meant by telling her that *being with her a little while* meant his explanation of her symptoms, feelings, and their causes; i.e., he had compassion and sympathy for her momentarily, but he could not remain in that mental state. The next step was *to go to Him that sent us*, which, as Quimby pointed out, was the creative power of God in all of us.

Quimby immediately traveled in his mind and contemplated the divine ideal; i.e., the vitality, intelligence, harmony, and power of God functioning in the sick person. This is why he said to the woman, "Therefore, where I go you cannot come, for you are in your narrow, restricted belief, and I am in health." This prayer and explanation produced an instantaneous sensation, and a change came over her mind. She walked without her crutches! Quimby said it was one of the most singular of all his healings. She was, as it were, dead to error, and to bring her to life or truth was to raise her from the dead. Quimby quoted the resurrection of Christ and applied it to her own Christ or health; this produced a powerful effect on her. He also explained to her that the truth, which she accepted, was the angel or idea, which rolled away the stone of fear, ignorance, and superstition, thereby, releasing the healing power of God, which made her whole.

THE DECREE METHOD

Power goes into our word according to the feeling and faith behind it. When we realize the power that moves the world is moving on our behalf and is backing up our word, our confidence and assurance grow. You do not try and add power to power; therefore, there must be no mental striving, coercion, force, or mental wrestling.

A young girl used the decree method on a young man who was constantly phoning her, pressing her for dates, and meeting her at her place of business; she found it very difficult to get rid of him. She decreed as follows: "I release . . . unto God. He is in his true place at all times. I am free, and he is free. I now decree that my words go forth into infinite mind and it brings it to pass. It is so." She said he vanished and she has never seen him since, adding, "It was as though the ground swallowed him up."

Thou shalt also decree a thing, and it shall be established unto thee: and the light shall shine upon thy ways. JOB 22:28.

SERVE YOURSELF WITH SCIENTIFIC TRUTH

1. Be a mental engineer and use tried and proven techniques in building a grander and greater life.
2. Your desire is your prayer. Picture the fulfillment of your desire now and feel its reality, and you will experience the joy of the answered prayer.
3. Desire to accomplish things the easy way—with the sure aid of mental science.
4. You can build radiant health, success, and happiness by the thoughts you think in the hidden studio of your mind.
5. Experiment scientifically until you personally prove that there is always a direct response from the infinite intelligence of your subconscious mind to your conscious thinking.
6. Feel the joy and restfulness in foreseeing the certain accomplishment of your desire. Any mental picture, which you have in your mind is the substance of things hoped for and the evidence of things not seen.

7. A mental picture is worth a thousand words. Your subconscious will bring to pass any picture held in the mind backed by faith.

8. Avoid all effort or mental coercion in prayer. Get into a sleepy, drowsy state and lull yourself to sleep feeling and knowing that your prayer is answered.

9. Remember that the thankful heart is always close to the riches of the universe.

10. To affirm is to state that it is so, and as you maintain this attitude of mind as true, regardless of all evidence to the contrary, you will receive an answer to your prayer.

11. Generate electronic waves of harmony, health, and peace by thinking of the love and the glory of God.

12. What you decree and feel as true will come to pass. Decree harmony, health, peace, and abundance.

HOW TO GET THE
RESULTS YOU WANT

The principle reasons for failure are: lack of confidence and too much effort. Many people block answers to their prayers by failing to fully comprehend the workings of their subconscious mind. When you know how your mind functions, you gain a measure of confidence. You must remember whenever your subconscious mind accepts an idea, it immediately begins to execute it. It uses all its mighty resources to that end and mobilizes all the mental and spiritual laws of your deeper mind. This law is true for good or bad ideas. Consequently, if you use it negatively, it brings trouble, failure, and confusion. When you use it constructively, it brings guidance, freedom, and peace of mind.

The right answer is inevitable when your thoughts are positive, constructive, and loving. From this it is perfectly obvious that the only thing you have to do in order to overcome failure is to get your subconscious to accept your idea or request by feeling its reality now, and the law of your mind will do the rest. Turn over your request with faith and confidence, and your subconscious will take over and answer for you.

You will always fail to get results by trying to use mental coercion—your subconscious mind does not respond to coercion, it responds to your faith or conscious mind acceptance.

Your failure to get results may also arise from such statements as: "Things are getting worse." "I will never get an answer." "I see no way out." "It is hopeless." "I don't know what to do." "I'm all mixed up." When you use such statements, you get no response or cooperation from your subconscious mind. Like a soldier marking time, you neither go forward nor backward; in other words, you don't get anywhere.

If you get into a taxi and give a half dozen different directions to the driver in five minutes, he would become hopelessly confused and probably would refuse to take you anywhere. It is the same when working with your subconscious mind. There must be a clear-cut idea in your mind. You must arrive at the definite decision that there is a way out, a solution to the vexing problem in sickness. Only the infinite intelligence within your subconscious knows the answer. When you come to that clear-cut conclusion in your conscious mind, your mind is then made up, and according to your belief is it done unto you.

EASY DOES IT

A house owner once remonstrated with a furnace repairman for charging two hundred dollars for fixing the boiler. The mechanic said, "I charged five cents for the missing bolt and one hundred ninety-nine dollars and ninety-five cents for knowing what was wrong."

Similarly, your subconscious mind is the master mechanic, the all-wise one, who knows ways and means of healing any organ of your body, as well as your affairs. Decree health, and your subconscious will establish it, but relaxation is the key. "Easy does it." Do not be concerned with details and means, but know the end result. Get the *feel* of the happy solution to your problem whether it is health, finances, or employment. Remember how you felt after you had recovered from a severe state of illness. Bear in mind that your feeling is the touchstone of all subconscious demonstration. Your new idea must be felt subjectively in a finished state, not the future, but as coming about now.

INFER NO OPPONENT, USE IMAGINATION
AND NOT WILLPOWER

In using your subconscious mind you infer no opponent, you use no willpower. You imagine the end and the freedom state. You will find your intellect trying to get in the way, but persist in maintaining a simple, childlike, miracle-making faith. Picture yourself without the ailment or problem. Imagine the emotional accompaniment of the freedom state you crave. Cut out all red tape from the process. The simple way is the best.

HOW DISCIPLINED IMAGINATION
WORKS WONDERS

A wonderful way to get a response from your subconscious mind is through disciplined or scientific imagination. As previously pointed out, your subconscious mind is the builder of the body and controls all its vital functions.

The Bible says, *Whatsoever ye shall ask in prayer, believing, ye shall receive.* To believe is to accept something as true, or to live in the state of being it. As you sustain this mood, you shall experience the joy of the answered prayer!

THE THREE STEPS TO SUCCESS IN PRAYER

The usual procedure is as follows:

1. Take a look at the problem.
2. Turn to the solution or way out known only to the subconscious mind.
3. Rest in a sense of deep conviction that it is done.

Do not weaken your prayer by saying, "I wish I might be healed." "I hope so." Your feeling about the work to be done is "the boss." Harmony is yours. Know that health is yours. Become intelligent by becoming a vehicle for the infinite healing power of the subconscious mind. Pass on the idea of health to your subconscious mind to the point of conviction; then relax. Get yourself off your hands. Say to the condition and circumstance, "This, too, shall pass." Through relaxation you impress your subconscious mind enabling the kinetic energy behind the idea to take over and bring it into concrete realization.

THE LAW OF REVERSED EFFORT AND WHY YOU
GET THE OPPOSITE OF WHAT YOU PRAY FOR

Coué, the famous psychologist from France who visited America about forty years ago, defined the law of reversed effort as follows: "When your desires and imagination are in conflict your imagination invariably gains the day."

If, for example, you were asked to walk a plank on the floor, you would do so without question. Now suppose the same plank were placed twenty feet up in the air between two walls, would you walk it? Your desire to walk it would be counteracted by your imagination or fear of falling. Your dominant idea, which would be the picture of falling would conquer. Your desire, will, or effort to walk on the plank would be reversed, and the dominant idea of failure would be reinforced.

Mental effort is invariably self-defeated, eventuating always in the opposite of what is desired. The suggestions of powerlessness to overcome the condition dominate the mind; your subconscious is always controlled by the dominant idea.

Your subconscious will accept the strongest of two contradictory propositions. The effortless way is the better.

If you say, "I want a healing, but I can't get it," "I try so hard," "I force myself to pray," "I use all the willpower I have," you must realize that your error lies in your effort. Never try to compel the subconscious mind to accept your idea by exercising willpower. Such attempts are doomed to failure, and you get the opposite of what you prayed for.

The following is a rather common experience. Students, when taking examinations and reading through their papers, find that all their knowledge has suddenly deserted them. Their minds become appalling blanks, and they are unable to recall one relevant thought. The more they grit their teeth and summon the powers of the will, the further the answers seem to flee. But, when they have left the examination room and the mental pressure relaxes, the answers they were seeking flow tantalizingly back into their minds. Trying to force themselves to remember was the cause of their failure. This is an example of the law of reversed effort whereby you get the opposite of what you asked or prayed for.

THE CONFLICT OF DESIRE AND IMAGINATION MUST BE RECONCILED

To use mental force is to presuppose that there is opposition. When your mind is concentrated on the means to overcome a problem, it is no longer concerned with the obstacle. MATTHEW 18:19 says, *If two of you shall agree on earth as touching anything that they shall ask, it shall be done for them of my Father which is in heaven.* Who are these two? It means the harmonious union or agreement between your conscious and subconscious on any idea, desire, or mental image. When there is no longer any quarrel in either part of your mind, your prayer will be answered. The two agreeing may also be represented as you and your desire, your thought and feeling, your idea and emotion, your desire and imagination.

You avoid all conflict between your desires and imagination by entering into a drowsy, sleepy state which brings all effort to a minimum. The conscious mind is submerged to a great extent when in a sleepy state. The best time to impregnate your subconscious is prior to sleep. The reason for this is that the highest degree of outcropping of the subconscious occurs prior to sleep and just after we awaken. In this state the negative thoughts and imagery, which tend to neutralize your desire and so prevent acceptance by your subconscious mind no longer present themselves. When you imagine the reality of the fulfilled desire and feel the thrill of accomplishment, your subconscious brings about the realization of your desire.

A great many people solve all their dilemmas and problems by the play of their controlled, directed, and disciplined imagination, knowing that whatever they imagine and feel as true *will* and *must* come to pass.

The following will clearly illustrate how a young girl overcame the conflict between her desire and her imagination. She desired a harmonious solution to her legal problem, yet her mental imagery was constantly on failure, loss, bankruptcy, and poverty. It was a complicated lawsuit and there was one postponement after another with no solution in sight.

At my suggestion, she got into a sleepy, drowsy state each night prior to sleep, and she began to imagine the happy ending, feeling it to the best of her ability. She knew that the image in her mind had to agree with her heart's desire. Prior to sleep she began to dramatize as vividly as possible her lawyer having an animated discussion with her regarding the outcome. She would ask him questions, and he would answer her appropriately. He would say to her over and over again, "There has been a perfect, harmonious solution. The case has been settled out of court." During the day when fear thoughts came into her mind, she would run her mental movie with gestures, voice, and sound equipment. She could easily imagine the sound of his voice, smile, and mannerism. She ran this mental picture so often, it became a subjective pattern, a regular train track. At the end of a few weeks her attorney called her and confirmed objectively what she had been imagining and feeling as true subjectively.

This is really what the Psalmist meant when he wrote, *Let the words of my mouth* [your thoughts, mental images, good], *and the meditations of my heart* [your feeling, nature, emotion] *be acceptable in thy sight, O Lord* [the law of your subconscious mind], *my strength, and my redeemer* [the power and wisdom of your subconscious mind can redeem you from sickness, bondage, and misery]. PSALMS 19:14.

IDEAS WORTH RECALLING

1. Mental coercion or too much effort shows anxiety and fear, which block your answer. Easy does it.

2. When your mind is relaxed and you accept an idea, your subconscious goes to work to execute the idea.

3. Think and plan independently of traditional methods. Know that there is always an answer and a solution to every problem.

4. Do not be overly concerned with the beating of your heart, with the breathing of your lungs, or the functions of any part of your anatomy. Lean heavily upon your subconscious and proclaim frequently that Divine right action is taking place.

5. The feeling of health produces health, the feeling of wealth produces wealth. How do you feel?

6. Imagination is your most powerful faculty. Imagine what is lovely and of good report. You are what you imagine yourself to be.

7. You avoid conflict between your conscious and subconscious in the sleepy state. Imagine the fulfillment of your desire over and over again prior to sleep. Sleep in peace and wake in joy.

MAGIC
OF FAITH
(1954)

CONTENTS

THE SONG OF TRIUMPH

"Tell me, O thou whom my soul loveth, where thou feedest, where thou makest THY FLOCK to rest at noon?"

"Behold, thou ART fair, my love; behold, thou ART fair,
thou HAST doves' eyes."

"He brought me to the banqueting house, and his banner
over me WAS love."

"His left hand IS under my head, and his right hand
doth embrace me."

"My beloved spake, and said unto me, Rise up, my love,
my fair one, and come away.

"For lo, the winter is past, the rain is over AND gone;

"The flowers appear on the earth; the time of the singing
of BIRDS is come, and the voice of the turtle is heard in
our land;

"Arise, my love, my fair one, and come away.

"My beloved IS mine, and I AM his: he feedeth among the lilies.

"Until the day break, and the shadows flee away."

It is inconceivable that any anthology could be written wherein *The Song of Solomon* would not be included. It is really one of the most inspired parts of the Bible. *The Song of Solomon* reveals God as the Great Lover. It is ecstatic and thrilling.

In order to lead the triumphant life, you must be moved by Love. You can go wild in the joy of being actually drunk with the Spirit. In other words by singing the Song of God, you become God-intoxicated, and fired with Divine enthusiasm, thereby expressing more and more of Divine love and joy every day.

You sing the Song of God, or the mood of triumph, when you subjectively feel that you are that which your five senses tell you, you are not; you are then God-intoxicated and seized with a Divine frenzy—a sort of mad joy.

Haven't you at times seen a person bubbling over with enthusiasm and intoxicated with joy? That person is singing the Song of God at that moment. "In thy presence *is* fulness of joy; at thy right hand *there are* pleasures for evermore."

When you sing a song, you are expressing your whole nature. Your mind and body enter into the song. When your heart is full of love and good will, and you are radiating peace, you are truly singing God's Song; It is the song of the jubilant soul.

The real You is a spiritual, eternal, perfect being. You are a living expression of God now. "I have said, Ye *are* Gods; and all of you are children of the most High."

When you pray, it is a romance with God or your Good. Your desire, when realized, brings you joy and peace. In order to realize the desire of your heart, which is depicted in *The Song of Solomon* as your beloved, you must woo it; let that desire of yours captivate, hold, and thrill you. Let it fire your imagination. You will always move in the direction of the desire which dominates your mind.

The majority of students of psychology know that *The Song of Solomon* is a beautiful description of the wonderful romance of the conscious and subconscious mind (Solomon and Sheba).

"Tell me, O thou whom my soul loveth, where thou feedest?" Your realized desire is he whom your soul loveth. You are asked, "Where thou feedest?" In other words what are you mentally dwelling upon? The *flock* represent your thoughts, ideas, opinions, and beliefs. You are to feast on nothing but the joy of the answered prayer.

If you are saying to yourself, "I can't. It is too late now. I am too old, and I don't know the right people"—in other words if you are mentally feeding on all the reasons why you cannot do something, or be what you want to be, you are not making "thy flock to rest at noon."

At noon the sun casts no shadow; likewise, when you pray, you are not to permit any shadow of fear or doubt to cross your path, or deflect you from your goal or aim in life. The world of confusion shall be rejected, and you shall mentally eat of, or meditate on the reality of your desire.

"Behold, thou *art* fair, my love; behold, thou *art* fair; thou *hast* doves' eyes." *The dove* is a symbol of God's inner peace.

Once I talked to an alcoholic who said, "Don't say anything about this God-stuff to me. I don't want God. I want a healing." This man was deeply resentful toward a former wife who had remarried; moreover, he was full of grudges against several people. He needed the *doves' eyes*, which means he needed to see the truth which would give him peace of mind.

I asked him, "Will you pray with me now? All I ask is that you be sincere; if you are, you will experience an inner peace which passeth all human understanding."

He relaxed his body, and I said to him, "Imagine you are talking to the Invisible Presence within you—the Almighty Power which created the Cosmos. It can do all things. Say, 'Thank you, thank you, for this inner peace.' Say it over and over again."

After ten minutes in silent meditation, he was blinded by an interior, Inner Light. It seemed to come from the floor where he was. The whole room was flooded with Light!

He exclaimed, "All I see is Light! What's wrong?" Then he relaxed into sleep in my office, and his face did truly shine as the sun. He awakened in about fifteen minutes, and was completely at peace saying, "God truly is! God is!" This man had found his Beloved; It had *doves' eyes*.

As you fall asleep at night, tell your desire how fair it is, and how wonderful you would feel in realizing it. Begin to fall in love with your ideal. Praise it; exalt it. "Arise my Love!" Feel that you are what you want to be. Go to sleep in the consciousness of being or doing what you long to do.

I told a man in one of the islands one time "to sleep" on the idea of success. He was selling magazine subscriptions. He became a great success by following this procedure: I suggested that he think of success prior to sleep; i.e., what success meant to him; what he would do if he were successful. I told him to use his imagination; then as he was about to go to sleep, fall in love with the idea of success this way: Repeat the one word, "Success," over and over again. He should get into the mood of success; then fall off to sleep in the arms of his Everlasting Lover. Your Lover—your Divine Presence—will bring to pass whatever you accept as true. The conditions, experiences, and events of your life are called children of your mind.

"He brought me to the banqueting house, and his banner over me *was* love." The *banquet house* is your own mind where you entertain the idea or desire of your heart.

I will illustrate at this point how to entertain in this *banquet house* of your own mind. A young girl having a special talent to sing was having great difficulty in getting anything to do in the motion picture field, television, or radio. She had been turned down so often she feared she was getting a rejection complex. She heard me state over one of our radio programs that whatever the mind of man could imagine and feel as true, he could realize. She wrote that down, and came to one of our classes, and began to practice entering into the *banquet house* by quieting the wheels of her mind, relaxing the body by simply talking to it, and telling it to relax; it has to obey you. In that quiet, relaxed, peaceful state, with her attention completely focused on an imaginary, movie contract in her hand, she felt the reality of the joy and wonder of it all. She was now in the *banquet house* and the banner over her was love. *Love* is an emotional attachment. She was definitely, mentally attached to this contract. "He calleth things that are not seen, as though they were, and the unseen becomes seen." The visible world comes out of the invisible. She caused the contract to become a reality by becoming emotionally attached to the imaginary picture of a contract in her mental, *banquet house*. She knew that what she imagined and believed must come to pass in the three-dimensional world.

"His left hand is under my head, and his right hand doth embrace me." *The left hand* is your deep, subjective feeling; the *right hand* is your disciplined imagination. As you begin to imagine and feel the reality of your desire, you are joining the right and left hands together in a Divine embrace; then a union of the idea and feeling takes place. Another way of saying this is: There is an agreement of the conscious and subconscious mind which denotes the answered prayer.

You know when there is no longer any argument or doubt in your conscious or subconscious mind, your prayer is answered, because the two have agreed as touching upon it, and it is so.

"My beloved spake, and said unto me, Rise up, my love, my fair one, and come away." Is not that what your goal, aim, ambition, or desire is saying to you? For instance the idea of perfect health is now beckoning to you, and saying, "Rise up, and come away from the belief in sickness, limitation, pain, and aches to health, harmony, and peace of mind."

I had a long talk with a man in England who had trouble with his leg. He had been confined to his home for nine months, and was unable to lean on his leg or walk. The first thing I did was to ask him what he would do if he were healed? He said, "I would again play polo, swim, golf, and climb the Alps which I used to do every year." That was the answer I was seeking.

I told him in the simplest way how to achieve the perfect use of his legs again. The first thing was to imagine he was doing the things he would do. I painted an imaginary picture for him. For fifteen or twenty minutes three times a day he sat in his study and imagined he was playing polo; he assumed the mental mood of actually performing the role of a polo player. He became the actor; an actor participates in the role.

Note carefully that he did not see himself playing polo; that would be an illusion. He *felt* himself playing polo. He actualized it by living the drama in his mind or *banquet house*.

At noon he would quiet the mind; still the body, and feel his Alpine clothes on him. He would feel and imagine he was climbing the Alps; he would feel the cold air on his face, and hear the voice of his old associates. He lived the drama and felt the naturalness and the tangibility of the rocks.

At night prior to sleep, before going into the Arms of his Beloved—His Deeper Self—he would play a game of golf. He would hold the club; touch the ball with his hand; put it in place, and tee off. He would swing his clubs, and delight in watching where the ball went. When he was in the mood of playing a good game, he would go off to sleep feeling very satisfied and happy about his experience.

Within two months this man's leg was healed. He did all the things he imagined he would do. The *idea* of climbing the Alps, plus the *desire* to play polo again, said to this man, "Arise, my love, my fair one, and come away," from your belief in a physical handicap; that is what he did.

The law of the subconscious is one of compulsion. When you subjectively feel you are swimming,—for example, when you feel the chill of the water, and the naturalness of your various swimming strokes,—you will sooner or later be compelled to swim. Whatever the handicap, whether fear or a physical condition, you will do what you subjectively felt you were doing.

Your desire, dream, ambition, goal, or aim is your savior! It is walking down the corridor of your mind, saying to you, "Arise, my love, and come away," and enjoy the good and glorious things of life.

No matter what the problem is, or its magnitude, you have really nothing to do but convince yourself of the truth which you are affirming. As quickly as you succeed in convincing yourself of the reality of your desire, results will automatically follow. Your subconscious mind will faithfully reproduce what you impregnated within it.

The Bible says, "Choose you this day whom ye will serve." You have the freedom to choose the tone, feeling, or mood you enter into. The manifestation of your feeling or conviction is the secret of your lover or subconscious mind. Your external actions are, therefore, determined by your subconscious beliefs and impressions.

Your thought and feeling determine your destiny. The knowledge of the truth is saying to you now, "The winter is past, the rain is over *and* gone." *The winter* represents that cold state when the seeds are frozen in the bosom of the earth and nothing is growing. The winter and all the seasons are in your mind.

Are your desires, dreams, visions, and aims in life frozen within you due to fear, worry, or false beliefs? You can resurrect them now by turning away from appearances, entering into the banquet *house* of God within you, and saying to yourself, "I can be what I want to be. All I have to do is impress my subconscious mind with my desire for health, wealth, companionship, or true place, and it will express that state with which I have impressed it."

The *winter* is now over for you; the rain is gone also. Your mind may have been flooded with negative thoughts causing the mood of despondency, dejection, and melancholia. This is what a flood or avalanche of negative thoughts, false beliefs, and erroneous opinions will do. Now you know that all you have to do is fill your mind with the truths of God which have come down to you from time immemorial. As you do this, you will crowd out of your mind everything unlike them.

The winter and the floods are over for you when regularly and systematically you fill your mind with the concept of peace, happiness, love, and good will. You can do this by reading one of the Psalms, such as the twenty-third or ninety-first, and feeling the truth of everything you say; or you can read aloud a good meditation of the real truths of God. As you do this, these truths go in through the eye and the ear; they release a tremendous, therapeutic vibration which courses through your entire mind and body. These curative, healing, soothing vibrations destroy, neutralize, and obliterate all the negative, fearful, diseased thoughts which caused all the trouble in your life; their embodiment must then disappear. This is prayer; do it often enough until it becomes a habit. Prayer should be a habit also.

Do everything from the standpoint of the One God and His Love. For instance, when you shop, pray before purchasing. Say, "God guides me in all my purchases." Say quietly to the saleslady or salesman, "God is prospering him."

Whatever you do, do it with love and good will. Pour out love, peace, and good will to all. Claim frequently that God's Love and Transcendent Beauty flow through all my thoughts, words, and actions. Make a habit of this. Fill your mind with the eternal verities; then you will see that "The flowers appear on the earth; the time of the singing of *birds* is come!" You will begin to *flower;* yes, you will begin to blossom forth.

The earth means your body, environment, social life, and all things necessary on this objective plane.

The flowers you witness will be the birth of God in your

mind. *The flowers* of God's guidance will watch over you, and lead you to green pastures and still waters. The flowers of God's Love will fill your heart. Now when you see discord anywhere, you will see the Love of God operating in all His Creation; as you realize It, you will see love come forth and flower in the other.

When you go into a home, and you see confusion, quarrelling, and strife, you will realize within yourself, that the peace of God reigns supreme in the minds and hearts of all those in this house; you will see the flower of peace made manifest and expressed.

Where you see financial lack and limitation, you will realize the infinite abundance and wealth of God forever flowing, filling up all the empty vessels, and leaving a Divine surplus. As you do this, you will live in the garden of God where only orchids and all beautiful flowers grow; for only God's ideas circulate in your mind.

As you go to sleep every night, you will clothe yourself with the garment of love, peace, and joy. From now on you always go to sleep feeling that you now are what you long to be. Your last concept as you fall asleep is etched on your deeper mind; you shall resurrect it. Always take into the *banquet house* of your Lover a noble, Christ-like concept of yourself; your Lover will always give you what you conceive and believe as true. Anything you can conceive, your Lover can give conception. Love gives birth to all things. Your tomorrows are determined by your concept of yourself as you fall asleep in the arms of your Lover (your ideal).

The time of the singing of birds is at hand for you when you cease singing that old song of lack. You have listened to people sing this kind of song: It is like an old gramophone record: "I'm so lonesome; things never went right for me. I never

had a chance. I have been cruelly treated." "I have been operated on three times." "You should hear about all the money I
lost." Yes, then they tell about the fear on the lonely road, plus
their likes, dislikes, pet peeves, and hates. Imbued with God's
love, you will no longer sing that song again. You will sing the
new song; for God's ideas and truths (birds) will sing in you.

Then you will *speak in a new tongue* which means the
mood of peace, joy, good will, and love. You will no longer
react to people and conditions like you did. The Song of God
is now heard. Now when someone says something mean or
nasty to you, you will immediately transform it by realizing
God's peace fills your soul. You will consume it with the fire of
right thoughts; the birds will truly sing in your mind and heart
as you do. You are happy; you are bubbling over with enthusiasm, and you are looking forward with a joyous expectancy
to all good things. Wherever you go, you carry peace with you;
all those who come within your orbit are blessed by your inner
radiance. You begin to see sermons in stones, tongues in trees,
songs in running brooks, and God in everything. *The voice of
the turtle* is now heard in your land!

Tennyson said, "Speak to Him thou, for he hears, spirit
with spirit shall meet, closer is He than breathing, and nearer
than hands and feet."

The voice of the turtle dove is the voice of peace, the voice
of intuition, and of God's inner guidance. You can hear it by
lowly listening. For instance one time as a boy I was lost in
the woods. I sat down under a tree, and remembered a prayer
which starts with, "Our Father, He will shows us the way; let
us be quiet, and He will lead us." I quietly repeated, "Father,
lead us."

A wave of peace came over me which I can still recall.
The voice of the turtle dove became real. *The turtle dove* is intuition

which means being taught from within. An overpowering feeling came over me to go in a certain direction as if I were being pushed ahead. Two of the boys came with me; the others did not. We were led out of that thick jungle, as if by an Unseen Hand.

Great musicians have listened and heard the music within; they wrote down what they heard inwardly. In meditation Lincoln listened to the principle of liberty; Beethoven heard the principle of harmony.

If you are intensely interested in the principle of mathematics, you are loving it; as you love it, it will reveal all its secrets to you.

Jesus heard *the voice of the turtle dove* when he said, "Peace, I leave with you; my peace I give unto you; not as the world giveth, give I unto you. Let not your heart be troubled; neither let it be afraid." How wonderful you will feel as you drink in these words and fill your mind with their therapeutic potency.

Job heard *the voice of the turtle* when he said, "Acquaint now thyself with Him, and be at peace." "Thou wilt keep *him* in perfect peace, *whose* mind is stayed *on thee:* because he trusteth in thee." "For God is not *the author* of confusion, but of peace."

You can hear *the voice of the turtle* by turning to the Infinite Intelligence within you, saying, "Father, this is what I want . . ."; then state specifically and clearly the thing you desire. You are now turning your desire over to the God-Wisdom within you, Which knows all, sees all, and has the "know how" of accomplishment. You always know whether you have really turned your request over or not. If you are at peace about it, you have turned it over. If anxious and worried, you have not subjectified your prayer; you do not fully trust the God-Wisdom within.

If you want guidance, claim Infinite Intelligence is guiding you now; It will differentiate Itself as right action for you. You will know you have received the answer, for *the dove of peace* will whisper in your ear, "Peace be still." You will know the Divine answer, for you will be at peace, and your decision will be right.

A girl recently was wondering whether to accept a position in New York for considerably more money or remain in Los Angeles in her present position. At night as she went to sleep, she asked herself this question, "What would be my reaction if I had made the right decision now?" The answer came to her, "I would feel wonderful. I would feel happy having made the right decision." Then she said, "I will act as though I had made the right decision," and she began to say, "Isn't it wonderful! Isn't it wonderful!" over and over again, as a lullaby, and lulled herself to sleep in the feeling, "It is wonderful."

She had a dream that night, and the voice in the dream said, "Stand still! Stand still!" She awakened immediately, and knew of course that was *the voice of the turtle dove*—the voice of intuition.

The fourth dimensional-self within her can see ahead; it knows all and sees all; it can read the minds of the owners of the business in the east. She remained in her present position. Subsequent events proved the truth of her Inner Voice; the Eastern concern went into bankruptcy. "I the Lord will make myself known unto him in a vision, *and* will speak unto him in a dream."

"My beloved *is* mine, and I *am* his; he feedeth among the

lilies." *The lilies* represent the poppies which grow in the East. To see the poppy field sway in the breeze is a very beautiful sight. Here the inspired Biblical writer is telling you to have a romance with God. As you turn to the God-Presence, It turns to you. You experience the mystic marriage, the wedded bliss, when you fall madly in love with truth for truth's sake; then you become full of the new wine, the new interpretation of life.

The lilies symbolize beauty, order, symmetry, and pro-portion. As you feed or feast on the great truth that God is In-describable Beauty, Boundless Love, Absolute Bliss, Absolute Harmony, and Infinite Peace, you are truly *feeding among the lilies.* When you claim that what is true of God is true of you, miracles will happen in your life.

By realizing and knowing these qualities and attributes of God are being expressed through you, and that you are a channel for the Divine, every atom of your being begins to dance to the rhythm of the Eternal God. Beauty, order, har-mony, and peace appear in your mind, body, and business world as you feed among the lilies; you feel your oneness with God, Life, and God's Infinite Riches. You are married to your Beloved, for you are now married to God; you are a bride of the Lord (I AM). From this moment forward you will bring forth children of your Beloved; they will bear the image and likeness of their Father and Mother.

The *father* is God's idea; the *mother* is the emotionalizing of the idea, and its subjective embodiment. From that union of idea and feeling come forth your health, abundance, happi-ness, and inner peace.

Sit down and feed among the lilies by realizing that every night of the year when you go to sleep, you go before the King of Kings, the Lord of Lords, and the Prince of Peace. Be sure you are dressed properly as you enter into His Holy

Presence. If you were going before the President, you would put on your best clothes. The clothes you wear as you enter into the heavens of your own mind every night represent the mood, or the tone you wear. Be sure it is always the wedding garment of love, peace, and good will to all.

Be absolutely sure that you can say, "Behold, thou art fair." There must be no resentment, ill-will, condemnation of self or others, and no criticism of any person. God's Love must really fill your heart for all men everywhere. You must sincerely wish for everyone what you wish for yourself; then you can say to your mood or feeling, "Behold, thou *art* fair." "And when ye stand praying, forgive, if ye have ought against any."

"My beloved is mine." All that God is, is yours, for God is within you. All you can possibly desire is already yours. You need no help from the outside to *feed among the lilies.*

When you go to sleep tonight, forgive everyone, and imagine and feel your desire is fulfilled. Become absolutely and completely indifferent to all thought of failure, because you now know the law. As you accept the end, you have, as Troward so beautifully stated, willed the means to the realization of the end. As you are about to enter sleep, galvanize yourself into the feeling of being or having your desire. Your mental acceptance or your feeling as you go to sleep is the request you make of your Beloved; then She looks at your request (conviction in the subconscious mind), and being the Absolute Lover, she must give you what you asked.

"You feed among the lilies until the day breaks and the shadows flee away." The *shadows* are fear, doubt, worry, anxiety, and all the reasons why you cannot do something. *The shadows* of our five senses and race belief hover over the minds of all as we pray.

When you pray, accept as true what your reason and five senses deny and reject. Remain faithful to your idea by being full of faith every step of the way. When your consciousness is fully qualified with the acceptance of your desire, all the fear will go away. Trust in the reality of your ideal or desire until you are filled full of the feeling of being it; then *the day will break and all shadows will flee away.* Yes, the answer to your prayer will come, and light up the heavens of your mind bringing you peace.

No matter what the problem is, how acute, dark, or hopeless things seem to be, turn now to God, and say, "How is it in God and Heaven?" The answer will softly steal over your mind like the dew from heaven: "All is peace, joy, bliss, perfection, wholeness, harmony, and beauty"; then reject the evidence of your senses, and *feed among the lilies of God and Heaven,* such as peace, harmony, joy, and perfection. Realize what is true of God must be true of you and your surroundings. Continue in this abiding trust and faith in God "until the day breaks and the shadows flee away."

THE PRACTICE OF THE PRESENCE OF GOD

"Whither shall I go from thy Spirit? or whither shall I flee from thy presence? If I ascend up into heaven, thou ART THERE; If I take the wings of the morning, AND dwell in the uttermost parts of the sea; Even there shall thy hand lead me, and thy right hand shall hold me."

This one hundred and thirty ninth Psalm is one of the most beautiful Psalms in the Bible. It is a matchless, priceless gem of truth. The language of this Psalm is unsurpassed for beauty and elegance. David's marvelous conception of the Omnipresence of God was found in this passage.

The religion outlined in the Bible is the practice of the Presence of God. To understand and to intelligently practice this truth, you will find is the way to health, harmony, peace, and spiritual progress. The practice of the Presence is powerful beyond imagination. Let us not overlook it, because of its utter simplicity.

The first step is to realize that God is the Only Power.

The next thing to become aware of is that all things—no matter what they are—represent God in manifestation. The whole world is God in infinite differentiation, as God never repeats Himself; this is the whole story, and the greatest of all truths. It is really the all-inclusive, all-encompassing truth.

I know many students who sit down for five or ten minutes every day, and meditate on the fact that God is the Only Presence and the Only Power. They let their thoughts dwell on this profound truth; they look at it from all angles; then they begin to think that every person they meet is an expression of God; that in fact everything they see is God made manifest; it is God dramatizing Himself for the joy of expressing Himself. As they do this, they find their whole world changing; they experience better health; outer conditions improve, and they are possessed of a new vitality and energy.

Your whole world will change as you really begin to see God in everything and in everyone. "For thou shalt be in league with the stones of the field: and the beasts of the field shall be at peace with thee. And thou shalt know that thy tabernacle *shall* be in peace." This means that the man who begins to see God everywhere, and who follows and practices the good, will not be afraid of anything. As a matter of fact the whole world will be his friend, and everything will extend the offer of help whether animate, or what the world calls inanimate.

The only way to magnify the Presence of God in the eyes of others, is to radiate at all times the sunlight of God's Love. Love God or Truth, and you will be under a Divine compulsion for good. You cannot go wrong. You will find that you will never make any real mistake or a wrong choice. Love of all things good, or of the truth, is really the touch of Midas.

In a building the superstructure depends upon the foundation. Let *your* foundation be God and Him alone. You are always practicing the Presence of God when you activate your mind with true ideas which heal and strengthen you. Your mind needs constant cleansing, disciplining, and direction. By practicing the Presence of God, you are constantly cleansing your mind; this is prayer.

Think all day long from the standpoint of the One God about every person and every situation you meet. Pray at work by realizing God is your partner, and God is in action through all your associates.

Pray driving your car, by realizing the vehicle is God's idea moving from point to point freely, joyously, and lovingly.

Pray when you go into a store by realizing God directs your purchases, that God is prospering the clerk who waits on you, and that the store is being governed and directed by God's Wisdom.

Let prayer be the orderly, right way of doing everything. Practice the Golden Rule in all your transactions; then you are writing God's Law in your heart.

It is essential for you to get the right concept and understanding of God. Have you meditated? or have you asked yourself what God is? Your concept of God molds, fashions, and shapes your whole future. Your real belief about God is of supreme importance. It is done unto you as you believe. If you say and believe God is the only Presence, the only Power, Infinitely Good, Perfect, Boundless Love, and Limitless Life, your whole life will be transformed.

If you say, "Oh, I do not know what I think of God; my thoughts are confused and muddled," confusion will reign in your life. It does not really matter whether you call God: Reality, Infinite Intelligence, Being, Life, Allah, or Brahma; the real Name of God, in so far as you are concerned, is your concept or your belief about God.

A man said to me one time, "I believe in God, and that is all that matters."

I asked him, "But tell me, what sort of God do you really believe in?"

He said, "I believe in the laws of nature."

That was his idea of God, and he cannot transcend this belief. He is subject to that belief, thereby limiting his Inner Powers. He had no idea that God was his own Life, that he could contact this Presence with his thought, that he could be guided, and that he could heal his body by prayer. He was bound by his limited belief about God. Many have said to me that God is some kind of a man in the skies—a sort of a glorified man. Others say and believe there are three persons in God. You will always manifest the result of your belief. If you believe that God is some sort of a tyrannical, inscrutable being living in the skies, ready to judge and punish you for your mistakes and violations of man-made laws and religious taboos, you are bound by that belief, and you cause pain, misery, guilt-complexes, and so forth to follow. This is why Quimby said, "Man is belief expressed."

Your concept of God enters into all departments of your life; it is bound to have its effect upon you. God is Life, and Life seeks to express Itself as Love, Light, Truth, and Beauty. Life cannot wish death, sickness, or disease. To say that Life wishes death would be a violation of its own nature. Life cannot have a tendency toward limitation of any kind. Life is a Oneness, a Wholeness, a Unity, and It seeks to express that Unity in the formed universe.

In order to practice the Presence, you must do the will of God. What does this mean? *The will of God* must always be the nature of God. You can rest assured the will of God must always be something wonderful and glorious. "His name shall be called Wonderful, Counsellor, The Mighty God, The Everlasting Father, The Prince of Peace."

If your desire, idea, or intention is constructive, if it will bless others, and if it is in keeping with the universal principle of harmony, your will or desire is God's will. Your desire for wealth, true place, abundance, security, and better living conditions conforms to the will or tendency of Life or God.

Life is forever seeking to express Itself through you along higher levels. Enthrone in your mind the concept that God is the Only Presence, the Only Power, and that God is Infinitely Good and Perfect. Think of some of God's qualities and attributes, such as Boundless Love, Infinite Intelligence, Indescribable Beauty, Omnipotence, Omniscience, and Omnipresence. Believe these truths about God, and your whole life will change. You will begin to express more and more God-like qualities every day. Believe that God is All Life, All Love, All Truth, and All Beauty; accept It in the same way as you accept the sun in the heavens each morning; then you will find a great sense of peace and good will stealing over your mind and heart.

Do you believe in a vengeful, capricious, anthropomorphic Deity who sends sickness, trials, and tribulation to you? Watch the effect of such a belief. If you do, you will be like the man who said to me one time, "God sent this arthritis to me for a good purpose, and I suppose I must just bear it." This is superstition; such an attitude of mind has no foundation. He had arthritis for fifteen years, and he could not overcome it.

When this man with arthritis got a new concept of God, and he learned to forgive those whom he deeply resented, by realizing the Love of God was dissolving in his mind and body everything unlike Itself, he was healed, even though it took some months. This man's concept of God worked out, and made Itself manifest in his body according to his belief.

It is not your theoretical belief about God that manifests itself, but it is your real, deep, subconscious belief.

There are people who forget to practice the Presence when a lawsuit or verdict goes against them. Even though the judge rendered a verdict which seems unjust to you, continue to believe that it is God in action, and that there is a Divine, harmonious solution for all concerned; the matter will come right in due season. You cannot lose; you can only win by practicing the Presence.

If you believe that God is a man in the skies, you must experience the result of such a concept; consequently you experience confusion and trouble, just the same as if some human being with all his whims were running the world.

God is Pure Spirit, Infinite Mind, and Infinite Intelligence. The Bible calls the Name of God, "I AM," meaning Pure, Unconditioned Being. No one can, of course, define God, for God is Infinite, but there are certain Truths which the illumined of all ages have perceived as true of God, and that is why the Bible says, "I AM THAT I AM." What is "I AM?" It is your True Being—your Real Self; nobody can say, "I AM," for you. That is the Presence of God in you, and your Real Identity. Whatever you affix to "I AM," and believe, you become. Always claim, "I am strong, powerful, radiant, happy, joyous, illumined, and inspired"; then you are truly practicing the Presence, for all these qualities are true of God.

When you say, "I am weak," "I am inferior," "I am no good," you are denying God in the midst of you, and lying about Him.

Brother Lawrence of the 17th century was a monk. He was a saintly man, and wholly devoted to God. The book entitled *The Practice of the Presence of God* reveals a great humility, simplicity, and a mystic touch with God. "To do the will of God was," as he said, "his whole business." Brother Lawrence practiced the Presence when washing the dishes or scrubbing the floor. His attitude was that it was all God's work. His consciousness and awareness of the Divine Presence was no less when employed in the kitchen, than when he was before the altar. The way to God was to Brother Lawrence through the heart and through Love. His superiors marvelled at the man who, though only educated to the point of reading and writing, could express himself with such beauty and profound wisdom. It was the Voice of God within him that prompted all his sayings.

This is how he daily practiced God's Holy Presence: He said in effect, "I have put myself in Your Keeping; it is Your Business I am about, and so everything will be all right." How beautiful! How simple, yet how soul-stirring is this prayer! He said the only sorrow he could experience would be the loss of the sense of God's Presence, but he never feared that, being wholly aware of God's Love and Absolute Goodness.

In his early life he feared he would be damned; this torture of his mind persisted for four years; then he saw the whole cause of this negativity was lack of faith in God; seeing that, he was freed and entered into a life of continual joy.

Brother Lawrence schooled himself whether cooking, baking, or washing pans in the kitchen to pause, if only for a moment, to think of God in the center of his being, to be conscious of His Presence, and to keep a hidden meeting with Him. Due to his inner illumination, when he enjoyed the raptures of the Spirit, he emerged into a realm of profound peace.

Begin now to practice the Presence by keeping your eyes on God, or all things Good, by seeing God in everyone you meet, and by constantly affirming, "It is God in action in all departments of my life." Calmly trust God's Holy Presence to lead you to green pastures and still waters. Love the Truth with a love that leaves no room for care or doubt. No matter what your work may be, as you go to your business say, "God walks and talks in me. I rely on God's guidance and wisdom completely." Give thanks for the perfect day. Do as Brother Lawrence suggests whenever your attention wanders away on fear or doubt, bring it back to the contemplation of His Holy Presence.

To secure and know the life of peace and joy, school yourself daily to have an intimate, loving, familiar, humble conversation with God all day long. In this way you will draw upon God's grace abundantly. You shall become illumined by an Inner Light, and you will behold the inner vision of God, your Beloved.

CASE HISTORIES

Case History Number One

This interesting case from my files may bless many of you. This man invested a large sum of money in a certain organization. He had a very high regard for the two men who were active partners in this business. They appropriated the money which he gave them for themselves, and a little later they went into bankruptcy. He was very bitter and resentful, because he had practically put his life's savings into this venture. He was also ill, due to the hatred in his heart.

I explained to this man that resentment is never justified, and that many people make investments in land, stocks, bonds, etc., and have lost their money, but that it is absurd to blame the broker or the real estate man, because we erred in judgment. In a great measure this man's resentment was caused by a feeling of guilt for his own mistake, which he refused to admit. He was blaming the other men by an active resentment for his own shortcoming and failure. He prayed his way through it by the practice of His Presence in this way: "I now radiate love and goodwill to these two men. I humbly, sincerely, and honestly wish for them God's guidance, inner peace, and Divine Love. I wish for each one of them: prosperity, success, and a richness of life. It is God in action in all departments of their life. I mean this; I am sincere. My mind is now clear, clean, poised, serene, and expectant of happiness. God is guiding me in all ways. Nobody can take happiness, peace, or wealth away from me. I am one with God, and my business is God's Business. I am now minding my own business. The money I gave these men comes back to me in peace and harmony." He prayed like this night and morning, and during the day when hateful thoughts would come, he would say, "God is with me now."

In two weeks he was at peace with the world. All the resentful thoughts were burned up in his deeper mind; they were withered away by realizing God in action in his own life, and the life of those whom he said wronged him. A relative died in the interim, and a most interesting thing happened: He was bequeathed the exact amount he lost in that business venture. "For as the heavens are higher than the earth, so are my ways higher than your ways."

Case History Number Two

A young girl in our recent Bible Class practiced the Presence in this way: She said, "A man was constantly annoying her by calling her on the phone, and meeting her at her place of employment. One day she decided to do something about it. She relaxed; quieted the wheels of her mind; focused all her attention on the God-Presence within by realizing It was there.

She quietly said to herself, "God never made a man like that. Only the God in him is expressed to me. God is all, and only God can be expressed through him." This man completely disappeared out of her life; she never saw him again. She said it was as if the earth swallowed him! Undoubtedly, he was healed and blessed by her prayer; she had a healing also.

Prayer always prospers. It is like the gentle rain from heaven; it is twice blessed; it blesses him that gives and him that receives. She saw this man in a new light; then he felt this change within him; he was healed and ceased to annoy her.

"Love your enemies, bless them that curse you, do good to them that hate you, and pray for them which despitefully use you, and persecute you."

REALIZING YOUR DESIRE

Desire is the power behind all action. We could not lift our hand or walk unless we had the desire or urge to move. Desire is the gift of God. As Browning said, "Tis thou, God, who giveth, 'tis I who receive."

It is man who receives—not a few of the gifts of life, but all of them! "Son thou art ever with me, and all that I hath is thine." All things whatsoever the Father hath are mine. *Our Father* holds within Himself all things we require, such as peace, harmony, abundance, guidance, joy, and infinite expression. We must grow unceasingly. We can never exhaust the Infinite Storehouse.

Let us realize a few simple truths: It is due to desire that we jump out of the way of an oncoming bus. The reason we do this is because we have a basic desire to preserve our life. Self-preservation is the first law of nature.

By example, the farmer plants seed due to his desire to attain food for himself and his family. Man builds airplanes due to his desire to collapse time and space. Similar illustrations are found throughout our whole course of life.

Desire pushes man; it is the goad of action. It is behind all progress. Desire is really the cosmic urge in all of us, impelling us to go forward, onward, upward, and Godward.

Desire is the angel of God—the messenger of the Divine—saying to each one of us, "Come on up higher."

Desire is behind all progress. It is the push of life. We

find that we follow the desire which captivates and holds our attention. All of us find ourselves moving in the direction of the idea which dominates our mind for the time being.

Desire is an angel of God, telling us of something which, if accepted by us, will make our life fuller and happier. *The greater the expected benefit from the desire, the stronger is our desire*. Where there is no expected benefit, gain, or advancement accruing, there is no desire; consequently no action is found.

"I am alpha and omega, the beginning and the end, saith the Lord." Our ideal murmuring in our hearts is the alpha; in order that it become the omega, we must enter into the feeling that it is ours *now,* and walk the earth knowing that it is so.

Failure to realize our desire over a long period of time results in frustration and unhappiness. I have talked to many men in different parts of the country; their frequent complaint is that for years they have tried in vain to attain a certain ideal or position in life, and that they have failed miserably. They did not know that the desire to be, to do, and to have was the Still Small Voice speaking to them, and all that was necessary was for them to say, "Yes, Father, I accept and believe it"; then walk the earth knowing that, "It is done."

By illustration take the seed which draws all that it requires, such as water, chemicals, etc. from the ground, and when it comes above the ground, it extracts from the rays of the sun through a process of photosynthesis all the light and other elements necessary to form a complex substance called chlorophyll. It also has the intelligence within it to make the most complex, chemical compounds in its bark and leaves beyond the ken of man to discover.

In like manner when man becomes as the seed, and knows that all things necessary for the unfoldment of his ideal will be given to him, he will attract to himself whatsoever things he needs for the complete realization of his dream, for instance: friends, funds, introductions, ideas, etc.

All men, women, and children that help us on the road of life are servants of the law which we set in operation within us. "My ways are not your ways." This Infinite Intelligence, which we set in motion when we pray aright, inspires in others the actions, words, and movements necessary to aid us in the grand unfoldment of our ideal or in the great drama of our life.

It is foolish to blame or accuse others, as we must realize that others are witnesses telling us who we are—"As within, so without." If there is discord within, there will be discord without. If we dwell in a mood of lack and limitation, others must come and testify to our lack.

I knew a woman in London one time, and on three occasions her purse was snatched from her by a thief in the tube of London; she was a wealthy woman. The explanation for this is that she was living in the fear of having her purse stolen; this was really an expectancy. "What I fear most has come upon me."

The mood, feeling, or conviction in which we walk determines the movements and actions of others towards us. In the eleventh chapter of Mark it says, "All things whatsoever ye shall ask in prayer, believe that ye receive them, and ye shall receive them."

The word *whatsoever* in the above quotation means anything you wish; it is all inclusive. There are no specific conditions set forth; you do not have to be a church-goer, or belong to a certain creed, or make any sacrifices. "I rejoice not in the sacrifices of man, not by power, not by might, but by the spirit saith the Lord." "For what purposes is the multitude of thy sacrifices. I am full of the blood of rams and the fat of beast, I rejoice not in the blood of rams or he goats." The only requisite is to believe that you have it now, or that you are the being you long to be.

Believe means to live in the state of being it; this means a complete mental acceptance where there is no longer any doubt or question in your mind. This is the state of consciousness called "a conviction." All other procedures as cited by Isaiah are foolishness and superstition. The only prerequisite is to believe that you have received; then comes the manifestation of your ideal.

We grow through desire. It is desire that pushes us forward, for it is the cosmic urge.

Let us realize that we are all channels of the Divine— individualizations of God-consciousness. The desire that lingers in your heart, that murmurs quietly—perhaps it has been there for months making itself known to you—is the Voice of God speaking to you, telling you to come on up higher— to arise and shine. Maybe you have looked around you and said to yourself, "What chance have I?" "Mary can, but I can't." "Perhaps, someday!" "It is just wishful thinking, etc." Have many such expressions come to your mind? Remember it is your five senses and worldly reason arguing with your Higher Self. We must remember that in prayer we always shut out the evidence of our senses and reason, plus everything that contradicts or denies what we truly want; then, as Jesus commands, we go within; shut the door, and pray to our Father in secret; the Father who seeth in secret will reward thee openly. Let us now proceed to enter into this Secret Place, and perform the spiritual, creative act in our own mind.

Sit down in an armchair, relax, and let go. Practice the Nancy School technique by getting into a drowsy, meditative state, a state of effortless effort, wherein effort is reduced to a minimum.

By example if you want to be a singer on the radio, imagine you are before a microphone; the microphone is now in front of you, and you see the imaginary audience; you are the actor. ("Act as though I am, and I will be.") You *feel* yourself into the situation; you are singing now (in your imagination); enter into the joy of it; feel the thrill of accomplishment! Continue to do this in your imagination until it begins to feel natural for you; then go off to sleep. If you have succeeded in planting your desire in your subconscious mind, you will feel a great sense of peace and satisfaction when you awaken. An interesting thing will have happened: You will have no further desire to pray about it, because it is fixed in consciousness. The reason for this is that the creative act has been finished, and you are at rest.

After true prayer when you have reached an inner conviction, there steals over you a sense of inner peace, calm, and certitude which tells you, "All is well." This is called *the sabbath* in the Bible, or period of stillness, or rest; it is the interval that elapses between the subjective realization of your desire and its manifestation. The manner of manifestation is not known to you; that is the secret of the subjective. "My ways are past finding out."

The answer or manifestation comes as a thief in the night. You know a thief comes when you least expect him; there is always an element of surprise; perhaps when you are sound asleep, the thief will come. If you sit up watching and waiting for the intruder, he will not come. Likewise we must go about our daily business, and the moment we think not, the answer will come. You are now at peace, made whole so to speak. You do not have to assist this Infinite Intelligence; It is All Powerful. It would be foolish to try to add power to Power.

The trouble with many people is this: When they pray, they are tense, anxious, and impatient. They say, "I wonder when it will come?" Others say, "Why has it not happened yet?"

If I say, "Why?" it means I am anxious and lack faith. If I *know* a thing is true, I do not question my prayer. Let us remember, therefore, anytime we ask, "Why?" to ourself or another, it means we have not reached a conviction within ourselves.

When we possess something in consciousness, we do not seek it; we have it! Another point I want to stress here is: When the student questions, "How will it come?" he shows lack of faith and conviction.

By illustration, I am now in Los Angeles, I do not ask, "How will I get there?" I *am* there. Similarly when our ideal is fixed in consciousness, we do not wonder, "How will I get there?" I am there already. Where your consciousness is, you are. "Where I am there you will be also."

CASE HISTORIES

Case History Number One

Several years ago the author was lecturing in the Park Central Hotel in New York City. A man spoke to me at the end of the meeting saying, "I desire desperately to go to Pittsburgh, and I have no money."

I said to him, "Did you hear the lecture?"
He said, "Yes, but—."

I told him to ignore the doubts in his mind. We made a simple statement of truth together in that lovely, lecture room. The statement was, "I am now at home in Pittsburgh with my people. All is peace and harmony." He was at home with them during those few minutes of silence in his imagination and feeling.

He phoned me later saying, "I went to the restaurant, and a man who sat next to me said, "You know I am driving to Pittsburgh. I would love to have someone share in the driving; I would pay him also. Do you know anyone? You look like a mechanic." This was the way Infinite Intelligence answered this man's prayer.

Case History Number Two

I want to tell you of another experience I had in the army. A young soldier said to me, "You know before the war I tried to get into Bellevue Medical School for several years; I was always turned down; yet my marks were very high."

This boy believed he was a victim of racial prejudice. He was attached to my battalion. We chatted one night about the laws of life. I discussed with him the relationship of the conscious and subconscious mind which is given in detail in my book, *The Miracles of Your Mind*. I explained to him that his subconscious mind had the answer; it knew all, and had the "know how" of accomplishment.

I reviewed with him some experiments that I had conducted several years previously with a refugee Psychologist from Berlin. In one instance a boy under these experiments became clairvoyant, and described things taking place at a distance, which we subsequently verified. This boy also gave the location of missing articles, and predicted accurately certain international incidents. We discussed the fact that Infinite Intelligence and Wisdom is lodged in the subliminal mind of man; it is possible to tune in with It, and to get It to work for us.

Accordingly and apropos to the above conversation, the following experiment was suggested to him: At night as he was about to fall asleep, he would imagine he saw a medical diploma inscribed with his name stating he was a physician and surgeon. He felt this diploma with his hand, and imagined the joy of it all. He made it real and natural by focusing his attention on one thing—the diploma—the finished thing; then he contemplated the reality of it.

"Believe that you have it now, and ye shall receive it." "Call things that be not, as though they were, and the unseen becomes seen." "I told you before it came to pass, that when it is come to pass, ye might believe." These are perfect formulas for prayer.

This boy went to the end; he asked himself this question: "What actually would I receive to prove to the world that I am a doctor?" The answer came, "A diploma!" In his imagination, he saw the diploma, and made it real. He went to sleep feeling the diploma in his hand.

By example, you can close your eyes now and feel silk, mohair, or a fur coat on you. As you feel the naturalness of the fur coat, you will receive it.

The sequel to this soldier's prayer is very interesting: This man said to me one morning, "You know I have a feeling that something is going to happen, and that I won't be around here long." This was the subconscious mind telling him, "All is well."

We know sometimes by a hunch, an inner awareness, or feeling that our prayer is answered. Technically we would say the idea has been sub-subjectified or embodied in the subconscious. In truth we would say the soldier accepted the idea in consciousness, and his inner knowing brought it to pass. The many words or phrases we use all illustrate the same thing, namely, he felt the reality of it; that is all that is necessary. The technique he used aided him in its fulfillment.

The commanding officer called him in, and informed him that in view of his pre-medical training, he was to take an examination; if he received good marks, he would be sent to the Medical College at the expense of the Army. It ensued that he was sent to Stanford, and not to Bellevue. "My ways are past finding out." (It had been explained to him that he did not have to go to Bellevue to be a doctor; let Infinite Intelligence be the guide.)

In prayer go to the end. Feel that you are now what you desire to be; then Infinite Intelligence takes charge, and acts on the thoughts, ideas, and actions of others, so that they aid us in the realization of our desire. (In the same manner a seed attracts to it all things, such as chemicals, water, sunshine, air, etc., necessary for its growth.)

We are always using this Principle, Power, Intelligence, and Wisdom all the days of our life. When we lift our hand to write, we use this Power and Energy. In the same manner when we breathe, we are using the same air.

For example, I am writing now. The ideas expressed come from the One Mind, common to all individual men. There is only One Source, and That is God. We do not originate anything; for all ideas live, move, and have their being in God. This Infinite Being, Consciousness, Awareness, or whatever we choose to call It is the only Originator—the Fountain of all. All men drink from this One Source or Spring. You will understand from these truths that when we look at the sun or a tree, we all see a sun and a tree, which shows that all of us are using the One Mind.

There is, therefore, no such thing as an atheist; there could not be, because he is using the Mind, the Power, and the Intelligence which is of God. He is alive, and the very Life of him is God, for God is Life. When he says, "I do not believe in God," you can see how absurd it is. He knows, and he believes, he is alive. Aliveness, Awareness is God.

As a teacher I wish to point out that there is no teacher who could give you anything new; he could not; neither can he give you truth. All any teacher can do is to awaken that which is already within you. You house God. As the Book of Revelation says, "The tabernacle of God is with man." A teacher causes you to see the truth which was always there; he kindles a fire if he is a good teacher; then you warm yourself by its glow. But the fire, the glow, and the warmth, thereof, were always within you. The real teacher, if he has a good knowledge of truth, will teach you freedom, and tell you frankly that you do not owe him any personal allegiance, since your heart belongs to God or the Truth. "To thine own self be true, as the night the day, thou canst then be false to no man." The teacher of truth will tell you if you do not get anything from him, to go elsewhere where you will be blessed. We call our own; there is no competition in truth.

You do not have to strive toward a goal; for the goal you seek already is, and through your treatment work you appropriate it by accepting the state desired in consciousness. All states co-exist in the Greater Now, or other dimensions of your mind. It is like the keyboard of a piano; the music you wish to play is already in the piano; all you do is to strike the proper keys and chords to bring it forth, but the tune or the sonata was always there; you do not create it. All you did was to recognize a certain composition and to bring it forth. You can play on the piano *Pop Goes The Weasel* or a Beethoven *Sonata;* the piano does not care.

Similarly look at the English alphabet; you did not create it; it always existed in Infinite Mind. With this alphabet you can write a beautiful, magnificent drama of life, or you may write a gossip column that may cause some misguided person to die by suicide.

We must strike the key to bring forth our music also; our music is: harmony, health, peace, true place, or expression in life. We strike the proper key by contemplating the reality of the state sought now, feeling, and believing ourselves to possess it.

A simple illustration is as follows: Suppose you wish to sell a home for $20,000. This is the price you would pay for it if the tables were reversed. You are satisfied this is the correct price, and there is no quarrel in your consciousness. The next step is, as Troward says, "to see the end." A simple way to do this is to take a little phrase that is easily graven on the memory, for instance, "It is sold," or "It is done," and repeat it over and over again like a lullaby until you feel the naturalness and reality of it. (This latter procedure is suggested by the New Nancy School. See Baudouin's book on autosuggestion.)

The author has instructed many people in the sale of property as follows: See the check in your hand, and feel the joy of accomplishment. Imagining that you have the check in your hand is seeing the end, and having seen the end as Troward says, you have willed the means to the realization of the end. Infinite Spirit will attract to you the person who wants what you have to offer; the price and the time will be right, and you will find the place will be sold in peace and harmony for all concerned. "Let him that is athirst come and drink of the waters of life freely."

THE MAGIC OF FAITH

The purpose of this chapter is to teach you the spiritual truth of your dominion and freedom. "In all thy ways acknowledge him, and he shall direct thy paths." (Prov. 3:6). "I will lift up mine eyes unto the hills, from whence cometh my help." (Psalm 121:1).

In the above verse from proverbs you are told to acknowledge the Infinite Intelligence within you, and that It shall direct you in all ways. The answer to your problem will come when you turn in faith and recognition to the Divine Principle within.

It was Shakespeare who said, "Our doubts are traitors, making us lose the good we oft might win, by fearing to attempt." Fear holds us back. *Fear* is a lack of faith in God or the Good.

A man told me one time that he was a member of a sales force for a large, chemical organization which had two hundred men in the field. The sales manager died, and the vice president offered him the position; however he turned it down. He realized later that the only reason he rejected the offer was due to fear. He was afraid to attempt the responsibility. This man lacked faith in himself and his Inner Power. He hesitated, and the wonderful opportunity passed him by.

This salesman came to me for consultation, and I learned he was condemning himself, which was like a destructive, mental poison. In place of condemnation, he began to realize there were other opportunities. I explained to him that faith is a way of thinking, a positive mental attitude, or a feeling of confidence that what you are praying for will come to pass.

For example, you have faith that the sun will rise tomorrow. You have faith that the seed you deposited in the ground will grow. The electrician has faith that electricity will respond to his proper use of it. A scientist has an idea for an ediphone; he proceeds to bring it to pass by having faith in the execution of the invisible idea.

Opportunity is always knocking at your door. The desire for health, harmony, peace, and prosperity is knocking at your door now. Perhaps you are offered a promotion; are you going to act like Peter of old who walked on the waters? ("And when Peter was come down out of the ship, he walked on the water, to go to Jesus. But when he saw the wind boisterous, he was afraid; and beginning to sink, he cried, Lord, save me.")

Besides being historical, this drama of Peter and Jesus takes place in your own mind. *Peter* means faith, perseverance, and determination. *Jesus* means your desire which, if realized, would be your savior. Jesus comes into your mind as an idea, desire, plan, purpose, vision, or some new undertaking. The realization of your dreams, plans, or purpose would bring you and others great satisfaction and inner joy; this would be your Jesus. You must now call Peter which is faith in the God-Power to bring all things to pass. Look at Peter and Jesus as dramatizations of the power of truth within you.

Oftentimes as you attempt something new—for example, a new position—doubt comes into your mind; this is *Peter* in you looking at the *boisterous wind and sinking*. This represents the impingement in your mind of the race belief in failure, lack, and limitation.

You must cremate, burn up, and destroy that negative

thought immediately. You must not suffer a witch to live; meaning you must supplant the negative feeling with the positive thoughts of success, peace, and prosperity immediately, and give your love and feeling to these concepts. As you sustain this mood of confidence, you will become victorious.

Doubt and fear hold men in bondage of sickness and failure. These false concepts cause you to vacillate, waver, equivocate, and hesitate to go ahead. The way to overcome is to increase your faith and awareness of your deep, spiritual potencies. Be like Peter; he succeeded, because he went forward; he had faith and confidence, knowing he would succeed.

A general in the field cannot afford to vacillate and waver on the battlefield. He has to come to a decision. Failure to come to a decision, plus a constant wavering in the mind, leads to a nervous breakdown and mental confusion. When you find yourself being pulled two ways, that is a sign of doubt and fear.

Your good comes to you in the form of your desire. If you are sick, you wish health. If you are poor, you desire wealth. If you are full of fear, you desire faith and confidence. Jesus comes as your desire walking down the streets of your mind.

There is another part of your mind which says, "No, it can't be. It is too late now." "It is impossible." This is the time to lift up your eyes unto the hills from whence cometh your help; i.e., you lift up your eyes when you focus your attention on your good. Remember faith can do all things. "Thy faith hath made thee whole." "According to your faith is it done unto you." You must appreciate the fact that your desire, idea, or dream is real, though it is invisible. To know that the idea is real, that it is a fact of consciousness, gives you faith, and enables you to move over the waters of confusion, strife, and fear to a place of conviction deep in your own heart. Peter said, "Lord, if it be thou, bid me come unto thee on the water."

Ideas are our lords and masters. Ideas govern and rule us. The dominant idea which you now entertain is your lord; it generates its own emotion. Emotions compel you to express them. The dominant idea of success enthroned in the mind generates its own mood or feeling. This feeling compels you to right action, so that whatever you do under the mood of faith and confidence will be successful. The desire or idea of yours now is your lord. "Lord, if It be thou, bid me come to thee upon the water." Mentally appropriate your desire, kiss it, love it, let it captivate your mind; feel the reality of it.

Is your desire lofty, inspiring, and wonderful enough to lead you forward? This ideal of yours is real, just the same as the idea of a radio was real in the mind of the inventor; or the idea of an automobile was real in the mind of Ford; or the idea of a house is real in the mind of an architect. It is not idle fancy or a daydream.

Peter is within you; i.e., *Peter* is faith, perseverance, stick-to-it-iveness, and an abiding trust in an Almighty Power which responds to man's thought and belief. This Formless Awareness within you takes the form of your belief and conviction. It is really all things to all men. It is strength to you, if you need strength. It is guidance, if you need guidance. It is food and health also.

Everyone has faith in something. What is *your* faith? Let it be faith in all things good, a joyous expectancy of the best, and a firm belief inscribed in your heart that Infinite Intelligence will lead you out of your difficulty, and show you the way. You have a firm conviction now in the Power of God to solve your problems and heal you. This faith in God enables you to walk over all the waters of fear, doubt, worry, and imaginary dangers of all kinds. You now know that error and fear are false beliefs without power. You know these negative states are false and groundless. Paul says, "Faith is the substance of things hoped for, the evidence of things not seen." It is from faith or feeling that all things flow.

When you look down, you see mud, but when you look up, you see the stars! Similarly, when you say, "There is no way out. I have no chance," you are looking like Peter at the winds of confusion, fear, and human opinion; but when he remembers where his power is, he *looks up at Jesus*, meaning that he looks at the solution, the way out, the happy ending, and ignores the winds of human intellect and the waves of race mind.

The man of faith puts his trust in the Invisible Power within him. He knows this is the Kingdom of the Real. He knows that his ideal is real in the Inner Kingdom, and that his faith or feeling will cause the formless or the invisible to take on form as a condition, event, or experience. This is why the man of faith walks upon the waters, and moves in confidence and understanding to the promised land—his cherished goal. Faith is accepting as true what your reason and intellect deny.

All great scientists, mystics, artists, poets, and inventors are gifted or possessed by an abiding faith and trust in the Invisible Powers within.

Faith is trust. You trusted your mother when you were in her arms; you looked into her eyes, and you saw love there. Your *Peter* is your faith and trust in God, the Absolute Lover, and it should be greater than faith in your mother.

As you read this, turn your desire or request over to the subjective mind within you, acknowledging in your heart it has the answer and the "know how" of accomplishment, and that its ways are past finding out. When you are relaxed and peaceful, you will know you have succeeded in impregnating your deeper mind. Signs follow; the wave of peace is the sign; this is inner conviction. You now walk above all the waters of confusion, chaos, and false beliefs, because in a little while what you felt as true will be experienced.

Troward says if a thing is true, there is a way in which it is true. Look at the magic and miracle-working power of faith in your own life. Behold the miracle which takes place as you drink a glass of milk; it is transformed into tissue, muscle, bone, hair, and blood cells in your body by the Master Chemist within. Look within for your savior. Your true savior is your thought and feeling. Blend these together, and you have a holy covenant, a wedded bliss, the mystic marriage. Any idea or desire impregnated with love is invincible; this is working faith. Blend Peter (faith) and Jesus (desire) together, and the miracle will happen.

CASE HISTORIES

Case History Number One

I visited a man in prison a few months ago. The first thought in his mind was freedom; this is symbolized in the Bible as Jesus walking on the waters of your mind. This prisoner was very bitter and cynical. I explained to him that he had placed himself in prison by his actions which were contrary to the golden rule. He was living in a psychological prison of hatred and envy. He changed his mental attitude by calling forth Peter which was his faith in an Almighty Power to bring to pass the cherished desire of his heart.

I gave detailed instruction to this prisoner. He began to pray for those he hated by saying frequently, "God's love flows through them, and I release them." He began to do this many times a day. At night prior to sleep, he imagined himself home with his family. He would feel his little daughter in his arms and hear her voice saying, "Welcome, daddy." All this was done in his imagination. After a while he made this so real, natural, and vivid, that it became a part of him. He had impregnated the subconscious with the belief in freedom.

Another interesting thing happened; he had no further desire to pray for his freedom; this was a sure psychological sign to him that he had embodied the desire for freedom subjectively. He was at peace, and though he was behind bars, he knew subjectively that he was free. It was an inner knowing. You no longer seek that which you have. Having realized his desire subjectively, he had no further desire to pray about it.

A few weeks passed by, and this young man was liberated from prison. Friends came to his rescue, and through the proper channels, the door was opened to him for a new life.

Case History Number Two

A student in our Bible class stated that there was no way to save her boy-friend from losing his store. He could not meet the bills; even his automobile was attached.

She was saying, "It isn't possible. I see no way out. It is just hopeless." She listened to one of our lectures on prayer, and applied it that night.

She said, "I will walk upon the waters of doubt and negativity, and 'I will say of the Lord, He *is* my refuge, and my fortress: my God; in him will I trust.'" She anchored her mind on the following great truth: "God's peace floods his mind, and God answers him."

She remained in a quiet, passive state; she got into the mood or feeling that there was a solution for her boy-friend, and went off to sleep, dwelling on the following, wonderful words of truth: "I stand still, and I see the salvation of the Lord." This young girl knew that the savior was in her own faith; she turned her eyes to the hills; these *hills* are always of an inner range; they are the hills of faith and trust in God which moves mountains. Reject mentally all sense-evidence, and look into the eyes of your savior; this means to live in the emotional embodiment of your desire or ideal.

The following day her boy-friend called her, and told her that a miracle had happened. A check was presented to him the following day for $2,000 by a man who had borrowed this amount ten years previously. It came out of the blue as a perfect response to her prayer of faith.

STEPS TO HAPPINESS

Happiness is a state of consciousness. Faith and fear are moods of the soul. Your faith is a joyous expectancy of the best. Fear comes to challenge your faith in God or the Good. You must look upon fear as man's ignorance or his false beliefs which try to overcome his conviction in the good.

Never entertain or accept the suggestions of sickness, weakness, or failure. If you listen to negative suggestions and become fearful, begin to affirm the Truths of God, such as Love, Peace, Joy, etc. Know that thought and feeling are the causes of conditions and experiences.

Fear is based on the false beliefs that there are other powers, and that external things and conditions can hurt you. Fear must leave you, because it has nothing to sustain it; there is no reality behind it; its claims are false. Come back to the simple truth: "Only your thought has power over you, and the One Almighty Power now moves on your behalf, because your thoughts are in tune with the Infinite One.

The man full of faith in God is never concerned about the future. When worry or fear knock at the door of his mind, faith in God opens the door, and he is at peace.

I met a farmer one time on the west coast of Ireland. I lived in his house for a few days. He seemed to be always happy and joyful. I asked him to tell me his secret of happiness. His answer was, "It is a habit of mine to be happy." This is the whole story! Prayer is a habit; happiness is likewise a habit.

There is a phrase in the Bible which says, "Choose ye this day whom ye will serve." You have the freedom *to choose* happiness; this may seem extraordinarily simple—and it is. Perhaps this is why people stumble over the way to happiness; they do not see the simplicity of the key to happiness. You can choose unhappiness by entertaining these ideas: "Today is a black day; everything is going to go wrong." "I am not going to be successful." "Everyone is against me."

Perhaps you say to yourself, "Business is bad. It is going to get worse." Furthermore, you may say to yourself, "The worst is yet to come!" If you have this attitude of mind the first thing in the morning, you will attract all these experiences to you, and you will be very unhappy.

On the other hand you can choose happiness. This is how you do it: When you open your eyes in the morning, say to yourself, "All things work together for good to them that love God." Remember that in all languages God and Good are synonymous.

Love is an emotional attachment. Continue to become attached to the good in the morning in this way: Look out the window, and say, "This is God's day for me. I am Divinely guided all day long. Whatever I do will prosper. I cast the spell of God around me. I walk in His Light. Whenever my attention wanders away from God or the Good, I will immediately bring it back to the contemplation of God and His Holy Presence. I am a spiritual magnet attracting to myself all things which bless and prosper me. I am going to be a wonderful success in all my undertakings today. I am definitely going to be happy all day long."

Start each day in this manner; then you are choosing happiness, and you will be a radiant, joyous person.

You can experience nothing outside your own mentality.

Your dominant, mental mood is the way you think and feel inside about yourself, others, and the world in general. What is your present mental attitude? How do you feel inside? Are you worried, confused, angry, or concerned about other people's actions? If you are, you are not happy, because you are dwelling mentally on limitation.

Begin to anchor your mind on thoughts of peace, success, and happiness; this is really prayer. Do this frequently; then you will be like the Irish farmer who said, "It is a habit of mine to be happy." Your dominant mental attitude rules and governs all your experiences; therefore nothing can come into your world but the out-picturing of your mental attitude. Love all things good, and even your so-called "enemies" will be constrained to do you good.

Oftentimes you read in psychological and metaphysical literature that the world you behold is the world you are; this means you can control your relationship with the world. The world you really live in is a mental world of thoughts, feelings, sensations, and beliefs. As a matter of fact every person, circumstance, and experience you meet becomes a thought in your mind. How you mentally feel and react to life and conditions depend on what you believe about life and things in general. If your knowledge about life and the world is false, you can be very unhappy. If you have true knowledge and the right ideas, you can control your emotional reactions to life and have inner peace.

You are now awakening to the truth that happiness is determined by what goes on in your mind. There is one very important point about being happy: You must sincerely *desire* to be happy. There are people who have been depressed, dejected, and unhappy so long, that were they suddenly made happy by some wonderful, good, joyful news, they would actually be like the woman who said to me, "It is wrong to be so happy!" They long for the former, depressed, unhappy state.

I knew a woman in England who had rheumatism for twenty years. She would pat herself on the knee, and say, "My rheumatism is bad today. I can't go out; my rheumatism keeps me miserable." This dear, elderly lady got a lot of attention from her son, daughter, and the neighbors. She really wanted her rheumatism; she enjoyed her "misery," as she called it. This person did not really want to be happy.

I suggested a curative procedure given in the Bible. I wrote down some biblical verses, and said if she gave her attention to these truths, she would be healed, but she was not interested. There seems to be a peculiar, mental streak in many people, whereby they seem to enjoy being miserable and sad.

Jesus said, "If you know these things, happy are ye if ye do them." "We should become as little children." The reason for this is that a child is happy, because it is close to God. The child knows intuitively where to find happiness. You do not have to become old, dull, crotchety, petulant, and cantankerous; neither do you have to become jaded and depressed in spirit. The simple truths of life, and not the opinions of man, produce and generate happiness within us. There are a great number of people trying to buy happiness through the purchase of radios, television sets, automobiles, and a home in the country, but happiness can not be purchased or procured that way.

The Kingdom of God is within you, and the kingdom of happiness is in your thought and feeling. Too many people have the idea that it takes something artificial to produce happiness. Some people say, "If I had a million dollars, I would be happy." Others say, "If I was elected mayor, or the president of the organization, I would be happy." The answer is, "We must *choose* happiness." We must make it a habit to be happy. It is a mental and spiritual state. Happiness comes through your daily visits with God and in silent communion with His Holy Presence.

Begin now to eat the bread of the silence; you do this by meditating on the fact that, "In Him there is fullness of joy." As you dwell on these words, imagine the joy and the love of God are flowing through your mind and heart as a living current or stream; then you are stirring up the gift of God within you.

The Savior is within you, but He is asleep. Awaken Him! It takes only thought to stir God into action. Every time you mentally reject the power of conditions and circumstances, and recognize the Presence of God in you, you are stirring up the gift of God within you. "Wherefore I put thee in remembrance that thou stir up the gift of God, which is in thee."

When your mind is clean and wholesome, when your eyes are dedicated and focused on God or the Good, and when you have a child's heart, your mind is at peace; then you are full of good will, and you are happy.

Say to yourself every day when you awaken, "God is my partner." If the day is raining, say with joy, "How wonderful it is to see God in action!" When you see snow falling, give thanks. When the sun shines, know it is blessing everyone.

Within you is the Power to overcome any situation. You were born to win, to succeed, and to conquer. There is a great thrill in mastering a difficult assignment; the joy is in overcoming. Stand up against the problem now. Take up that shining sword of truth, and say, "I go forth conquering and to conquer!" The Power of the Almighty is within you; It will reveal to you the perfect solution. It will show you the way

you should go. Conquer and overcome every negative emotion within you. Love casts out fear. The peace of God casts
out pain. Good will casts out envy. In the midst of all kinds of
adversity, look for that which is good, and that which is right;
in other words look for the Divine answer.

Turn within you now, and say, "Every morning I will
say, 'There is something happy on my way.'" Evil has no reality; for your evil is your disorganized mind.

God is Life, and Life is forever seeking to express Itself
in ways of pleasantness and paths of peace. Its tendency is
Lifeward. The urge of Life is progression. Life is seeking to
express through you as harmony, health, peace, joy, and happiness; these are the truths you are seeking. There is nothing
but Good in God's universal, cosmic design. Enthrone in your
mind the thought of the complete Omnipotence of God, and
that God is watching over you, guiding you in all your ways.
Let your mind be imbued with this idea, and the waters of
healing will flow through you. As you focus your attention
on these truths, you are making it a habit to be happy.

CASE HISTORIES

Case History Number One
I knew an alcoholic in London who had sunk to the
depths of degradation. When I met him, he was begging pennies on the street for drink. At one time he
was a highly respected lawyer. I spent some time
with him in Hyde Park, London, telling him a few
simple truths. I wrote these words for him to repeat: "I surrender myself completely to God and His
Boundless Love and Goodness. My mind and heart

are now open to the Spirit of Almighty God which flows through me now. God fills my mind and heart with His Joy and His Love. I do not see the wind, but I feel the breeze upon my face; likewise I feel God's Presence stirring in my heart. God's river of Love flows through me, and I am clean and made whole."

I told him to relax, and slowly articulate the above meditation fifteen minutes, three times a day. All that was necessary was sincerity and humility on his part; then he was assured he would be free from the habit and blessed beyond his wildest dreams. This man became childlike in his simplicity. He fulfilled his promise. In less than a week he was engaged in a romance with God. Truly he touched the hem of His garment. As he meditated aloud, he imagined that the words were seeds sinking down into his soul. On the sixth day his whole being and his room were flooded with an Interior Light which seemed to blind him temporarily. He was completely healed.

Case History Number Two

Lecturing in San Francisco some years ago, I interviewed a man who was very unhappy and dejected over the way his business was going. He was the general manager. His heart was filled with resentment toward the vice president and the president of the organization; "They opposed him," he claimed. Because of this internal strife, business was declining; he was receiving no dividends.

This is how he prayed and solved his business problems: The first thing in the morning, he used the following meditation, "All those working in our corporation are spiritual, wonderful, God-like links in the chain of its growth, welfare, and prosperity. I radiate good will in my thoughts, words, and deeds to my two associates, and all those in the company. God's Love and good will fill my heart for the president and the vice president of our company. Infinite Intelligence and Divine Wisdom make all decisions through me. There is only right action taking place in our life. I send the messengers of peace, love, and good will before me to the office, and the peace of God reigns supreme in the minds and hearts of all those in the company including myself. I now go forth into a new day full of faith, confidence, and trust."

This business executive repeated the above meditation slowly three times in the morning feeling the truth behind the words. He put life, love, truth, and beauty into the words, and they went deep down into his subconscious mind. When fearful or angry thoughts came into his mind during the day, he would say, "God is within me now." After a while all the harmful thoughts ceased to come, and peace came into his mind. He wrote me in New York saying that at the end of the two weeks, the president and the vice president called him into the office, apologized, and shook hands with him saying that the organization could not get along without him. He was so happy again. His happiness resulted from seeing God in the other fellow, and in radiating love and good will to all. True happiness came to him as he began to practice the Presence of God.

Love frees; it gives; it is the spirit of God. Love is the Universal Solvent; for Love dissolves everything unlike Itself.

HARMONIOUS HUMAN RELATIONS

"All things whatsover ye would that men should do unto you, do ye even so to them."

The first thing you learn is that there is no one to change but yourself. The above truth has outer and inner meanings: As you would that men should *think* about you, think you about them in like manner. As you would that men should *feel* about you, feel you also about them in like manner. As you would want men to *act* toward you, act you toward them in like manner. This Biblical passage is the key to happy, human relationships in all walks of life.

Do you observe your "inner talking"? For example, you may be polite and courteous to someone in your office, but when his back is turned, you are very critical and resentful toward him in your mind. Such negative thoughts are highly destructive to you; it is like taking poison; you are actually taking a mental poison which robs you of vitality, enthusiasm, strength, guidance, and good will.

The suggestion you give to the other, you give to yourself. Ask yourself now, "How am I behaving internally toward this other fellow?" This interior attitude is what counts. Begin now to observe yourself; observe your reactions to people, conditions, and circumstances. How do you respond to the events and news of the day? It makes no difference if all the other people were wrong, and you alone were right, if the news disturbs you, it is your evil, because your bad mood affected and robbed you of peace and harmony. You do not have to react negatively to the news or the comments of the broadcaster. You can remain unmoved, undisturbed, and poised, realizing he has a right to his expression and beliefs. It is never what a person says or does that affects us; it is our reaction to what is said or done that matters.

Mentally divide yourself into two people: Your present mental state and that which you desire to be. Look at the thoughts of envy, jealousy, and hatred which may have enslaved and imprisoned you. You have divided yourself into two people for the purpose of disciplining yourself: One is the race mind working in you, the other is the Infinite or the God-Self seeking expression through you. Be honest with yourself and determine which mood shall prevail.

For example, if someone gossips about you or criticizes you, what is your reaction? Are you going to engage in the typical way by getting excited, resentful, and angry? If you do, you are letting the world-mind work in you. You must positively refuse to react in this mechanical, stereotyped, machine-like way. Say positively and definitely to yourself: The Infinite One thinks, speaks, and acts through me now; this is my Real Self. I now radiate love, peace, and good will to this person who criticized me. I salute the Divinity in him. God speaks through me as peace, harmony, and love. It is wonderful. You are now a real student of truth. Instead of reacting like the herd who returns hate for hate, you have returned love for hatred, peace for hurt, good will for ill will. You have come into truth to think and react in a new way. When you come into truth, you make a new set of reactions to supplant the old. If you find yourself always reacting in the same way to people and conditions, you are not growing. Instead you are standing still, deeply immersed in the race mind.

You know that you do not have to accept negative thoughts. You can become what you want to be by refusing to be a slave to old thought patterns.

Become the real observer, and practice observing your reactions to the events of the day. Whenever you discover that you are about to react negatively, say firmly, "This is not the Infinite One speaking or acting"; this will cause you to stop your negative thinking; then the Divine Love, Light, and Truth will flow through you at that moment. Instead of identifying yourself with anger, resentment, bitterness, and hatefulness, identify immediately with peace, harmony, poise, and balance; with this attitude you are really practicing the art of separation. You are separating yourself from the old (your present, mental state), and you are identifying yourself with the new (that which you desire to be).

You want to be the Christed one, the Anointed individual, the Illumined one, the God-man—who does not? In order to become the ideal, you must identify yourself with all the qualities and attributes you wish to manifest.

Remember this great truth: You do not have to go along with, believe in, nor consent to negative thoughts or reactions. Begin to positively refuse to react mechanically as you formerly did. React and think in a new way. You want to be peaceful, happy, radiant, healthy, prosperous, and inspired;

therefore, from this moment forward you must refuse to identify with negative thoughts which tend to drag you down.

Many women say, "How can I change my husband?"
Another frequent statement is, "I would like to change Mary
in the office; she is the cause of all the trouble." Many have
heard the metaphysical phrase, "See the Christ in the other,
and all is well." However most people do not know exactly
what that means. It really means to become aware of the Presence of God in the other, and to realize that God is actually
being expressed through the thoughts, words, and actions of
that person. To really know, accept, and believe these truths is
to see the Christ in the other.

There is no problem in human relations that you cannot solve harmoniously and for the benefit of all concerned.
When you say that your associate in the office is very difficult
to handle, that he is cantankerous, mean, and obstreperous,
do you realize that in all probability he is reflecting your own
inner mental states? Like attracts like; birds of a feather flock
together. Is it not possible that your associate's crotchety, petulant, critical attitude is a reflection of your inner frustrations
and suppressed rage? What this person says or does cannot
really hurt you, except you permit him to injure you. The only
way he can annoy you is through your own thoughts.

For example, if you get angry, you had to go through four
stages in your mind: You began to think about what he said;
you decided to get angry and generate a mood of rage; then
you decided to act—perhaps you talked back and reacted in
kind. You see that the thought, emotion, reaction, and action all
took place in your mind.

You are the cause of your own anger. If someone called
you a fool, why should you get angry? You know you are not a
fool. The other person is undoubtedly very disturbed mentally;

maybe his child died during the night, or perhaps he is very ill psychologically. You should have compassion on him, but not condemn him. Realize God's peace fills his mind, and that His Love flows through him; then you would be practicing the Golden Rule. You would be identifying not with anger or hatred but with the law of goodness, truth, and beauty.

Would you condemn a person who had tuberculosis? No, you would not. In all probability if he told you, you would realize the Presence of God, harmony, and perfection where the trouble was; that would be compassion. *Compassion* is the Wisdom of God functioning through the mind of man, shown when you forgive all men, and see the God in them.

A person who is hateful, spiteful, envious, and jealous, and who says nasty, mean, scandalous things is very ill psychologically; he is just as sick as the man who has tuberculosis. How are you going to react to such a man? Where is your truth? Where is your wisdom and understanding? Are you going to say, "I am one of the herd; I react in kind; I return spite for spite, hate for hate, and anger for anger?" No, you would stop, and say, "This is not the Infinite One acting through me. God sees only perfection, beauty, and harmony. I see, therefore, as God sees." "Thou art of purer eyes than to behold evil, and canst not look on iniquity." I am going to see all men and women as God sees them. When your eyes are identified with beauty, you will not behold the distorted picture.

Information or news is constantly brought to your attention all day long through the medium of your five senses. You are the one who determines what your mental responses are going to be to the news conveyed. You can remain poised, serene, and calm, or you can fly into a rage, and as a result get an attack of migraine or some other form of pain.

The reason two men react differently to the same situation

is based on their subconscious conditioning. Your personality is based on the sum total of all your opinions, beliefs, education, and early religious indoctrination; this inner attitude of mind conditions your response.

One man will fly into a rage when he hears a certain religious program, but his brother may enjoy it, because one is prejudiced and the other is not. Our subconscious convictions and conditioning dictate and control our conscious actions. You can recondition your mind by identifying yourself with the eternal verities. Begin now by filling your mind with the concepts of peace, joy, love, good humor, happiness, and good will. Busy your mind with these ideas; as you do, they will sink into the subconscious level, and become orchids in the garden of God.

No matter where the problem is, how acute it may be, or how difficult the person may be, there is in the final analysis no one to change but yourself! When you change yourself, your world and environment will change. Begin with number one—*yourself!*

You are not living with people, you are living with your concept about them. How are you now responding to John Jones who is next to you on the bench? The fellow who works next to him likes him; his wife loves him; his children think he is wonderful. Perhaps members of his club believe he is generous, kind, and cooperative. Are you thinking of him as mean and petty? Are you resenting him? Who is this fellow? Is he *your* concept, or are all the others wrong? Would it not be wise to look within yourself and determine what it is in you that is causing him to be ugly or a stumbling block to you? I am sure you will find it within yourself.

Maybe you are saying to your son or father when you go home, "That fellow Jones annoys the life out of me. He irritates me beyond words." You are so upset, you cannot digest your dinner properly. According to your description he is impossible.

Where was Jones during the time you were saying all these things? Perhaps he was at the opera with his family; perchance he was out fishing in the stream having a wonderful, glorious time. As a matter of fact if someone said to you, "Where is Jones now?" You would answer, "I do not know." Be honest with yourself now, and admit he is in your own mind as a thought, a concept, or a mental image. You are revealing yourself and your own perturbed state of mind.

Surely he is not responsible for your anger, tension, or upset stomach. You know in your heart, which is the place that matters, that you are responsible for your own thoughts about him; it is your negative, hostile, reaction to him that is the cause of your trouble. You are the cause of your negative state. Ask yourself, "Who is thinking these things, and who is feeling them?" You are!

Quimby used to say that the suggestion we give to the other, we give to ourselves. You can now see how true that is. As a matter of fact, that is the basis of the Golden Rule. Never suggest to another, or think anything about another, that you would not wish the other to think, suggest, or feel about you.

Watch your hidden conversation to yourself. How do you meet people in your mind when they are thousands of miles away? You may be nice to their face, but the way you think about them is what counts. If you are negative, you are poisoning yourself. Does it make any sense to go to a corner drug store, and say, "I do not like that fellow Jones; give me some poison. I want to take small doses of it several times a day." You are answering now, "Oh, that is absurd!" But that is what you do when you resent or are antagonistic towards others; you are actually taking mental poison which saps your vitality, destroys your enthusiasm, and brings about a debility of the entire organism.

There are mental, corrosive poisons, just the same as there are physical, corrosive poisons; they are just as destructive also. If you are now disturbed, agitated, and angry over the way someone has acted toward you, it means you have a very negative thought pattern in your consciousness which you should heal instantly.

Be sure that you are not one of those people who will give all the reasons why they should be angry. Stop giving alibis; cease all self-justification. How could you be justified in hating or resenting someone? Do you have a special license? If you do, who gave you this authority? If you are agitated toward another, you are responsible for your unhappiness.

You should not defile the temple of the Living God. Your mind should be a house of prayer; do not make it a den of thieves. The thieves who rob you of peace, joy, health, and happiness are: envy, jealousy, hatred, resentment, and anger. Refuse to harbor these gangsters and assassins.

You do not have to go down the dark alleys and corridors of your mind to consort with thieves and ruffians. Go down the beautifully lit streets of your mind. Jesus or the Truth is always walking down the streets of your mind saying, "Come to God, and find peace, rest, joy, long life, and happiness." As you identify with these truths of God, you have found your savior. What you identify with, you become. You are transfigured into the image of what you contemplate and feel as true.

When you go to the factory tomorrow, and you meet that fellow or girl whom you say irritates you beyond words, quiet the mind, and say, "He is God's son, and God's Love flows through him. I see the Christ or the Presence of God in him.

I see him through the eyes of God, and he is perfect, loving, peaceful, and cooperative." Repeat it quietly to yourself a few times, and go on about your business. Do not bother looking for results. You know results follow your changed mental attitude.

If the old, vicious thought of resentment or anger comes to you during the day, say to yourself quietly, lovingly, and positively, "What is true of God is true of him. I see him as God sees him; it is wonderful to behold God in action in myself, and in him also." You are now observing yourself, because you are refusing to yield to the evil thought; you are identifying with God or the Good only. A complete healing will follow as you persist in your new way of thinking and reacting. You are, as the Bible tells you, transformed by the renewal of your mind. You have changed your mental and emotional reaction towards others; as a result you have dominion over yourself.

Now you can decree how your thoughts and emotions shall be directed. You are now a king over your own household (mind). Your thoughts, ideas, and feelings are your servants. You issue the command; their mission is to obey. You are here to control, and not to be controlled by angry, wild emotions.

Now when you say to yourself, "Who is the thinker in me?" you must answer, "I am!"

When you are thinking on whatsoever things are true, honest, just, lovely, and of good report, you are truly thinking. If you find yourself thinking negatively, it is the world-mind thinking in you; then you have lost control.

The next time you are prone to resent someone, or when you say that you cannot get along with another, say to yourself, "When I look into his face, I am looking into the face of

God; he is an incarnation of God walking this earth. I see God in him, and all is well."

> *"That thou seest man,*
> *That, too, become thou must;*
> *God, if thou seest God;*
> *Dust if thou seest dust."*

HOW TO CONTROL
YOUR EMOTIONS

The ancient Greeks said, "Man, know thyself." As you study yourself, you seem to be made up of four parts: Your physical body, emotional nature, intellect, and the Spiritual Essence which is called the Presence of God. The I AM within you, the Divine Presence, is your Real Identity Which is Eternal.

You are here to discipline yourself, so that your intellectual, emotional, and physical nature are completely spiritualized. These four phases of your nature are called the four beasts of *The Book of Revelation*. (*The Revelation of St. John* means God revealing himself as man.)

The real way for you to discipline and bridle your intellectual and emotional nature is by the Practice of the Presence of God all day long.

You have a body; it is a shadow or reflection of the mind. It has no power of itself, no initiative, or volition. It has no intelligence of itself; it is completely subject to your commands or decrees. Look upon your body as a great disc upon which you play your emotions and beliefs. Being a disc, it will faithfully record all your emotionalized concepts and never deviate from them; therefore, you can register a melody of love and beauty, or one of grief and sorrow upon it. Resentment, jealousy, hatred, anger, and melancholia are all expressed in the body as various diseases. As you learn to control your mental and emotional nature, you will become a channel for the Divine, and release the imprisoned splendor that is within you.

Think over this for a moment: You cannot buy a healthy body with all the money in the world, but you can have health through riches of the mind, such as thoughts of peace, harmony, and perfect health.

Let us dwell now on the emotional nature of man. It is absolutely essential for you to control your emotions if you want to grow spiritually. You are considered grown up or emotionally mature when you control your feelings. If you cannot discipline or bridle your emotions, you are a child even though you are fifty years old.

You must remember that the greatest tyrant is a false idea which controls a man's mind holding him in bondage. The idea you hold about yourself or others induces definite emotions in you. Psychologically speaking, emotions compel you for good or evil. If you are full of resentment toward someone or possessed by a grudge, this emotion will have an evil influence over you, and govern your actions in a manner which has nothing to do with what you say is the original cause. When you want to be friendly and cordial, you will be ugly, cynical, and sour. When you want to be healthy, successful, and prosperous in life, you will find everything going wrong. Those of you reading this book are aware of your capacity to choose a concept of peace and good will. Accept the idea of peace in your mind, and let it govern, control, and guide you.

Quimby pointed out that ideas are our masters, and that we are slaves to the ideas we entertain. The concept of peace with which you now live will induce the feeling of peace and harmony. Your feeling is the Spirit of God operating at the human level; this feeling of peace and good will will compel you to right action. You are now governed by Divine Ideas which are mothered by the Holy Spirit.

Uncontrolled or undisciplined emotion is destructive. For example, if you have a powerful automobile, it will take you through the roughest country, or to the top of a high hill; however, you must control the automobile. If you do not know how to drive, you may hit a telegraph pole or another car. Should you step on the gas instead of the brake, the car may be destroyed.

It is wonderful to posses a strong, emotional nature provided you are the master. Your emotions are controlling you if you permit yourself to get angry over trifles or agitated over practically nothing. If you get upset over what you read in the newspapers, you are not controlling your emotions. You must learn to blend your intellect and emotions together harmoniously. The intellect of man is alright in its place, but it should be anointed or illumined with the Wisdom of God.

There are many people who are always trying to intellectualize God. You cannot define the Infinite. Spinoza said that to define God is to deny him. You have met the highly intellectual man who says that man cannot survive death, because he does not take his brain with him. Somehow he is so clever he really believes the brain thinks by itself. Such a man is looking at everything from a three-dimensional standpoint; that is where the intellect ceases.

The intellect, as I said previously, is alright in its place—for example, in our everyday work, and in all kinds of science, art, and industry. However as we approach the Living Spirit Almighty within, we are compelled to leave the world of the intellect, and go beyond into the realm of spiritual values which are perfection, and where dimension is infinity.

When man's intellect is blended with the emotions of love, peace, and goodwill, he will not use explosives and knowledge of chemistry for the destruction of mankind. The reason man uses the atomic bomb, submarine, and other implements of warfare to destroy his fellow creature is because his spiritual awareness and knowledge lag so far behind his intellectual achievements.

Let us see how emotions are generated. Suppose you observe a cripple; perhaps you are moved to pity. On the other hand you may look at your young, beautiful child, and you feel an emotion of love welling up within you. You know that you cannot imagine an emotion, but if you imagine an unpleasant episode or event of the past, you induce the corresponding emotion. Remember it is essential to entertain the thought first before you induce an emotion.

An emotion is always the working out of an idea in the mind. Have you noticed the effect of fear upon the face, eyes, heart, and other organs? You know the effect of bad news or grief on the digestive tract. Observe the change that takes place when it is found the fear is groundless.

All negative emotions are destructive and depress the vital forces of the body. A chronic worrier usually has trouble with digestion. If something very pleasant occurs in his experience, the digestion becomes normal, because normal circulation is restored, and the necessary gastric secretions are no longer interfered with.

The way to overcome and discipline the emotions is not through repression or suppression. When you repress an emotion, the energy accumulates in the subconscious and remains snarled there. In the same manner as the pressure increases in the boiler, if all the valves are closed, and you increase the heat of the fire, finally there will be an explosion.

Today in the field of psychosomatics we are discovering that many cases of ill health, as arthritis, asthma, cardiac troubles, and failure in life, etc., may be due to suppressed or repressed emotions, perhaps occurring during early life or childhood.

These repressed or suppressed emotions rise like ghosts to haunt you later on. There is a spiritual and psychological way to banish these ghosts which walk in the gloomy gallery of your mind. The ideal way is the law of substitution. Through the law of mental substitution, you substitute a positive, constructive thought for the negative. When negative thoughts enter your mind, do not fight them; just think of God and His Love; you will find the negative thoughts disappear. "I say unto you, That ye resist not evil." (Math. 5:39) If a person is fearful, the positive emotion of faith and confidence will completely destroy it.

If you sincerely wish to govern your emotions, you must maintain control over your thoughts. By taking charge of your thoughts, you can substitute love for fear. The instant you receive the stimulus of a negative emotion supplant it with the mood of love and good will. Instead of giving way to fear, say, "One with God is a majority." Fill your mind with concepts of peace, love, and faith in God; then the negative thoughts cannot enter.

It is far easier to cremate, burn up, and destroy negative thoughts at the moment they enter the mind, rather than try and dislodge them when they have taken possession of your mind. Refuse to be a victim of negative emotions through controlling your thought and thinking of God and His Attributes.

You can be master of all emotions and conditions. "He that *is* slow to anger is better than the mighty; and he that ruleth his spirit than he that taketh a city."

The Book of Revelation deals with the control of the intellectual and emotional life of man. It says in Chapter 4, verses 6, 7, and 8: "And before the throne *there was* a sea of glass like unto crystal: and in the midst of the throne, and round about the throne, *were* four beasts full of eyes before and behind.

"And the first beasts *was* like a lion, and the second beasts like a calf, and the third beast had a face as a man, and the fourth beast *was* like a flying eagle.

"And the four beasts had each of them six wings about *him*; and *they were* full of eyes within: and they rest not day and night, saying, Holy, holy, holy, Lord God Almighty, which was, and is, and is to come."

The sea of glass before the throne means the inner peace of God, for God is peace. Deep in the center of your being, the Infinite One lies stretched in smiling repose. It is the Living Presence of God within you. You stand before this throne. The throne is a symbol of authority. Your emotional conviction of a deep, abiding faith in the God-Power is your authority in consciousness. To say it simply: Your inner conviction is your throne in heaven, because therein lies your power. "According to your faith is it done unto you." Faith is a positive, emotional attitude knowing that the good I seek is mine now.

The four beasts forever before the throne are the four phases of your being: spiritual, mental, emotional, and physical. In order to get your emotional nature on a spiritual basis, it is necessary to understand these four beasts; in doing so you learn the gentle art of scientific prayer which in the final analysis is the answer to all problems. Study these four potencies of consciousness.

The lion is the king of the jungle; it means God, your I AMNESS.

Taurus means the bull or beast of burden. *Your burden* is your desire. You labor in your imagination to make your desire a part of your consciousness.

Aquarius means the water bearer; it means meditation. The word meditation means to eat of God or your good, to feast upon your ideal. You pour water on your ideal, meaning you dwell upon and pour love on it which is the water of life. Something happens as you mentally feast upon your ideal; you generate an emotion; the latter is the spirit of God moving on your behalf. Your emotion is the Holy Spirit moving at human levels. God is a reactive, reciprocal Power within you. Your emotion responds according to the nature of the idea. As you emotionalize your idea, it sinks into the subconscious mind as an impression; this is called the Eagle or *Scorpio,* meaning the Divine impregnation. These are the four stages of the unfoldment or manifestation of an ideal or desire. Whatever is impressed is expressed.

The four beasts had each of them six wings. *The six wings* refer to the mental, creative act. When idea and feeling blend together in harmony and faith, there has taken place a wedding ceremony in the mind. Knowledge of this mental, creative act gives you wings; enables you to soar aloft above the storms and struggles of the world, and find peace and strength in your own mind.

Let us take an illustration explaining the story of spiritual and mental creation: In the name *Jehovah* is concealed the perfect way to pray scientifically; thereby bringing all discordant emotions under scientific control. Jehovah, Yod-He-Vau-He, is composed of four letters. *Yod* means God, or I

AM; *He* means desire or idea; *Vau* is feeling or conviction; the final *He* is the manifestation of what you felt as true inside. The third letter *Vau* is considered the most important of all. It enables you to feel you are that which you desire to be. Walk in the mental atmosphere that you now are what you want to be; this mood will jell within you, and you will experience the joy of the answered prayer. The word *Vau* also means nail. *To nail* your desire is to fix it in consciousness, so that you are at peace about it.

Remember you do not have to live in a world of sickness and confusion created by your own errors or ignorance. You have the power and the capacity to imagine and feel you are what you desire to be. As you completely accept your desire mentally, that you now are what you wish to be, through mental absorption, you have completed the name or the creative way of God as portrayed in the name: *Yod-He-Vau-He*. In other words you have completed the creative process in your own mind as outlined by Troward in his *Bible Mystery and Bible Meaning*. To know how to pray scientifically is to be able to control your emotions. "More things are wrought by prayer than this world dreams of."

CASE HISTORIES

Case History Number One

Let us take some cases histories. A soldier who has returned from Korea told me that when he was seized with fear, he would say to himself over and over again, "God's Love surrounds me, and goes before me." This affirmation impressed his mind with the feeling of love and faith. This mood of love supplanted his fear. "Perfect Love casteth out fear." This procedure is the answer to the process of freedom from fear.

Case History Number Two

A mother, whose only child died, was grief stricken. The grief was affecting her vision, and she suffered from migraine headaches. She was in a deep state of depression. I suggested to her that she go to a hospital, and offer her services in the children's ward. She was a former nurse. In offering her time at a local hospital, she began to pour out love on the children; she coddled them; cared for them, and fed them. The love was no longer bottled up within her; she became a channel for the Divine, and began to release the sunshine of God's Love. She practiced sublimation which was a redirection of the energy lodged within her subconscious mind. In this manner she drained off the poison pockets of her subconscious mind.

Case History Number Three

A woman who comes to our meeting told me that she was accustomed to fits of temper and anger periodically by the action of neighbors. Instead of letting the anger and hatred affect her mentally and physically by pushing it back into the subconscious, she transmuted it into muscular energy by getting a gallon of water and washing the windows or the floor. Sometimes she would begin to dig in the garden, saying to herself aloud, "I am digging in the garden of God, and planting God's ideas." She would do this for fifteen minutes at a time. When washing the windows, she would say aloud, "I am cleansing my mind with the waters of love and life." The above illustrations are simple methods of working off negative emotions in a physical way.

CHANGING THE FEELING
OF "I"

If you say, "I," to everything you think, feel, say, or imagine, you cannot transform your emotional life. Remember all kinds of thoughts can enter your mind; all kinds of emotions may enter your heart. If you say, "I," to all negative thoughts, you are identifying yourself with them, and you cannot separate internally from them. You can refuse to attach "I" to negative emotions and thoughts.

You make it a practice to avoid muddy places as you walk along the road; likewise you must avoid walking down the muddy roads of your mind where fear, resentment, hostility, and ill-will lurk and move. Refuse to listen to negative remarks. Do not touch the negative moods, or let them touch you. Practice inner separation by getting a new feeling about yourself, and about what you really are. Begin to realize that the real "I" in you is the Infinite Spirit, the Infinite One. Begin to identify yourself with the Qualities and Attributes of this Infinite One; then your whole life will be transformed.

The whole secret in transforming your negative, emotional nature is to practice self-observation. To observe, and *to observe* oneself are two different things. When you say, "You observe . . ." you mean you give your attention to external things. In self-observation the attention is directed inwards.

A man may spend his whole life-time studying the

atom, stars, body, and the phenomenalistic world—namely, knowledge of the external world; this knowledge cannot bring about an interior change. Self-observations is the means of interior change—the change of the heart.

You must learn to differentiate, to discern, to separate the chaff from the wheat. You practice the art of self-observation when you begin to ask yourself, "Is this idea true? Will it bless, heal, and inspire me? Will it give me peace of mind, and contribute to the well-being of humanity?"

You are living in two worlds: the external and the internal; yet they are both one. One is visible and the other invisible (subjective and objective). Your external world enters through your five senses, and is shared by everyone. Your internal world of thought, feelings, sensations, beliefs, and reaction is invisible and belongs to you.

Ask yourself, "In which world do I live? Do I live in the world revealed by my five senses, or in this inner world?" It is in this inner world you live all the time; this is where you feel and suffer.

Suppose you are invited to a banquet. All you see, hear, taste, smell, and touch belong to the external world. All that you think, feel, like, and dislike belong to the inner world. You attend two banquets recorded differently: namely, one the outer, and one the inner. It is in your inner world of thought, feeling, and emotion in which you rise and fall and sway to and fro.

In order to transform yourself, you must begin to change the inner world through the purification of the emotions, and the correct ordering of the mind through right thinking. If you want to grow spiritually, you must transform yourself.

Transformation means the changing of one thing into another. There are many well-known transformations of matter. Sugar through a process of distillation is changed into alcohol; radium slowly changes into lead, etc. The food you eat is transformed, stage by stage into all substances necessary for your existence.

Your experiences coming in as impressions must be similarly transformed. Suppose you see a person you love and admire; you receive impressions about him. Suppose on the other hand you meet a person you dislike; you receive impressions also.

Your husband or daughter sitting on the couch as you read this is to you what you conceive him or her to be. In other words impressions are received by your mind. If you were deaf, you would not hear their voices. You can change your impressions of people. To transform your impression is to transform yourself. To change your life, change your reactions to life. Do you find yourself reacting in stereotyped ways? If your reactions are negative, that is your life. Never permit your life to be a series of negative reactions to the impressions that come to you every day.

In order truly to observe yourself, you must see that regardless of what happens, your thought and feeling are fixed on this great truth: "How is it in God and Heaven?" This will lift you up, and transform all your negative thoughts and emotions. You may be inclined to say that other people are to blame, because of the way they talk or act, but if what they say or do makes you negative, you are inwardly disturbed; this negative state is where you now live, move, and have your being.

You cannot afford to be negative; it depletes your vitality; robs you of enthusiasm, and makes you physically and mentally ill. Do you live in the room where you are now? or do you live in your thoughts, feelings, emotions, hopes, and despair?

Is it not what you are feeling about your environment now, that is real to you? When you say, "My name is John Jones," what do you mean? Is it not a fact that you are a product of your thinking, plus the customs, traditions, and the influence of those around you as you grew up? You are really the sum-total of your beliefs, opinions, plus what you have derived from your education, environmental conditioning, and the countless other influences acting upon you from the external world and entering through your external senses.

Perhaps you are now comparing yourself with others. Do you feel inferior in the presence of a person who seems to be more distinguished than you are? Suppose you are a great pianist—when someone praises another pianist, do you feel inferior? If you have the real feeling of "I," this would not be possible; for the true feeling of "I" is the feeling of the Presence of the Infinite One in you, in Which there are no comparisons.

Ouspensky used to point out that people became upset easily, because their feeling of "I" was derived from negative states of consciousness. The feeling of "I" was one of his favorite expressions, and some of his ideas are incorporated in this chapter.

I said to a man in our Bible class recently, "Have you observed your typical reactions to people, newspaper articles, and radio commentators? Have you noticed your usual, stereotyped behavior?"

He replied, "No, I have not noticed these things." He was taking himself for granted, and not growing spiritually. He began to think about his reactions; then he admitted that many of the articles and the commentators irritated him immensely. He reacted in a machine-like manner, and was not disciplining himself. It makes no difference if all the writers and commentators were wrong, and he, alone, was right; the negative emotion aroused in him is destructive; it shows lack of mental and spiritual discipline.

When you say, "I think this . . ." "I think that . . ." "I resent this . . ." or "I dislike this . . ." which "I" is speaking? Is it not a different "I" speaking every moment? Each "I" is completely different. One "I" in you criticizes one moment; a few minutes later another "I" speaks tenderly. Look at and learn about your different "I's," and know deep within yourself that certain "I's" will never dominate, control, or direct your thinking.

Take a good look at the "I's" you are consorting with. With what kind of people do you associate? I am referring to the people that inhabit your mind. Remember your mind is a city; thoughts, ideas, opinions, feelings, sensations, and beliefs dwell there. Some of the places in your mind are slums and dangerous streets; however Jesus (your savior) is always walking down the streets of your mind in the form of your ideal, desire, and aim in life.

One of the meanings of Jesus is your desire; for your desire, when realized, is your savior. Your aims and objectives in life are now beckoning to you; move toward them. Give your desire your attention; in other words take a lively interest in it. Go down the streets of love, peace, joy, and good will in your mind; you will meet wonderful people on the way. You will find beautifully lighted streets and wonderful citizens on the better streets of your mind.

Never permit your house, which is your mind, to be full of servants which you do not have under control. When you were young, you were taught not to go with what your mother called, "bad company." Now when you begin to awaken to your inner powers, you must make it a special point that you do not go with wrong "I's" (thoughts) within you.

I had an interesting chat with a young man who studied mental discipline in France. His procedure was to take, as he said, "mental photographs of himself from time to time." He would sit down, and think about his emotions, moods, thoughts, sensations, reactions, and his tones of voice; then he would say, "These are not of God; they are false. I will go back to God and think from that Standard or Rock of Truth." He practiced the art of inner separation. He would stop when he got angry, and say, "This is not the Infinite One, the real 'I' speaking, thinking, or acting; it is the false 'I' in me."

Return to God like this young man. Every time you are prone to get angry, critical, depressed, or irritable, think of God and Heaven, and ask yourself, "How is it in God and Heaven?" *There* is the answer to becoming the new man; this is how you become spiritually reborn or experience what is called the second birth. (*The second birth* is internal discipline and spiritual understanding.)

The saint and the sinner are in all of us; so are the murderer and the holy man; likewise are God and the world mind. Every man basically and fundamentally wants to be good, to express good, and to do good. This is "the positive" in you. If you have committed destructive acts, as for example, if you have robbed, cheated, and defrauded others, and they condemn you, and they hold you in a bad light, you can rise out of the slum of your mind to that place in your own consciousness where you cease to condemn yourself; then all your accusers must still their tongues. When you cease to accuse yourself, the world will no longer accuse you; this is the power of your own consciousness; It is the God in you.

It is foolish to condemn yourself; you do not have to. It is idle to keep company with the thoughts of self-accusation.

Suppose you committed acts of injustice, criminal acts, or other dastardly crimes. It was not the God in you that did those things; it was not the real "I" or the Infinite One, it was the other self (the world-mind) in you. This will not, of course, excuse you from your responsibility, no more so than if you put your hand in the fire, you get burned; or if you pass a red light, you will get a ticket for a traffic violation.

The other self represents the many "I's" in you, for instance the many negative ideas and beliefs that there are powers outside your own consciousness; the belief that others can hurt you; the elements are unfriendly, plus the fears, superstitions, and ignorance of all kinds. Finally prejudices, fears, and hates drive and goad you to do that which you would not otherwise do. The ideal way to change the feeling of "I" is to affix to the real "I" within you everything that is noble, wonderful, and God-like.

Begin to affirm, "I am strong. I am radiant. I am happy. I am inspired. I am illumined. I am loving. I am kind. I am harmonious." Feel these states of mind; affirm them, and believe them; then you will begin to truly live in the Garden of God. Whatever you affix to the "I AM" and believe, you become. The "I AM" in you is God, and there is none other. "I AM" or Life, Awareness, Pure Being, Existence, or the Real Self of you is God. It is the Only Cause. It is the Only Power making anything in the world. Honor It; live with the feeling, "I AM Christ," all day long. *Christ* means the Anointed One, the Awakened One, the Illumined One. Feel you are this Anointed One; continue to live in that mental atmosphere; then you will draw out the Christ (Wisdom, Power, and Intelligence of God) within you, and your whole world will be transformed by that Inner Light shining in your mind. Every-time you feel, "I AM the Christ"; "I AM illumined"; "I AM inspired"; you are praying and qualifying your consciousness with the thing you are praying about, and with the thoughts you are thinking.

As you continue to change the feeling of "I" as outlined above, you will populate the heavens of your mind with God's Eternal Verities: "Fear not for I am with thee; and through the rivers, they shall not overflow thee: when thou walkest through the fire, thou shall not be burned." Who is That One? It is your own I AMNESS; It is the Light or Awareness within you which always goes before you whithersoever thou goest. Your dominant mental attitude or atmosphere is going ahead of you all the time, creating the experiences you will encounter.

Keep in mind that when you pray about any specific thing, it is necessary to qualify your mind with the consciousness or *feeling of having or being that thing*. You mentally reject completely the arguments in your mind against it; that is prayer. Qualify your consciousness with the thing you are praying for by thinking about it with interest. Do this quietly and regularly until a conviction is reached in your consciousness. As you do this, the problem will no longer annoy you. You will maintain your mental poise, plus the feeling of: "I now feel that I am what I long to be," and as you continue to feel it, you will become it.

Here is the law: "I am that which I feel myself to be." Practice changing the feeling of "I" every day by affirming: "I am Spirit; I think, see, feel, and live as Spirit, the Presence of God. (The other self in you thinks, feels, and acts as the race mind does.) As you continue to do this, you will begin to feel you are one with God. As the sun in the heavens redeems the earth from darkness and gloom, so will the realization of the Presence of God in you reveal the man you always wished to be—the joyous, radiant, peaceful, prosperous, and successful man whose intellect is illumined by the Light from above.

God causes the sun to shine on all men everywhere. No man can take away the sunshine of God's Love from you. No one can place you in the prison of fear or ignorance when you know the Truth of God which sets you free.

The feeling that the "I AM" in you is God reveals to you that there is nothing to be afraid of, and that you are one with Omnipotence, Omniscience, and Omnipresence. No one can steal health, peace, joy, or happiness from you. You no longer live with the many "I's" of fear, doubt, and superstition. You now live in the Divine Presence, and in the consciousness of freedom.

Ask yourself, "Who is it that takes charge of me at every moment, and speaks in His Name, calling Itself "I"? Never identify with this other man (fear, prejudice, pride, arrogance, condemnation, etc.). You now realize you need not go in the direction of negative "I's." You will never again say, "Yes," to any idle, negative thought; neither will you give it the sanction and signature of yourself.

Become the observer by keeping your eyes fixed on God—the real "I"—the Infinite One within you. Feel the sense of "I" on the observing side, and not in what you are observing. Feel that you are looking out through the eyes of God; therefore, "*Thou art* of purer eyes than to behold evil, and canst not look on iniquity."

HOW TO USE YOUR HEALING POWER

THE MEANING OF THE HEALINGS OF JESUS

(1957)

CONTENTS

INTRODUCTION

This book is written in response to thousands of requests from students in many parts of the world. One of the largest classes I have ever given was at the Wilshire Ebell Theatre, Los Angeles, California, on the healing miracles of Jesus and what they mean to men everywhere. This book is an attempt to elaborate on the inner meaning of the recorded healings in the New Testament and to show the reader that he can apply the Healing Principle today in the same way that Jesus did about two thousand years ago.

The stories of mental and physical illnesses recorded in the Bible have reoccurred from time immemorial to the present moment. You may see the conditions and symptoms of diseases described in the Bible in almost any hospital in the country. It is true, of course, that the diseases described today have scientific names derived from medical terminology.

All over the world today men and women of various creeds are awakening to the tremendous therapeutic results following the application of mental and spiritual laws. In the fields of medicine, psychiatry, psychology, and other related fields, evidence is being adduced and articles written on the effect of destructive mental and emotional conflicts as the cause of all kinds of disease. This is prophetic of the termination of the power of the five senses, the reign of so-called *matter*, and the reestablishment of the reign of Divine Intelligence and of the Infinite Healing Presence behind all things.

The Bible is a psychological textbook which teaches us how to overcome all problems. It explains how we get into trouble; then teaches us how to get out of trouble. It teaches a science of life. A knowledge of the meaning of symbols, the science of the Hebrew alphabet, and the meaning of the various names in the Bible forms the key to all the stories in the Bible. You may find the meaning of the various names given in the bible in *Strong's Concordance* or *Young's Concordance*. There are many other reference books but the above two are generally used by all Bible students interested in the inner meaning of the Bible.

To fully understand what another speaks or writes, it is necessary to tune in with the writer, claiming and knowing that his ideas, thoughts, words, and feelings are reproduced in our mind. We do not really know who wrote the Gospels, and as I write or speak on these wonderful Bible stories, I say to my Deep Self in meditation, "What did I as the writer of these stories mean when I wrote them?" Then I get quiet and still, feeling the Living Intelligence within flowing through my conscious mind revealing to me everything I need to know. There is only one mind. A memory of everything that has ever transpired is within your subjective mind, and it is possible for you to tune in. In a state of intercommunion of mind with mind, it is possible to have transmitted to your mind all the thoughts, ideas, and feelings of another mind with which you are in tune or *en rapport*. This is possible without the ordinary channels of sensuous communication. There is but one mind common to all individual men.

The purpose of this book, so far as possible, is to divest and strip these stories of the Bible of all mystery so that it will be an open book for all mankind. The same Healing Presence which Moses, Elijah, Paul, and Jesus used is available to you now. Use it and go forward in the Light, moving from glory to glory *until the dawn appears, and the shadows flee away.*

HEALING OF MENTAL DISORDERS

The following quotation is taken from the fourth chapter of Luke. It forms the sound basis for all healing, and tells all of us what we are here for.

> *The Spirit of the Lord is upon me, because he hath anointed me to preach the gospel to the poor; he hath sent me to heal the broken-hearted, to preach deliverance to the captives, and recovering of sight to the blind, to set at liberty them that are bruised. And he closed the book, and he gave it again to the minister, and sat down. And the eyes of all them that were in the synagogue were fastened on him. And he began to say unto them, This day is this scripture fulfilled in your ears.*
>
> Luke 4:18–21.

Here is one of the most remarkable and extraordinary statements in the whole Bible. *This day is this scripture fulfilled in your ears.* Not tomorrow or next week or next year, but NOW, this minute. *God is the Eternal Now.* Your good is this moment. Claim your health now, your peace now. The Healing Principle and the Peace of God are within you. Someone asked me in our class on

"The Healing Miracles" if the healing stories in the Bible were true. The answer to the question is very simple. If the use of the Healing Principle is going on all the time and is applicable to all people all of the time everywhere, it is certainly truer, more interesting, and more fascinating than if it were an historic event of a certain date, a definite geographical location, and confined to just certain people.

In order to understand your Bible see it as a great psychological drama taking place in the consciousness of all people everywhere when they pray scientifically. Look upon the following dramatic episodes recorded in the Bible as stories about yourself and your friends awakening from darkness to the Light within. You can call Jesus in the Bible, as Robert Taylor of Cambridge, England, in 1829 did, *illumined reason*. Your concordance gives you many meanings for Jesus such as "God is savior," or "God is your solution, or salvation." In other words the names Joshua and Jesus are identical. The meaning is that your awareness or faith in the God-Wisdom can do all things. Look upon Jesus as yourself possessed of faith and confidence looking at the thoughts, beliefs, and opinions of your mind (your synagogue) rejecting all the false beliefs, theories, and ideas and announcing the presence of your ideal or the state desired. You do this in the present tense.

The Bible writer tells you that no matter what you are seeking, it exists now. Why wait for a healing? Why postpone it? Why say, "Some day I will have peace." The God of peace is within. The Power of the Almighty is within, and you will receive energy and strength. Love is here this moment, and you can experience the Divine Love welling up in your heart for all people. You can also attract your divine companion now. What you are seeking in the future is present now, right where you are. Your knowledge of the laws of your mind is your savior.

And they were astonished at his doctrine: for his word was with power. And in the synagogue there was a man, which had a spirit of an unclean devil, and cried out with a loud voice, Saying, Let us alone; what have we to do with thee, thou Jesus of Nazareth? art thou come to destroy us? I know thee who thou art; the Holy One of God. And Jesus rebuked him, saying, Hold thy peace, and come out of him. And when the devil had thrown him in the midst, he came out of him, and hurt him not. Luke 4:32–35. *Related passages*, Mark 1:23–27, 3:11, 7:25–30.

There was a belief in ancient times that when a man was insane he was possessed by demons or devils. This had its corollary in the belief that all psychotic or mentally deranged people were demon possessed. In Bible days exorcism in its varied forms became the regularly accepted form of therapy for the mentally disordered patients. Even today in some parts of America and even here in Los Angeles a student will say, "Oh, I think he or she is possessed by a demon." At one time people tried varying methods in order to drive demons out of the mind or body of the person. Today the psychiatrist, psychologist, and spiritual leader tries to bring about an adjustment of the personality and a cleansing of the mind of all negative thoughts and false beliefs. You are very familiar with the sudden and miraculous change often seen nowadays when a manic-depressive condition of an individual is managed by shock therapy.

Many years ago when a boy traveling on an ocean liner to India, I saw a raving maniac completely healed by an American woman who prayed aloud for him. He had a remarkable, instantaneous healing. Being curious, I asked her what she did. She replied, "I claimed that God's love and peace filled his mind." Today I understand much better what she meant. Her realization of the presence and power of God in the man was instantaneously resurrected in his mind, and a healing followed. Her faith made him whole. This is the whole story from a spiritual standpoint.

All *demons* or *devils* are negative states of mind that have been developed because the creative power of man has been used in an ignorant and destructive manner. The work of every man is to go into his own *synagogue* (mind) and through spiritual awareness cast out of his own mind the false theories, dogmas, beliefs, opinions, as well as all negative states such as resentment, ill will, hatred, jealousy, etc. These are the devils which bedevil us. Obsessions, dual personalities, and all other mental aberrations are the result of habitual negative thinking, crystallizing into definite states of mind such as complexes and other various poison pockets in the subconscious.

You are empowered to cast out demons by affirming your unity and oneness with the indwelling God; then you silently or audibly with feeling and faith speak the word of health, harmony, and peace. Pray with confidence like the woman on board the ship referred to previously by silently concentrating on the dissolving Power of God's Love upon the person. Thus the hold of evil thoughts will be broken.

The supposed devil cries out, *Let us alone, what have we to do with thee.* And he rebuked him saying, *Hold thy peace, come out of him.*

To rebuke means that you completely reject, once and for all, the power of any so-called negative or evil force. You do not admit for one moment that demons have any power, or that there are such entities.

He suffered not the demons to speak. Mark 1:34.

This means that you, who are illumined by the Light, will not, under any circumstances, permit negative race thoughts to dissuade you to turn away from the belief in One Supreme Power which is One and Indivisible. The method of healing used by Jesus here was the word of authority, . . . *for with authority and power he commandeth the unclean spirits, and they came out.* Luke 4:36.

Your word is your awareness, your feeling, your conviction. Psychologically it is the union of the conscious and subconscious mind; *i.e.,* you have reached the point of agreement or complete mental acceptance of that which you affirm as true. The moment you accept it completely without reservations, the healing takes place in the person for whom you are praying. If you are praying for a mentally deranged person, follow the teachings of the Bible herein set forth.

Go boldly into your synagogue, which means the temple of your own mind; there gather your thoughts together rehearsing in your mind the Truths about God in the presence of your assembled thoughts and opinions; and therein feel the mental atmosphere of freedom and peace of mind for the sick person. Become Jesus (illumined mind) now; *i.e.,* you are full of faith and confidence as you enter the realm of your mind, giving no power to symptoms, or the nature of the mental blocks. Reject completely the verdict and opinions of those around you. Do this emphatically and with a sense of inner knowing. Know that you have the authority to speak the word; *i.e.,* to feel and know that your thought is authoritative inasmuch as it is the Infinite thinking through you.

Quimby, the great American healer, knew that when he thought of his patient he was in command of the other person's mind and body; then he contemplated his divine perfection. He duplicated many of the miracles recorded in the

Bible. Quimby's inner conviction that what was true of God was true of his patient was the *word* that he sent. *He sent his word and healed them.*

There are many evil spirits (negative emotions) such as hatred, resentment, revenge, jealousy, etc. It could be said that a man with intense hatred is obsessed by an evil spirit. Your mood or emotion is the spirit operating at the human level. The law governing your subjective mind is that it is amenable to suggestion. In ancient times, the idea was current that any one was liable at any time to be taken possession of by a devil. Many persons who easily entered the subjective condition through fear found themselves possessed by devils, *i.e.*, the power of their own fearful thoughts.

In ancient times and even today in some parts of the world the profession of exorcism was and is a very profitable one. The general belief was that the demons were afraid of holy water, the Bible, and of hearing the name of God pronounced. Accordingly it came to pass that, upon the verbal command of the exorcist the so-called devil would often incontinently fly, leaving the patient free. Sometimes the patient would go into convulsions on hearing the magic name pronounced, and more exorcists were then employed. You can see that the whole procedure is one of belief, and according to the belief of the exorcist is it done unto him.

Doctors and scientists are conducting experiments in hypnosis; they know, for example, that they can cause a subject under hypnosis to act like an insane person by suggestion. For instance, in a trance state a man can be told he will jump with one foot in the air when he sees a dog, and he will jump. If given a posthypnotic suggestion, he will repeat the performance after being awakened. This is a compulsion. He can be told he is possessed by a bad spirit or devil, and his subconscious mind which acts upon suggestion, faithfully reproduces the role of a devil with the same extraordinary acumen that it would personate any other character suggested. The subconscious mind which is all things to all men will exhibit as many different kinds and degrees of deviltry as there are devils embraced in the suggestion. Experimentally any type of insanity can be brought about by appropriate suggestions given to subjects in the trance state. In experiments when the suggestion is relieved, the subject being instructed that it was only a suggestion, the mental aberrations disappear. The schizophrenic, psychotic, depressive type, manic type of insanities can be demonstrated by suggestion. It is easy to see where the so-called devils come from.

The ceremony of exorcism which is even today in use by certain organizations constitutes a most powerful suggestive command to the subjective mind; according to the faith of the operator the desired result is achieved. The fact that the trouble is susceptible of cure by a ritual or ceremony points clearly to its mental origin, precluding the possibility of its being attributable to extramundane causes or external entities.

Many people come to see me and write me saying that they hear voices all the time, and what terrible things these voices are saying. They believe they are possessed by evil spirits. I tell them that I hear voices also. Clairaudience is a faculty of the human mind. It is that faculty of intelligence within you which enables your objective mind to receive communications from your own subjective mind, or from another by means of spoken words.

A few weeks ago I clearly heard an answer to a question which had perplexed me for some time. I heard the words clearly. These words did not come from some discarnate entity but they came from my own subjective self which is one with Boundless Wisdom and Infinite Intelligence. When you receive ideas from the subjective, or when the answer comes, it is necessarily by such means as can be understood by you, *i.e.*, by means which appeal to your senses. There are many people who hear clairaudiently; some attribute it to imagination, others regard it as a subjective hallucination. Some attribute this phenomenon of hearing words from the subjective mind to spirits of the departed; needless to say, the same law of suggestion applies and governs the character of their clairaudient manifestation.

The subconscious mind will assume the characters suggested by the conscious mind. If, for example, you believe it is a guardian angel speaking to you, or the voice of a disembodied spirit, the subconscious will follow the suggestion given, and all further communication will be conducted on the basis assumed by you. Your subconscious will assume the character of an angel or devil according to the suggestion given.

Some months ago a young man from a local university came to see me with the complaint that he was constantly hearing spirit-voices, that they made him do nasty things, and that they would not let him alone, neither would they permit him to read the Bible or other spiritual books. He was convinced that he was talking to supernatural beings. This young man was clairaudient, and not knowing that all people possess this faculty, he began to think it was due to evil spirits. His superstitious beliefs caused him to ascribe it to departed spirits. Through constant worry he became a monomaniac on the subject. His subconscious mind dominated and controlled by an all-potent but false suggestion, gradually took over control and mastery of his objective faculties, and his reason abdicated its throne. He was what you would call mentally unbalanced, as all men are who allow their false beliefs to obtain the ascendancy.

We must not place gangsters, assassins, and murderers in charge of our mind. Place Wisdom and Divine Love in charge of your mind. Let faith in God, and all things good take charge of your mind. The subjective or subconscious mind within each of us is of tremendous importance and significance, but it can be influenced negatively and positively. Be sure that you influence it only positively, constructively, and harmoniously. The subconscious possesses transcendent powers, but it is at the same time amenable to good and bad suggestions. The explanations which I gave him made a profound impression on him.

I gave him the following written prayer which he was to repeat for ten or fifteen minutes three or four times a day: "God's Love, Truth, and Wisdom flood my mind and heart. I love the Truth, I hear the Truth, and I know the Truth. God's River of Peace floods my mind, and I give thanks for my freedom."

He repeated the above prayer slowly, quietly, reverently, and with deep feeling, particularly prior to sleep. By identifying with harmony and peace, he brought about a rearrangement of the thought-patterns and imagery of his mind, and a healing followed. He knew that what was true of God was true of himself. He brought about a conviction by repetition, faith, and expectancy.

My prayer for him night and morning was as follows: "John is thinking rightly. He is reflecting Divine Wisdom and Divine Intelligence in all ways. His mind is the perfect mind of God, unchanging and eternal. He hears the Voice of God which is the Voice of Peace and Love. He understands the Truth, he knows the Truth, and he loves the Truth. God's River of Peace floods his mind. His mind is full of God's Wisdom and Understanding. Whatever is vexing him now is leaving him, and I pronounce him free and at peace."

I meditated on these words of Truth night and morning, getting the "feel" of peace and harmony; at the end of a week this young man was completely free. I fasted from the poisoned feast of sense-evidence and fear-symptoms. I had to cure myself of the belief in a diseased state, and outer results necessarily followed. I think my explanation was a great help to this young man. The ill state is conditioned in us as long as we see that state of illness portrayed. Our failure is due to absence of faith in the disciples (our mental faculties). We must contemplate the Infinite Perfection within us, and keep on doing so, until the day breaks and the shadows flee away.

He suffered not the demons to speak.

HOW YOUR MIND HEALS
THE SICK

And he arose out of the synagogue, and entered into Simon's house. And Simon's wife's mother was taken with a great fever; and they besought him for her. And he stood over her, and rebuked the fever; and it left her: and immediately she arose and ministered unto them.

Luke 4:38–39.

Related passage, Matt. 8:14–15.

Some time ago, a woman told me her child had a very high fever and was not expected to live. The doctor had prescribed small doses of aspirin, and had administered an antibiotic preparation. The mother was involved in a contemplated divorce action and was terribly agitated and emotionally disturbed. This disturbed feeling was communicated subconsciously to the child, and naturally the child got ill.

Children are at the mercy of their parents and are controlled by the dominant mental atmosphere of those around them. They have not yet reached the age of reason where they can take control of their own thoughts, emotions, and reactions to life. This mother, at my suggestion, decided to get quiet and still by reading the *Twenty-third Psalm*, praying for guidance, also praying for the peace and harmony of her husband, and pouring out love upon him instead of resentment and rage. The fever of the child was the suppressed anger and rage of the mother which was felt by the child and expressed as a high fever, or a state of excitation of the mind.

Having quieted her own mind, she began to pray for the child in this manner: "Spirit which is God is the life of my child. Spirit has no temperature; it is never sick or feverish. The peace of God floods my child's mind and body. The Harmony, Health, Love, and Perfection of God are made manifest in my child's mind and body now. She is relaxed and at ease, poised, serene, and calm. I am now stirring up the gift of God within her, and all is well."

She repeated the above prayer slowly, quietly, and lovingly for about ten minutes. She noticed a remarkable change in the child, who awakened, and asked for a doll and for something to eat. The temperature became normal. What happened? The fever left the child because the mother was no longer feverish or agitated in her mind. Her mood of peace, harmony, and love was instantaneously felt by the child, and a corresponding reaction was produced in the child. She took her child by the hand, biblically speaking.

The *hand* means the Power of God. With the hand you fashion, mold, shape, and direct. It is symbolic of the Creative Power or Intelligence in all of us. She lifted her child by the *hand* in the sense that she lifted up the idea of health, harmony, and peace in her mind to the point of acceptance, and the Power of the Almighty responded accordingly. It is the nature of the Deeper Mind to respond to the nature of your thought. When the mother focused her attention on the idea of perfect health for her child, the Power of the Almighty flowed through her focal point of attention, and a healing followed.

When the Bible speaks of *entering into Simon's house*, it refers to what you are hearing. The word *Simon* means to hear, and *Simon's wife's mother* means the emotional state which follows what you have been hearing or giving attention to. If disturbed by some news, or if you become unduly excited, you must rise up in your *synagogue* (mind); *i.e.*, you should contemplate the Inner Presence as saturating every atom of your being. Then a wave of inner peace will follow, and all will be well. You *rebuke the fever* or sick state by contemplating the Omnipresence of God. This is Divine Science in action.

Great peace have they who love thy law and nothing shall offend them.

And it came to pass, when he was in a certain city, behold a man full of leprosy: who seeing Jesus fell on his face, and besought him, saying, Lord, if thou wilt, thou canst make me clean. And he put forth his hand, and touched him, saying, I will: be thou clean. And immediately the leprosy departed from him. And he charged him to tell no man: but go, and shew thyself to the priest, and offer for thy cleansing, according as Moses commanded, for a testimony unto them.

Luke 5:12–14.

Related passages, Mark 1:40–44. Matt. 8:2–4.

A leper, biblically speaking, is a person who through erroneous thoughts has separated himself from the real Source of life. It means a man who is governed by the five senses, and is psychologically and spiritually separated from his Divine Center. A leprous or impure condition is the result of being governed by the five senses with its fears, superstitions, and erroneous thoughts.

He put forth his hand, and touched him, saying, I will: be thou clean. You have seen men lay hands on people, and pray over them, and a healing followed; this has occurred from time immemorial. Sometimes people refer to the man who practices the laying on of hands as a "natural born healer." Of course, we are all "natural born healers" for the simple reason that the Healing Presence of God is within all men. All of us can contact It with our thoughts. It responds to all. The Healing Principle is in the dog, the cat, the tree, and the bird. It is Omnipresent and is the Life of all things.

There are different degrees of faith. There is the man who, through faith, heals his ulcers, and another who heals a deep-seated, so-called incurable malignancy. It is as easy for the Healing Presence to heal a tubercular lung as a cut in the finger. There is no great or small in the God that made us all; there is no big or little, nor hard or easy. Omnipotence is within all men. The prayers of the man who lays his hand on another appeals to the cooperation of the unconscious; a response takes place, and *according to your faith* (feeling) *is it done unto you.* This is the time-honored procedure of healing.

And he charged him to tell no man. It is a wise procedure to refrain from going around telling everyone you had a spiritual healing. Many of your friends will pass derogatory and skeptical remarks which might undermine your faith, causing you to doubt and hence undo the benefits you received from the prayers of the healer and your own mental acceptance.

Shew thyself to the priest. When you pray, you are the *priest* offering up the *sacrifice.** Your feeling, mood, or attitude of receptivity is the connecting link between the Invisible and the visible. Your desire is your *offering;* you cleanse yourself by forgiving everyone, by sincerely wishing for all those who may have seemed to hurt you all of God's blessings such as peace, love, joy, and happiness. Having cleansed your mind of all impurities (negative imagery and destructive thoughts), you offer your gift (desire) to God by galvanizing yourself into the feeling of being one with your ideal. Become engrossed and absorbed in the joy of having heard the good news, or the joy of the answered prayer; this consumes the old state and gives birth to the new.

If you want a healing of your body, withdraw mentally from symptoms and evidence of senses and begin to think of God's Healing Presence within you. The five outward senses are now turned inward and focused on health and harmony. All your attention is on your health and peace of mind. The Almighty Creative Power flows through the focal point of attention. You feel the response of the Spirit flowing through you. The Healing Presence touches every atom of your being and you are spiritually enriched. Dwelling in conscious communion with the Divine, man oftentimes becomes intoxicated with the Spirit. A state of exhilaration of the whole being takes place. This spiritual awakening builds up the entire man, makes him new, so that each day

---

* See *Prayer Is the Answer.*

adds a new joy. As we continue to pray scientifically, we are lifted up so that an outpouring of Spirit takes place, and our whole being is revivified and recharged.

Dr. Alexis Carrel, in *Man The Unknown*, points out the marvelous effects produced by prayer. He cites a case of a cancerous sore which shriveled to a scar in front of his eyes. He recounts seeing wound-lesions heal in a few seconds, and pathological symptoms disappear in a few hours. Extreme activation of the processes of organic repair had set in. These healings of tumors, burns, etc., were due to nothing more than the release of the Healing Power within each one. God or Infinite Intelligence is the only Healer, the only Presence, the only Power. When we call on this Presence within, giving It supreme recognition, claiming that the Healing Power saturates our mind and body, we receive a corresponding flood of the Healing Power which permeates every atom of our body, cicatrizing wounds and making us whole. Our body begins to function harmoniously; its atomic and molecular formation once more is transformed into the way it is in the Divine Center within us; then we know the truth of the saying, *yet in my flesh shall I see God.*

When the Bible says, *offer for thy cleansing, according as Moses commanded,* you are to look at the word *Moses,* as Troward points out, as the Law—the way your deeper mind works. As you exalt your thought-patterns claiming and affirming your good, your deeper mind (the Law) automatically responds to the new mental pattern and mental imagery and a healing follows. The Law holds no grudges, no more so than the law of electricity. All you do is conform to the principle of electricity and results follow. You may have misused the principle for making water for fifty years; the moment you follow the correct procedure, you will get water.

And, behold, men brought in a bed a man which was taken with a palsy: and they sought means to bring him in, and to lay him before him. And when they could not find by what way they might bring him in because of the multitude, they went upon the house-top, and let him down through the tiling with his couch into the midst before Jesus. And when he saw their faith, he said unto him, Man, thy sins are forgiven thee.

Luke 5:18–20.

Related passage, Mark 2:3–5.

I say unto thee, Arise, and take up thy couch, and go into thine house.

Luke 5:24.

I remember a case of palsy and tremors being treated some years ago. The man's legs would become locked so that inability to move was experienced. Panic would ensue, and the man would be frozen to the spot even in the middle of a busy street. This condition of constant fear, panic, and fore-boding was wearing him down. The following procedure was adopted. The first step was to get him out of nature's way. After *agreeing quickly with thy adversary* he was told he must not continue in a state of quarrel, fear, and panic as to why he was beset with such a physical condition, causes which brought it about, etc. He admitted to himself that the condition was present and quite a problem, but that he didn't have to have it. He said to himself, "I am going to deny the worst and return to the Rock from whence I came."

He turned to the God-Presence within which created him

and knew what to do. This Healing Presence is Omnipresent, Omniscient, and Omnipotent. He aligned himself with the Infinite, realizing that the Healing Presence was saturating every atom of his being and flowing through him as harmony, health, peace, wholeness, and perfection. As he gradually filled his mind with these Eternal Verities, he became reconditioned to health and harmony. As he changed his mind, he changed his body, for the body is a shadow of the mind.

The Bible story says *men brought in a bed a man which was taken with a palsy*. The *bed* in which a man lies is his own mind. He lies down there with fear, doubt, condemnation, guilt, and superstition. These thoughts paralyze the mind and body.

In *Mark* 2:1–12 where we have a slightly different version of the same story, it says the man was *borne of four*. The numeral *four* represents the manifested world, the objective manifestation of subjective states of consciousness. *Four* means termination, the end result, the completion of a cycle of consciousness, negative or positive.

We are told that Jesus (awareness of the Power of God) healed him by *forgiving his sins*. *To sin* is to miss the mark, the goal of health, of happiness, of peace. We forgive ourselves by identifying mentally and emotionally with our ideal and continuing to do so until it jells within us as a conviction or subjective embodiment. We are, of course, sinning also when we think negatively or when we resent, hate, condemn, or fear another person. If we think there is some power to challenge the One Power (God), we are also sinning because we are cohabiting mentally with evil, thereby attracting all manner of calamity, trouble, and loss. We sin when we deviate or turn away from our announced goal or aim in life which should always be peace, harmony, wisdom, and perfect health. To indulge in morbid imagery and destructive thoughts, we mar our happiness and miss the target of a full and happy life.

Jesus forgave the paralytic by saying, *Arise, and take up thy couch*, which means that Truth or God never judges or condemns. The Absolute does not judge—all judgment is given to the son. All men are sons of the Infinite. Your mind is the son or offspring of the Spirit; with that mind you claim, choose, select, and arrive at decisions and conclusions. If you err in your judgment or decision, you experience the automatic or compulsory reaction from your unconscious mind. Your mind is always forgiving you, because the moment you present it with new mental imagery and lovely patterns of thought, it responds accordingly. It is perpetually forgiving you; this is called the love of God or the mercy of God.

The paralytic could not be cured until his sins had been cancelled; but once the inner state of mind is changed through contact with the Healing Power and his sense of oneness with It, he now rises through the Power of the Almighty (the One Power) and he no longer is carried around by four men, symbolic of worldly beliefs and erroneous impressions of all kinds. The outer change conforms to the inner, spiritual awakening.

And when they could not find by what way they might bring him in because of the multitude, they went upon the housetop. The multitude refers to man's mental accusers such as fear, self-accusation, remorse, and condemnation. When he realizes that Truth or God or the law of life never condemns, he ceases to condemn and forgives himself. Then instead of lying down prone in a bed of false beliefs and fears of all kinds, through his contact with the Almighty Power he stands upright in the law, visioning and imagining his perfect health and wholeness.

You must go on the *housetop* if you want an answer to your prayer. You must climb. You do this by reminding yourself of the One Omnipotent Power and your faith in It. We climb by faith; we soar aloft above our problem with wings of faith and disciplined imagination. Faith means to look up to the One, giving all your allegiance, devotion, and loyalty to God. Truth means to go in one direction only, knowing that the Great Physician is within, that He is healing you now, and that there is none to oppose, challenge, or thwart Him in any way. Fear is a denial of God and is nothing but a conglomeration of sinister shadows, without reality and with nothing to sustain it.

It is said they climbed up and opened the roof and let the paralytic down through the roof before Jesus. All this means is that in contemplating God and His Holy Presence, you are lifted up, your mind is open and receptive, and you let your deep, abiding conviction in the idea of perfect health sink down to subliminal levels within you. Jesus means God is your deliverer, the I AM within you, which receives the impress of your conviction and responds accordingly. If you break the roof of a house, you can see the heavens above, the sun, moon, and stars. Don't let the press of worldly thoughts prevent you from receiving a healing. If your loved one is sick, open up the roof of your mind and let in the Healing Light, surrender your loved one to God and realize that he is now immersed in the Holy Omnipresence; see him as he ought to be, radiant, happy, and free. Claim what's true of God is true of your loved one. As you continue to do this, your loved one will rise up from his bed of pain, misery, and suffering, and walk the earth glorifying God.

And it came to pass also on another sabbath, that he entered into the synagogue and taught: and there was a man whose right hand was withered. And the scribes and Pharisees watched him, whether he would heal on the sabbath day: that they might find an accusation against him. But he knew their thoughts, and said to the man, which had the withered hand, Rise up, and stand forth in the midst. And he arose and stood forth.

Luke 6:6–8.

And looking round about upon them all, he said unto the man, Stretch forth thy hand. And he did so: and his hand was restored whole as the other.

Luke 6:10.

Related passage, Mark 3:3–5.

Elsie H. Salmon, a missionary's wife in South Africa, tells in her book *He Heals Today* about a child with a deformed left hand. Three fingers were missing and in their place were tiny stumps. After prayer there was a growth of the whole hand at the end of the arm, and they began to unfold like a flower in front of their eyes. She also states that there is absolutely no doubt in the minds of people who have followed developments that a perfect hand is forming.

We must not look upon this as miraculous or something supernatural. We must begin to realize that the Creative Power which forms, molds, and shapes the body can certainly grow a hand, a leg, or an eye. After all where do the organs of our body come from? If you made an ice-box, couldn't you fix it if it were out of order, or if broken, couldn't you mend it and supply the missing parts?

When Jesus said, *Stretch forth thy hand,* you must look upon it as a drama taking place in your own consciousness. You are Jesus in action when you know that the realization of your desire would save you from any predicament, be it what it may. You are Jesus or the spiritual man in action when your conscious and subconscious mind agree on the realization of your wish or prayer. When there is no further argument, and you have reached an agreement, you are Jesus Christ in action. Jesus represents your illumined reason, and Christ means the power and wisdom resident in your subjective self.

Elsie H. Salmon's faith in the Creative Power of God to form a new hand for a child caused the stunted arm to grow. Her faith is her savior or her Jesus. She is aware of the reality of what she prays for and knows that the nature of the Infinite Intelligence is responsiveness.

In the correct esoteric interpretation of the Bible, it must be understood that principles are personified as persons in order to make portrayal and interaction vivid and forceful. *Know ye not your own selves, how that Jesus Christ is in you, except ye be reprobates?* 2 Cor. 13:5.

We must not however confine the story of the man with the withered hand to its literal meaning. *The hand* is a symbol of power, of direction, of effectiveness. With your hand you fashion, mold, create, and design. *The hand* of the Almighty means the Creative Power of God focused or directed on some objective. Symbolically a man has a *withered hand* when he has an inferiority complex, feels guilty, inadequate, or is a defeatist. Such a man does not function efficiently and is not expressing his God-given powers.

We *stretch forth our hand* when we release our Hidden Power and become channels for Divine Love, Light, Truth, and Beauty.

His hand was restored whole as the other means a healthy, happy, well balanced, and wholesome personality. Numbers of people are sick, unhappy, dissatisfied, inept, and inefficient. Their attitude toward life is all wrong; moreover their work is shoddy and desultory. They do not sing in their hearts at their work. Whenever you turn with confidence and trust to the Almighty Power within knowing that you are guided, directed by this Inner Light, and that you are expressing yourself fully, you will actually become a channel for the Divine and you will move from glory to glory.

The dreams, ambitions, ideals, plans, and purposes of many are withered and frozen in the mind because they do not know how to bring them to pass. The external world denies their desire. Not knowing the laws of mind and how to pray scientifically, they find their wonderful ideas die a-borning in their minds, resulting in frustration and neurosis. If you look around you in your office or factory, you will see many people with a *withered hand*. They are stagnating, literally dying on the vine. Life is progressive, life is growth. There is no end to our unfoldment or creativeness. We wither our hand (our ability to achieve and accomplish) by saying, "If I had Joe's brains or his wealth . . . his connections . . . I could advance and be somebody. But look at me, just a nobody. I was born on the wrong side of the tracks. I must be satisfied with my lot. I have a withered hand."

This is the way many people talk. They are constantly demoting and depreciating themselves. Liquidate, banish, and eradicate from your mind fear, doubt, and ill-will. Trust God completely, go all the way out on a limb and say with feeling and humility, "I can do all things through the God-Power and Awareness which strengthens, guides, comforts, and directs me." Watch the wonders you will perform. *Stretch forth your hand* by enlarging your concept or estimate of yourself. Aim high, raise your sights, realize you will always go where your vision is. You will be *stretching forth your hand* as you get a picture in your mind of what you wish to achieve. Touch this with faith in the God-Wisdom to bring it forth and you will see it made manifest on the screen of space. You will be satisfied for a while; then a divine discontent will stir you again, causing you to aim higher and higher and so on to infinity.

To *stretch forth your hand*, when psychologically understood, is the soundest, simplest, and most wonderful philosophy any man can have.

I say unto you now, *Stretch forth thy hand*.

ABSENT TREATMENT AND THE HEALING OF INSANITY

And when he was now not far from the house, the centurion sent friends to him, saying unto him, Lord, trouble not thyself: for I am not worthy that thou shouldest enter under my roof: Wherefore neither thought I myself worthy to come unto thee: but say in a word, and my servant shall be healed. For I also am a man set under authority, having under me soldiers, and I say unto one, Go, and he goeth: and to another, Come, and he cometh: and to my servant, Do this, and he doeth it. When Jesus heard these things, he marvelled at him, and turned him about, and said unto the people that followed him, I say unto you, I have not found so great faith, no, not in Israel. And they that were sent, returning to the house, found the servant whole that had been sick.

Luke 7:6–10.

Related passages, Matt. 8:5–13. John 4:46–53.

Here is the technique of absent treatment portrayed in a beautiful and simple way. You are told how to pray for another or send your *word* and heal him. When you pray for another, or give what is termed a mental and spiritual treatment, you

simply correct what you hear and see in your mind by knowing and feeling the other's freedom. Faith comes to you as you
leave the literal interpretation of life and enter into the psychological, spiritual interpretation of life.

Many of you, like the author, were no doubt in the United
States Army and you know how to take orders. A soldier is
conditioned to obey implicitly his superior officers. After con-
siderable training the soldier becomes disciplined; *i.e.*, his mind
and body are definitely bent to certain actions. The officer is a
man of authority. He has learned to command, but first he had
to learn to take orders himself; and he, too, is subject to authority from his superiors.

When you pray for another, you must be a good soldier; you must learn how to stand at attention and follow
the order, "Eyes right." You must give attention to the spiritual values or Truths of life and keep your "eyes right" by
seeing (spiritual perception) the other as he ought to be,
happy, peaceful, and free. You must begin to discipline your
thoughts, feelings, emotions, and faculties. You know very
well that you can begin now as you read these lines. If your
thoughts wander, bring them back and say to them, "I told
you to give attention to health, peace," or whatever it is you
are concentrating on.

The servants are your thoughts, ideas, moods, feelings, and
attitudes of mind. They serve you nobly or ignobly, depending
on the orders you issue. If you are an employer, you may order the employees to do certain things in the store. You expect
them to obey; you are paying them to conform to your business methods and processes. In the same manner, you order
your thoughts around. You are the master, not the serf or slave.
Surely you do not and will not permit the gangster-thoughts

of hate, fear, prejudice, jealousy, rage, etc., to order you around and make a football of you.

When you begin to discipline your mind, you do not permit doubt, anxiety, and false impressions of the world to browbeat, intimidate, and push you around. You are conditioning your mind so that you definitely issue orders to your thoughts to give attention to your aims in life, to your ideals; likewise, you direct and channel all your emotions constructively. You have complete dominion. You can't visualize an emotion. You must remember that emotion follows thought; and when you control your thoughts and mental imagery, you are in charge of your emotions.

No person, place, or thing can annoy you, disturb you, or hurt you—they do not have that authority. For example, another could call you a skunk. Are you a skunk? No. The suggestions or statements of the other could not affect you except through your thought. This is the only emotional power you have. Your thought in such an instance could be, "God's peace fills that man's mind." You are in charge of the movement of your mind. You can move in anger, hate, or revenge; also, you can move in peace, harmony, and good will.

The disciplined mind is accustomed to take a spiritual medicine called "In tune with the Infinite." The moment you are tempted to react negatively, identify immediately with your aim. Switch to your ideal immediately and you have overcome and are victorious. You are a man of authority, and you say to your thoughts (servants) *go and they go, come and they come.*

You can give your faculty of imagination to anything you wish, such as lack, loss, or misfortune. You can discipline, direct, and focus your imagination on success, health, and prosperity also. What you imagine and feel as true comes to pass. Let your imagination become the workshop of God, which is what it should be.

Let me cite the misuse of imagination. A mother whose son is rather late arriving home begins to imagine that he has met with some disaster. She sees in her vivid, distorted, twisted mind mental pictures of him on a hospital bed or she dramatizes an accident in her imagination. She can *send her word and heal him* and herself also. She must learn how to pray scientifically and become a good soldier who follows orders.

You are under *Holy Orders** when you pray. You have surrendered your ego and intellectual pride in your own thoughts, viewpoints, and perspective, yielding to the God-Wisdom within. You are under orders now to bring forth harmony, health, peace, joy, wholeness, and beauty in the world. You are here to let your light shine. You must have faith and complete trust in the Omnipotence, Omniscience, and Boundless Love of the Infinite which seeks only to express Itself. Identify yourself mentally and emotionally with God. You feel and know that you are a channel for the manifestation of all of God's attributes, qualities, and potencies, and that God flows through you as harmony, health, peace, joy, and abundance. As you make a habit of this kind of prayer by frequently repeating or affirming these Truths, your mind will become imbued with Eternal Verities, and you will find yourself under a Divine compulsion to bring forth only the good, the beautiful, and the true. You have placed yourself under *Holy Orders,* or Orders of the Only One—God. You become a God-directed man, a divinely ordained person whose

---

* See my book *Prayer Is the Answer,* chapter 5.

sole mission in the world is to follow the orders of the *Holy One who inhabiteth Eternity whose name is perfect.*

Whose orders are you carrying out? *Ye are servants to whom ye yield yourself, servants to obey.* Whatever idea I yield to, or give myself to, will dominate, control, and compel me to act it out as frustration and expression.

In the above instance, whose order do you think the woman was obeying when she had all kinds of misgivings about her boy—bombarding him with a barrage of negation and with dire forebodings which if continued would have had catastrophic implications? This woman was taking her orders from the thoughts of fear, worry, and anxiety. In other words the marauders and intruders in her mind were browbeating her and making her a nervous wreck.

Begin now to *stretch forth your hand* by realizing there is no limit to your possibilities. Feel and believe God is your Silent Partner, counseling, directing, and governing you. As you do this, your life will be wonderful and satisfying. It will be more useful and constructive than it is. Begin to know yourself. Try the amazing power of true prayer as outlined in each chapter of this book. As you yield yourself to the God-Wisdom, you will live a better life than you ever dreamed of.

Arise, take up thy bed (new mental attitude) *and walk* the earth radiant, happy, and free.

Now when he came nigh to the gate of the city, behold, there was a dead man carried out, the only son of his mother, and she was a widow: and much people of the city was with her. And when the Lord saw her, he had compassion on her, and said unto her, Weep not. And

he came and touched the bier: and they that bare him
stood still. And he said, Young man, I say unto thee,
Arise. And he that was dead sat up and began to speak.

Luke 7:12–15.

Here is a wonderful, psychological drama. The *dead man* is your desire which you have failed to manifest. As you claim you now are what you long to be, you are resurrecting the *dead man* within you.

According to your belief is it done unto you. To believe something is to accept it as true. We are told the dead man was the son of a widow. A *widow* is a woman whose husband is dead. When we are not married, mentally and emotionally, to God and His truths, we are truly dead to peace, joy, health, happiness, and inspiration. A true widow is one whose husband is God, or the Good, and who is not governed by sense-evidence and worldly belief. The *son*, the desire, of such a woman will not remain dead because she turns to her Lord, which is the Creative Power within her and, with the door of her five senses closed, she completely rejects all that her senses deny. Silently and lovingly she claims and feels herself to be what she longs to be, knowing in her heart that her Lord (the Spirit within) will honor and validate her claim. She lives, moves, and has her being in the mental atmosphere of complete acceptance; as she continues to qualify her consciousness in this way, she reaches an inner conviction, thereby resurrecting the *dead man* within her. Her inner mood of triumph is her *Lord* commanding the *dead man*. *Young man, I say unto thee, Arise.*

This is the external manifestation of her subjective embodiment or the joy of the answered prayer. Whatever we appropriate and assimilate in consciousness, we resurrect. When it says the *dead man sat up and began to speak,* it means that when your prayer is answered you speak in a new tongue. The sick man who is healed speaks in the tongue of joyous health and exudes an inner radiance. Our dead hopes and desires speak when we bear witness to our inner beliefs and assumptions.

As a corollary to this, I would like to relate about a young man I saw in Ireland a few years ago. He was a distant relative. He was in a comatose condition; his kidneys had not functioned for two days. I went to see him accompanied by one of his brothers. I knew he was a devout Roman Catholic and I said to him, "Jesus is right here now and you see him. He is putting his hand out and is this moment laying His hands on you."

I repeated this several times, slowly, gently, and positively. He was unconscious when I spoke and was not consciously aware of the presence of any of us. He sat up in bed, opened his eyes, and said, "Jesus was here; I know I am healed; I shall live."

What happened? This man's unconscious mind accepted my statement that Jesus was there and his subconscious projected that thought form; *i.e.,* this man's concept of Jesus was portrayed based on what he saw in church statues, paintings, etc. He believed Jesus was there in the flesh and that he had placed his hands upon him.

The readers of this book are well aware of the fact that you can tell a man in a trance that his grandfather is here now and that he will see him clearly. He will see what he believes to be his grandfather. His subconscious projects the image of his grandfather based on his subconscious, memory picture.

You can give the same man a posthypnotic suggestion saying to him, "When you come out of the trance, you will greet your grandfather and talk to him."

He does exactly that. This is called a subjective hallucination. The faith kindled in the unconscious of my Catholic relative, based on his firm belief that Jesus came to heal him, was the healing factor. It is always done unto us according to our faith or mental conviction. The subconscious is amenable to suggestion even though the subject is unconscious; the deeper mind can receive and act upon the suggestion of the operator. In a sense you could call such an incident the *resurrection of the dead*. It is the resurrection of health, faith, confidence, and vitality. We must never let hope, joy, peace, love, and faith in God die in us; that state of mind is the real death. We should die to fear, ignorance, jealousy, envy, hate, etc. We should starve these states to death by neglect. When fear dies, there is only room for faith. When hate dies, there is only room for love. When ignorance dies, there is only room for wisdom.

Now it came to pass on a certain day, that he went into a ship with his disciples: and he said unto them, Let us go over unto the other side of the lake. And they launched forth. But as they sailed he fell asleep: and there came down a storm of wind on the lake: and they were filled with water, and were in jeopardy. And they came to him, and awoke him, saying, Master, master, we perish. Then he arose, and rebuked the wind and the raging of the water: and they ceased, and there was a calm.

Luke 8:22–24.

Here we are told how to control our emotions and heal the turbulent soul. This is a story of everyone, not just about men in a ship, because we are always traveling somewhere psychologically speaking. When beset with a difficulty, we seek an answer, a solution. When fearful, we must move to faith. The journey is always first in the mind, the body follows where the mind goes. The body cannot do anything or go any place unless the mind agrees and directs. Consciousness is the only power and the only mover. The consciousness of man is perpetual motion. Our mind is always active, even when asleep.

Our *disciples* are our mental attitudes, moods, and faculties which go with us wherever we go. We must not let *Jesus go to sleep in the boat.* In order to understand the science of life in the Bible, you must regard—*Jesus,* the *boat,* the *wind,* the *waves,* and the *disciples,* as personifications of truths, faculties, moods, and thoughts of mankind. Your *Jesus* is your awareness of the Divine Power within you, enabling you to achieve, accomplish, and realize your objectives. Your knowledge of the laws of mind and your use of mental and spiritual laws is your *savior* or solution at all times, everywhere.

You must not permit *Jesus to sleep in the boat,* which means you must not go blithely along with the winds (opinions of man) and waves (fears, doubts, envy, hatred, etc.) of the race mind. The *lake* is your mind; when your mind is at peace, God's wisdom and God's ideas rise to the surface of your mind. The mind that stays on God feels God's River of Peace flowing through it and is full of poise, balance, and serenity. The *Storm* of *wind* represent the fear, terror, and anguish which seize man at times, causing him to vacillate, hesitate, and tremble with anxiety. He finds himself pulled two ways; his fear holds him back and prevents him from going forward.

What do you do when fear and limitation seize your mind? Realize that when you are looking at your desire, you see your *savior* or the solution in your mind. Your *savior* is always knocking at the door of your mind. Perhaps you are working for the government and you are saying, "Oh, I can't make any more money; I've reached the maximum." You are now seeing the *waters* of confusion and doubt welling up in you. Don't become submerged in these watery, negative emotions. Wake up your *savior*, stir up the gift of God within you.

Do it in this way. Realize first of all that the wish, desire, ideal, plan, or purpose you want to realize is definitely a reality of the mind, though invisible; then realize that by uniting with your desire mentally, you can definitely and positively move over the turbulent, noisy, and foaming waters of fear and hesitancy. Your faith is your feeling and your awareness that the thing you are praying for is a reality of the mind in the form of an idea or desire. Inasmuch as you thought about it, it is real. Trust the mental picture; it is real. By contemplating its reality you *walk over the waters* and you *quiet the waves* of fear. Your fear has abated because you know that when you focus your attention on your ideal, the Creative Power of God flows through that focal point of attention. You are now *stilling the waves*. You have disciplined your mind. You have reasoned it out and you know that the idea is always real. The thought is *the substance of things hoped for, the evidence of things not seen,* for the simple reason that you believe in the possibility of the execution of the idea.

Keep your eyes on your goal, your objective, knowing in your heart that there is an Almighty Power which supports you in all your ways. It never deserts you or leaves you. The subjective mind responds to your constructive thinking and feeling; thereby sustenance, strength, and power are given you. To look down at the *waves* of fear, false belief, and error is to sink. Look up and you will go where your vision is. Your ordered mind, your faith, and confidence enable you to walk over all the water of life to *green pastures and still waters*. You can *command the winds and waves*, and they will obey.

And when he went forth to land, there met him out of the city a certain man, which had devils long time, and ware no clothes, neither abode in any house, but in the tombs. When he saw Jesus, he cried out, and fell down before him, and with a loud voice said, What have I to do with thee, Jesus, thou Son of God most high? I beseech thee, torment me not. (For he had commanded the unclean spirit to come out of the man. For oftentimes it had caught him: and he was kept bound with chains and in fetters; and he brake the bands, and was driven of the devil into the wilderness.) And Jesus asked him, saying, What is thy name? And he said, Legion: because many devils were entered into him. And they besought him that he would not command them to go out into the deep. And there was there a herd of many swine feeding on the mountain: and they besought him that he would suffer them to enter into them. And he suffered them. Then went the devils out of the man, and entered into the swine: and the herd ran violently down a steep place into the lake, and were choked. When they that fed them saw what was done, they fled, and went and told it in the city and in the country. Then they went out to see what was done; and came to Jesus, and found the man,

out of whom the devils were departed, sitting at the feet of
Jesus, clothed, and in his right mind: and they were afraid.

Luke 8:27–35.

Related passages, Matt. 8:28–32. Mark 5:1–13.

In reading this account, it certainly reminds you of a manic-depressive type of psychosis. This is, of course, a form of mental derangement and is characterized by combativeness and destructivity. In the book of *Mark* we have a story similar to the above wherein the maniac is depicted as *living among the tombs.*

The *tombstones* are a record of the dead, which means here that the man is living in the dead past, nursing some old grudge or grievance until it becomes an obsession in his mind. The madman is a man who has allowed or permitted the gangsters of remorse, hate, revenge, or self-pity to take charge of his reasoning, discriminating mind. We must never abdicate and let destructive, negative emotions control us. Emotion follows thought; and by redirecting our thought life, we control our emotional life. Man cannot visualize an emotion. He has to construct the scene or event in his mind and relive it, thereby generating the emotion. In psychiatry the doctors endeavor to correct the basic conflicts of the patient and give him a new orientation.

Jesus addressing the insane man asks, *What is thy name? And he said, Legion: because many devils were entered into him.* I knew a man in New York who feared that whenever he went into a bar some evil entity was lurking in the shadows somewhere to take possession of him. I don't know where he heard or read of such rank superstition. This belief governed his mind and caused all kinds of trouble. His subjective mind, being dominated by this all-potent but false suggestion, gained control of his reasoning faculties and his reason abdicated. He had to experience the effects of such a false belief; this subjective false belief gained the ascendency. He began to hear what he supposed to be spirit voices, not knowing he was talking to himself. He thought he was conversing with supernatural entities. He began to realize that his subconscious mind was simply acting in obedience to the false suggestions of fear and belief in spirits which he had dwelt upon so long. The subconscious will assume a dozen different characters whose collective name is *Legion*. This man went to a clergyman who used the ritual of the Church to banish the tormentors. The procedure of the exorcist was, as the reader will readily conclude, a series of incantations or adjurations in the name of Jesus Christ. The ritual, ceremony, and prayers of the exorcist instilled great faith and confidence in the subconscious mind of the man. He was very receptive to the power of the Church and the priest to cast out his so-called devils. The exorcist had confidence in what he was doing also. This coupled with the faith of the so-called possessed man brought about a marvelous healing. The priceless ingredient in the whole process was simply faith, which brought about a basic change in the mental attitude of the patient that generated a healing. It was, of course, blind faith which is certainly better than no faith at all. The bones of saints, certain waters, the incantations of a witch doctor may affect the deeper mind and cause a psychological transformation inducing faith and receptivity.

Divine healing or Spiritual healing refers to the harmonious functioning of our conscious and subconscious minds.

Our mind contains within its conscious and subconscious areas all our desires, characteristics, tendencies, and urges with which we were born. Through the process of thinking, education, and experience we have acquired many attitudes and habits of various kinds. Man is a creature of habit. When we begin to think intelligently we deliberately reject all negative thoughts and opinions. When we fail to realize a desire or ideal, we become full of fear and frustration, this leads to unconscious impressions. These repressed urges and tendencies seek expression and an outlet. These destructive emotions manifest as inner conflicts; if those are not resolved, disorganization of the mentality takes place and a completely disordered mind is the result.

The subjective self in us is forever seeking to restore a balance in us; when our fears, tensions, and conflicts become unbearable, nature or the Divine Self in us causes us to lose all consciousness of the problems; this is called insanity. The mind is now deflected and detached from the strain and stress which caused the trouble. Imbalance results when we fail to choose between good and evil. We must not seek to solve our problems without Divine Wisdom and Divine Power. The mental derangement is simply the expression of deep, repressed urges and conflicts which are too great to bear. A complex is a group of ideas highly charged with emotion seeking expression.

If a man is full of hatred and prejudice, he is living in *the tombs*. When these are exposed and held up to the light of reason, they are dissipated. In Bible language, you are Jesus casting out the devils of hate, prejudice, and jealousy. These obnoxious complexes are always hiding in the *tomb* (subconscious mind). When men refuse to acknowledge and hold up their prejudices, peeves, and grudges to the light of reason, these ideas are forced down beneath the conscious level of personality and they are bound by the chains of fear, ignorance, and various mental obsessions. When we nurse grudges, prejudices, revenge, and remorse they sink into the unconscious area of mind like a smoldering fire ready to explode sooner or later. If we recognize these smoldering flames and handle them intelligently, we can be free and lead a normal life.

Our emotional side of life is the driving power. It would be a good thing for all of us to take a good look at ourselves and see if the qualities we criticize so harshly in others are not in ourselves. When our story says the insane man sat at the *feet* of the Master, it depicts our understanding of the laws of mind and how they work.

When you are asked to pray for an insane man in the hospital, you can't get his cooperation. He has ceased to reason and discriminate. Actually he is governed by the ghosts of the subconscious that walk the gloomy galleries of his mind. When you pray for such a type of person, it is necessary to do all the work yourself. You have to convince yourself of his freedom, peace, harmony, and understanding. You could pray two or three times a day in this way: "I now decree for John Doe that the intelligence, wisdom, and peace of God are made manifest in him and he is free, radiant, and happy. He is now clothed in his right mind. The Mind of God is the only Real and Eternal Mind; this is his mind, and he is poised, serene, calm, relaxed, and at ease. He is full of faith in God, in life, and all good things. I decree this, I feel it, and I see him whole and perfect now. Thank you, Father."

By repeating these Truths to yourself, realizing that there is but one mind, you will gradually, through frequent picturing in your mind, reach a dominant conviction; and the man you are praying for will at that moment be healed. In a case such as the above, all healing has to be done in the mind of the practitioner. The practitioner must not at any time give power to symptoms, or the prognosis of the case. He must rely exclusively on the operating Principle of Life which forever responds to his faith and trust in it. When you pray for another, you leave the realm of time and space, of appearances and circumstances, the verdict of the world, and you judge righteous judgment. This means that you come to a conclusion that the Inner Man (the Spiritual, Divine Presence) cannot be sick, confused, or insane. Nothing could ever happen to Wisdom, Peace, Harmony, Intelligence, or Divine Love. The inner man has all of these qualities and attributes, and the practitioner by meditating on the Eternal Life, perfect mind, and absolute peace of the mentally sick man, dissipates and dissolves the mist of fixed opinions and error thoughts that separate the man from God's River of Peace. Become aware now of the Almighty Power which is Invisible and Intangible. Don't struggle in your prayer-work; then you will find the outer coat of painting will fade away, and the masterpiece will be revealed in all its pristine glory.

The story says *the devils went out of the man and entered into the swine: and the herd ran violently down a steep place into the lake, and were choked.* Pigs were chosen symbolically as pigs decapitate themselves when swimming; likewise, when we begin to swim psychologically in the waters of life, our negative thoughts and confusions (devils) die from want of belief. The past dies for you when you no longer think of the past. If you feel you can't accomplish or cannot be healed, you are looking back at the past, you are living *among the tombs*. Don't listen to these messages of the past. The ideal or desire which beckons, which says to you, "Arise, go forth, achieve," is the savior walking down the corridors of your mind. Accept that ideal as real now and walk as though you possessed it. You are now *clothed* in your right mind, and a wave of peace moves over you because you realize that which you seek already is. This is why the Bible says, *Lift up your eyes, look on the fields; for they are already white to harvest.*

And, behold, there came a man named Jairus, and he was a ruler of the synagogue: and he fell down at Jesus' feet, and besought him that he would come into his house: For he had one only daughter, about twelve years of age, and she lay a dying. But as he went the people thronged him. And a woman having an issue of blood twelve years, which had spent all her living upon physicians, neither could be healed of any, came behind him, and touched the border of his garment: and immediately her issue of blood stanched. And Jesus said, Who touched me? When all denied, Peter and they that were with him said, Master, the multitude throng thee and press thee, and sayest thou, Who touched me? And Jesus said, Somebody hath touched me: for I perceive that virtue is gone out of me. And when the woman saw that she was not hid, she came trembling, and falling down before him, she declared unto him before all the people for what cause she had touched him, and how she was healed immediately. And he said unto her, Daughter, be of good comfort: thy faith hath made thee whole; go in peace. While he yet spake, there cometh one from the ruler of the synagogue's house, saying to him, Thy daughter is dead; trouble not the Master. But when Jesus heard it, he answered him, saying, Fear not: believe only, and she shall be made whole. And when he came into the house, he suffered no man to go in, save Peter, and James, and John, and the father and the mother of the maiden. And all wept, and bewailed her: but he said, Weep not; she is not dead, but sleepeth. And they laughed him to scorn, knowing that she was dead. And he put them all out, and took her by the hand, and called, saying, Maid, arise. And her spirit came again, and she arose straightway: and he commanded to give her meat.

Luke 8:41–55.

Related passages, Matt. 9:20–22, 14:35–36.

Mark 5:28–34.

All these stories are psychological and must be interpreted as such. You are *Jairus* which means the ruling thought in the mind; *you throw yourself at Jesus' feet; i.e.,* you begin to realize that based on your new understanding of the Power of God in you, you can resurrect the *dying child*. The *dying daughter* represents your unfulfilled ambition, the desire of your heart. *Jesus, Jairus*, the *daughter*, the *woman with the issue of blood, Peter, James*, and *John*—all these characters are within each of us. It is a story of everyman. Our *daughter* (desire) *is dying* because we lack the faith to resurrect it. *A woman with the issue of blood* cannot give birth, she cannot conceive. A bleeding womb cannot possibly give form to a body. *Woman* means emotion, feeling. When our emotions are running wild and undisciplined, we are symbolically *bleeding from the womb*. Energy and vitality are being wasted because of fear, worry, and doubt. The *womb* (mind) must be closed in order to procreate.

As you go within and shut the door of your senses to all objective evidence and assume that you are what you long to be, you are closing your *womb* (mind) and will succeed in giving form to your idea or plan. Your thought is creative; when you begin to think on what you wish to express, the Creative Power of God responds and by remaining faithful to the new mental focus, you will resurrect your *child*. You know in your heart that *the child is not dead* and that you can bring it forth. Your new attitude of mind which is your faith closes the *womb*.

Thy faith hath made thee whole. Faith comes through hearing that there is only One Sovereign and Supreme Power which can do all things for It is Almighty. As we give our attention to the Truth about this One Power, we are said to hear it. Let us hear the Truths about the Power of Love, faith, and good will, and let us trust our subjective wisdom to reveal to us the answer to any problem. Faith is going in one direction only. Many people give their ear or attention to lies, falsehoods, superstition, and erroneous concepts of all kinds. When we do this, confusion reigns supreme.

Somebody hath touched me: for I perceive that virtue is gone out of me. You can mentally and emotionally touch faith, love, joy, and peace. When you mentally appropriate the idea of perfect health, the Healing Presence responds, and you are made whole—this is the virtue that comes out of the depths of yourself.

We are told that *they laughed him to scorn*. Is it not true that your five senses mock and laugh at you? Do they not challenge you and say, "It can't be done," or "It is impossible." This is why you suspend your senses and direct your mind to give attention to the new mental picture, and as you envelop this desire with the mood of love, you become one with it. This is the meaning of taking *Peter, James, and John into the house with Him.* The *house* is your mind or consciousness. Your own I AM-NESS is the father and mother of all ideas, desires, concepts, and urges. *Peter* means faith in God; *James* means to judge righteously, *i.e.,* to hear the good news only; *John* is love or a sense of atonement, at-one-ment, with your ideal. We actually take these three qualities with us whenever we recognize a state as true that is not evident to the senses. Our reason and senses may question, ridicule, scoff, and laugh, but if we will only go within, knowing that when we feel something as true, Omnipotence moves in our behalf; then, though the whole world would deny it, we would demonstrate our desire because we are sealed in faith, and *according to our faith is it done unto us.*

YOUR HEALING
PRESENCE

And, behold, a man of the company cried out, saying, Master, I beseech thee, look upon my son: for he is mine only child. And, lo, a spirit taketh him, and he suddenly crieth out; and it teareth him that he foameth again, and bruising him hardly departeth from him. And I besought thy disciples to cast him out; and they could not. And Jesus answering said, O faithless and perverse gen-eration, how long shall I be with you, and suffer you? Bring thy son hither. And as he was yet a coming, the devil threw him down, and tare him. And Jesus rebuked the unclean spirit, and healed the child, and delivered him again to his father. And they were all amazed at the mighty power of God.

Luke 9:38–43.
Related passages, Matt. 17:14–21.
Mark 9:17–29.

There are similar stories in the *Book of Mark* and *Matthew*, which definitely seem to indicate a disease known as epi-lepsy today. Of course, looking at the story literally one would think of demon possession which was the popular belief in those days. The boy is thrown down; he foams at the mouth and wallows on the ground suffering from convulsions. The Bible does not mention the word epilepsy. The word is derived from the Greek word *epilepsia*, which means a falling sickness characterized by seizures. The Greeks called epilepsy the sacred disease because it was believed to be caused by the moon. As we all know, the term lunatic comes from the Latin word *lunaticus*. In ancient symbology the moon meant the subconscious mind. The sun was the illumined intellect or the conscious mind full of wisdom.

In other words the Bible is saying the child had a subconscious poison pocket which was the cause of his seizures and epileptic fits. *The sun shall not smite thee by day, nor the moon by night*. Psalms. 121:6. Modern psychology and psychiatry show definitely that mental and physical disorders have their roots in the depths of the deeper mind, called the subconscious or unconscious.

Negative subconscious patterns are called *pestilences of the darkness*. By turning to the God-Presence within and calling on the Power and Goodness of God, we bring the action of God to play in our life. We prove our allegiance, devotion, and love for God by identifying ourselves with His qualities and by absolutely refusing to recognize evil as having any power over us. Because of our faith in the One Power, we claim His Perfect Harmony and Perfect Peace which is His Will.

Hippocrates, about 400 B.C., recognized this type of mental disorder called epilepsy which in his time was believed to be caused by divine beings. He ridicules the superstitions of his day and points out that the disease could not be of divine origin for the simple reason that the condition was healed by purifications and various incantations which were in vogue at the time. A local psychiatrist told me that his study of Hippocrates showed that this famous physician had a wonderful knowledge of the causes underlying mental disorders of all kinds.

The ailment of the child in question doesn't matter. We must realize in praying for another that *with God all things are possible*. The *Book of Mark* says this type of case is healed by *prayer and fasting. Fasting* means, fasting from the sense evidence, symptoms, and race belief. We must *fast; i.e.,* mentally reject the poisoned feast of objective evidences.

Where did this healing take place? Jesus, as the story goes, had to heal himself of the disease, whether insanity or idiocy, and outer results necessarily followed. It is the *prayer of faith* which gets results. The mentally deranged state of consciousness is conditioned in us as long as we see that condition of illness portrayed. The failure to heal a child is not the child's fault but the absence of faith in the *disciples* (mind's faculties). The one praying must cure himself of the claim supposedly gripping the ailing child; the condition is actually gripping the practitioner who is unawakened yet to the Truth. When we fail in this type of case, we simply have failed to fix our mind's eye on the embodiment of health which the ailing one needs.

We are told the reason the disciples could not heal the sick boy was due to unbelief. There is a deep unconscious belief in the minds of people that certain diseases are difficult to heal; when they see a lunatic and his symptoms, their senses are deeply impressed with the difficulties. The *disciples* spoken of are our own attitudes, mental faculties, and viewpoints. We must completely detach ourselves from the evidence of senses and identify with the Omnipotent Healing Presence, paying no attention to appearances and symptoms. Power, faith, confidence, and elevation of consciousness will come as we consider the Divine Masterpiece within and not the appearance.

Here is a treatment I use in treating mental disorders: I go within myself, mention the name of the patient; then I think of God for three or four minutes by mentally dwelling on Infinite Peace, Harmony, Divine Intelligence, Divine Love, and Wisdom. At the same time I claim that that which is true of God is true of the one I am praying for. I try to get the *feel* that all is order, harmony, bliss, peace, and joy in the mind of the person being prayed for. In this way I induce the mood or mental atmosphere of peace, health, and harmony. When I feel that I have done the best I can, I leave it and pronounce the person whole. I may repeat this treatment two or three times a day or as often as I am led to do so, always praying as if I had never prayed before. If I have only a partial realization, the person in question will feel better. The main thing is to keep on keeping on until the *day breaks and the shadows flee away* in your own mind.

The main purpose of all our prayers for others is to get the feeling of inward joy, and God will do the rest. In prayer we must go to *heaven;* that means a state of inner peace and rest. As we enter this *heaven* frequently, we shall see heaven on earth.

And he was teaching in one of the synagogues on the sabbath. And, behold, there was a woman which had a spirit of infirmity eighteen years, and was bowed together, and

*could in no wise lift up herself. And when Jesus saw her,
he called her to him, and said unto her, Woman, thou art
loosed from thine infirmity. And he laid his hands on
her: and immediately she was made straight, and glorified God. And the ruler of the synagogue answered with
indignation, because that Jesus had healed on the sabbath day, and said unto the people, There are six days in
which men ought to work. in them therefore come and
be healed, and not on the sabbath day. The Lord then
answered him, and said, Thou hypocrite, doth not each
one of you on the sabbath loose his ox or his ass from the
stall, and lead him away to watering? And ought not this
woman, being a daughter of Abraham, whom Satan hath
bound, lo, these eighteen years, be loosed from this bond
on the sabbath day?*

Luke 13:10–16.

Healing by the laying on of hands has gone on for
countless generations. I have seen some remarkable healings
performed in that manner. Some say they are gifted and that
their hands are *healing hands*. Of course if they believe that
they have this divine gift of healing, it is done unto them
as they believe. The truth of the matter is that all of us have
the gift of healing. It is not a divine prerogative bestowed
on the few. The Healing Presence is operating within you
twenty-four hours a day. Did you ever consider all the cuts,
bruises, and scratches you experienced when young? Did
you not notice an Infinite Intelligence at work? It formed
thrombin, closed up the cut, gave you new cells, and a complete healing took place. This happened in all probability

without your being aware of it. The Intelligence within is constantly renewing your body. Faith causes this Healing Power to speed up tremendously, so much so that you can experience an instantaneous healing. As a matter of fact, a great number of churches of all denominations practice the laying on of hands.

We are told that the woman in the Bible story was healed on the *sabbath*. Many practice the *sabbath* from a literal standpoint, thinking it is a sin to drive a nail on the sabbath or do work of any kind. Some go to extremes and won't even handle money on the sabbath. All this is meaningless. *The sabbath* is an inner stillness, an inner certitude, whereby man reminds himself of the availability of the God-Presence in all emergencies, at all times, everywhere. You are *walking in the sabbath* when you accept in your mind that your prayer is answered. When you meditate and pray and succeed in reaching the point of inner peace; then your prayer is answered. You have reached the seventh day, the seventh hour, which psychologically means the moment of conviction. You are in the *sabbath* when your heart is aflame with the Glory of God and the certainty of His response, and at that moment you will experience an instantaneous, Divine transfusion of energy, power, vitality, and life.

We must realize that external acts, ritual, ceremony, and conforming to rites, precepts, and ordinances of some organization or church is not real religion or true worship. A man may observe all the rules and regulations of his church and at the same time violate all the laws of God in his heart. He could go to church every day of the week and yet be very unreligious. We must become aware of the fact that the only change that matters is the internal change, the change of the heart, where you have actually fallen in love with spiritual values; then all fear, enemies, and sickness will fall away.

When you walk in the consciousness of peace, health, and happiness, you are *in the sabbath* all day long. You are *in the sabbath* when you feel and know that it is impossible for your prayer to fail. You are unmoved, undisturbed, calm, serene, and tranquil because you are carrying in your subjective mind a divine impression, a subconscious embodiment of your ideal. You know that there is always an interval of time between the subjective embodiment and the objective manifestation. Your inner certitude and imperturbability is the sabbath, and *it was on the sabbath day that she was healed*.

The *ruler of the synagogue* mentioned in the Bible means the ruling thought or prevailing worldly viewpoint or opinion. *The synagogue* is your mind where the aggregation of thoughts, feelings, moods, and opinions gather. Jesus is always available, which means when you are looking at your desire, you are really looking at Jesus, or your solution, or that which saves. *The Woman who has the infirmity* means the feeling of weakness, the depressed state of consciousness, the subjective belief in some crippling disease. The word *woman* means emotional nature, the subjective side of life. Whatever our disease, it represents a negative pattern of thought, charged with emotion in our subliminal depths. The *ruler of the synagogue* represents the fear thoughts, the doubts, and arguments which come to your mind trying to dissuade you to turn away from the belief in the One Power which can do all things. There is an argument in your mind and you must psychologically slay these hypocritical thoughts, by asking them where they come from. Is there a principle behind them? Are they not shadows of the mind? The fear thoughts have no heavenly credentials. Take your attention away from them altogether and they die of neglect. Feast on God's Almighty Power, accept It, imagine that you are being healed now. Do this as often as necessary and you will experience *the sabbath*, or the fullness of acceptance; then you will rise and walk. *It is the sabbath day for you.*

THE INCURABLE ARE CURED

And it came to pass, as he went into the house of one of the chief Pharisees to eat bread on the sabbath day, that they watched him. And, behold, there was a certain man before him which had the dropsy. And Jesus answering spake unto the lawyers and Pharisees, saying, Is it lawful to heal on the sabbath day? And they held their peace. And he took him, and healed him, and let him go; And answered them, saying, Which of you shall have an ass or an ox fallen into a pit, and will not straightway pull him out on the sabbath day? And they could not answer him again to these things.

Luke 14:1–6.

The *Pharisee* is everywhere; he is the type of man who lays stress on external acts and observances. He adheres to the letter of the law and lacks the love and understanding behind the words of the Gospel. The *Pharisee* believes that the fan gives him a stiff neck, that germs are the cause of his cold, and that the hidden virus is the cause of his influenza. The weather, conditions, and circumstances influence the mind in a suggestive way only. Man is the only thinker in his world;

therefore it follows that the fan can't give him a cold except he thinks it does. A belief is a thought in the mind generally accepted as true. Many people can sit under a fan all day without getting a cold or a stiff neck. If one accepts the hypnotic suggestion that he will catch cold because of a draft, the fact still remains that the cold was due to his own thought. He had the power to reject or accept the suggestion. If accepted, the result is due to the movement of his own mind. He has no one to blame but himself. His mind accepted a false idea and produced the consequences.

The case of *dropsy* mentioned in the above Gospel story was due to a flood of negativity. When the mind is full of strain, stress, and tension, a corresponding effect is produced in the body, and there is a breakdown in the organs of elimination. If a man is possessed with hatred or deep-seated resentment, it could well bring on an internal flood which, if not checked, could terminate in disintegration of his vital organs due to the corrosive effect of these mental poisons. The conditions in the body are outpicturings of man's mental attitude or states of consciousness.

I knew a man in London who was very religious and completely free from any ill will or resentment. However, he saw his father die of dropsy, and it made a very deep impression on him; he told me that all his life he feared that the same thing would happen to him. He added that his father used to be tapped with an instrument and that the doctor would draw out large amounts of water from his abdominal area. This lingering fear, which was never neutralized, was undoubtedly the cause of his dropsical condition. He did not know the simple psychological truth which Quimby elucidated about a hundred years ago. Quimby said that *if you believed something, it will manifest whether you are consciously thinking of it or not.*

This man's fear became a belief that he would become a victim of the same disorder that troubled his father. This explanation helped the man considerably. He began to realize that he had accepted a lie as the truth. The truth began to dawn on him that his fear was a perversion of the truth, a fear which had no real power because there is no principle behind discord. There is a principle of health, none of disease; a principle of abundance, none of poverty; a principle of honesty, none of deceit; a principle of mathematics, none of error; a principle of beauty, none of ugliness. His belief was the only power which controlled him. One's mind can be moved negatively or positively and can be influenced by good or evil.

This man saw the truth about his situation and cast out the lie. He reasoned that the Healing Power which made him was still with him and that his disease was due to a disordered group of thoughts; thus he rearranged his mind to conform to the Divine pattern. Before going to sleep at night he would affirm with feeling and with a deep meaning behind each word, "The Healing Presence is now going to work transforming, healing, restoring, and controlling all processes of my body according to its Wisdom and Divine Nature. I rest secure in this knowledge. I know it is God in action. There is no other power and this Healing Power is working now." He repeated this prayer every night for about thirty days. At the end of that time his mind had reached a conviction of health. This was the *sabbath day* for him, which meant the moment of complete fulfillment in his mind.

I attended a church service some years ago during which the minister gave a very fine talk on Divine Healing. After the service a member of the minister's church board said to him, "It's all right to say, 'Jesus healed', but don't say we can do it!" Can you imagine a statement like that in this so-called enlightened age? The man who said that had had hundreds of healings all through his life. Life is forever healing our cuts, bruises, sprains, and scratches. It never condemns us. When we take some contaminated food, the same Life-Principle which seeks to preserve us causes us to regurgitate and tries Its utmost to heal us. A healing will take place if, as Emerson says, "we take our bloated nothingness out of the way."

I knew a Christian Scientist who swallowed a poisonous liquid by mistake one time. He was a splendid practitioner and had great faith in the God-Power. He told me that he was a hundred miles away from any kind of help so that he had to rely solely on the subjective power within him. He got very still and these are the words he used, "God is in His Holy Temple and His Presence fills every organ and cell of my being. Where God is there is only order, beauty, and perfect functioning. His Holy Presence neutralizes everything unlike Itself." He kept this up for an hour and, though in a very weakened condition, had a complete recovery.

Could one take a corrosive poison trusting the subjective power to nullify baneful effects? I don't suggest that anyone take on such a trial. I definitely believe that in an emergency or through a mistaken situation, the sincere truth student looking loyally to God for help could actually prove St. Mark's statement, *And if they drink any deadly thing it shall not hurt them,* and come out unscathed by the experience.

There are mental as well as physical poisons. The lawyers and the Pharisees are in all of us. They represent man-made laws and opinions, and the belief that we are being punished for our sins, that our *karma* is catching up to us, that we have sinned in a former life, and that now we are expiating our sins. Pharisaical thoughts come floating into our mind saying, "We must not question God, maybe it is God's

Will that we be sick. This is the cross we must bear." Others have a martyr complex and say, "God is testing me, this is a trial. I must accept my suffering as the Will of God."

God's *Will* is the will of life, and life wants to manifest itself as health, harmony, joy, wholeness, perfection, and abundance. The Will of God is the Nature of God, which is Boundless Love, Infinite Intelligence, Absolute Harmony, Perfect Peace, Infinite Joy, Boundless Wisdom, and Perfect Order, Symmetry, and Proportion. Life cannot wish death. Peace cannot wish pain. Joy cannot wish sorrow. Harmony cannot wish discord. Order cannot wish disorder. Love cannot wish punishment, misery, and suffering. People who say that God is punishing them would never dream of accusing or attributing to their own parents the things of which they accuse God. To such people the words *Infinitely Good* and *Perfect* seem to have no meaning.

Many diseases follow such false beliefs for all our beliefs tend to manifest themselves. To believe that God is testing you or punishing you sets in motion the law of your own mind bringing trouble, opposition, sickness, and difficulties of all kinds. That is why you hear a man say a jinx is following him. If man has a false premise, his conclusion or experience must conform with his false premise. Actually man punishes himself. He gives everything to himself, whether sorrow or joy, pain or peace.

Jesus means you, yourself, operating your conscious and subconscious mind synchronously and harmoniously. When you know the laws of your mind and apply them constructively, you are the Jesus of the Bible, raising the dead desires, healing the blind thoughts, and walking triumphantly toward your goal. You are no longer blind, halt, withered, or lame. This is why the Bible says, *And he took him, and healed him, and let him go.*

I have outlined for you in this chapter how a man healed a similar condition in himself. The same Healing Power is present in all men. It is not something that existed two thousand years ago. It is Omnipresent. You can lay hold of it and perform what we call miracles in your life. We must remember that a miracle cannot prove that which is impossible. It is a confirmation of that which is possible, always was, and always will be. For with God all things are possible.

Love, joy, and peace had no beginning and will have no end. Harmony always has been. The Principle of Life always has existed. It is not something that one man possessed. To say this would be the essence of absurdity. Don't wait for some angel or saint to heal you. Don't wonder whether God wants you to be healed or not. Realize that you are violating God's laws which are written in your heart and nature when you are sick, morose, hateful, or poor. Mental poisons are wrong thoughts which work underground in consciousness like a contaminated stream to emerge even after years of wrong experiences such as illness, loss, unhappiness, etc.

The first step in healing is not to be afraid of the manifest conditions from this very moment. The second step is to realize that the condition is but the product of past thinking which will have no more power to continue its existence. The third step is to *exalt the God who is in the midst of thee* (subjective self). This will stop the production of all toxins in you or your patient. You have now pronounced the condition false; in lifting yourself up, seeing the person as he ought to be, you draw the manifestation or the ideal state to you. Live in the embodiment of your desire and the *word* (your thought and feeling) will soon be made flesh. If you allow yourself to be swayed by the beliefs of man (mental poisons), you will not be able to live emotionally in your embodiment.

Among the most deadly mental poisons are the following: Hatred, which is really ignorance, and self-pity, which is really self-absorption. These drugs creep through the psychic bloodstream poisoning all springs of hope and faith, leading to dementia praecox, melancholia, and other forms of mental derangement. The spiritual antidote is to find your *other* real Self (God) and become God-intoxicated. You can fall madly in love with the new knowledge that thoughts are things and that by filling your mind with spiritual values, you will transform your whole life, bringing you health, happiness, love, and joy. You can fall in love and become wildly enthusiastic in knowing that there is a Principle of Life which flows through your mental patterns and imagery creating after their image and likeness. When you realize that the law of attraction is forever operating in your life, you are seized with a Divine frenzy at the wonder of it all. You are now in love (emotionally attached) with God, or all things good, pleasing, elevating, and uplifting. You now hunger and thirst for more Wisdom and you move forward in the light of the One Who Forever Is.

Old age is another mental poison. The Bible looks upon age *not as the flight of years, but as the dawn of wisdom.* Seek the Divine Frenzy which cleanses you of all toxins. Like Daniel, even in the lions' den, exalt the God within you—the Divine Anti-Body.

THE HEALING POWER OF THANKSGIVING

And it came to pass, as he went to Jerusalem, that he passed through the midst of Samaria and Galilee. And as he entered into a certain village, there met him ten men that were lepers, which stood afar off: And they lifted up their voices, and said, Jesus, Master, have mercy on us. And when he saw them, he said unto them, Go shew yourselves unto the priests. And it came to pass, that, as they went, they were cleansed. And one of them, when he saw that he was healed, turned back, and with a loud voice glorified God, And fell down on his face at his feet, giving him thanks: and he was a Samaritan. And Jesus answering said, Were there not ten cleansed? but where are the nine? There are not found that returned to give glory to God, save this stranger. And he said unto him, Arise, go thy way: thy faith hath made thee whole.

Luke 17:11–19.

This wonderful account of ten lepers being healed is a story of all of us. If you remove the stories of healings in the four Gospels, you have certainly emasculated one of the most important parts of the Gospels. The story of the lepers is telling all of us that sickness of the body has its origin in sickness of the soul.

I remember reading some time ago a report of a statement made by Dr. Elmer Hess as he was inaugurated president of the American Medical Association to the effect that a physician who does not believe in God has no business in a sick room. I believe that most physicians agree that faith in God has a profound effect in the maintenance of perfect health. Let us remind ourselves at this point of the famous saying, "The doctor treats the patient; God heals him."

As previously pointed out, the word *leper* in the Bible means a mind troubled with conflicting desires, emotions, and confused ideas. It means a sick mind, a man who is sick in his thoughts, his emotions, and his body. Leprosy is a wasting disease, therefore it typifies the state of a man who has lost his vitality, energy, enthusiasm, and vigor for life, because he has psychologically separated himself from the Source of all life. We have a leprous condition when we are full of envy, jealousy, anger, hatred, self-condemnation, etc.

When the Bible says *Jesus passed through Samaria and Galilee to reach Jerusalem*, it refers to a process of prayer or steps of prayer. *Jesus* represents the ideal, your desire, plan, or purpose which is always walking down the streets of your mind beckoning you onward and upward. Your ideal, picture, or vision is at this moment saying to you, "Rise up and accept me." When you raise your desire up in consciousness to the point of acceptance, you experience the truth of the statement, *Thy faith hath made thee whole.* Your desire must go through *Samaria*, which means confusion, double-mindedness, and conflict *in Galilee* (your mind).

The numeral *ten* mentioned here symbolizes the completion of a process. To look at it in a very simple way, the numeral *one* means the male or pressing aspect, namely your idea or desire. The naught or circle symbolizes a womb or receptive mind of man. *Woman* means the *womb of man*. In other words, *ten* means the interaction of the male and female elements of your own mind, thought and feeling, idea and emotion, the brain and heart. When these two are functioning harmoniously, constructively, and joyously, it is a happy marriage or union. Such a person is well integrated, healthy, vital, and courageous. The thoughts must be united with true feeling. Our thoughts must conform to the spiritual standard set forth by Paul, *Whatsoever things are true, whatsoever things are honest, whatsoever things are just, whatsoever things are pure, whatsoever things are lovely, whatsoever things are of good report; if there be any virtue, and if there be any praise, think on these things.* Phil. 4:8.

True emotion follows true thought. The heart or subjective feeling nature should be the chalice of God's Love as it is the sanctuary of His Holy Presence. It is called the *cup* in the Bible. As we meditate on the spiritual values of life we receive a transfusion of love, faith, confidence, and energy which courses through our veins transforming our whole being. Our faith is kindled when we realize that all things are done by faith, which is a movement of Omnipotence within ourselves. There is only one power and that is our own consciousness. When we think of something, we have at that moment pinpointed the flow of the Almighty Creative Power through one focal point of attention. Our faith is really our thought which, as Baudouin the French psychologist said, begins to execute itself immediately, taking form and function in your life.

All of us want to go to *Jerusalem*, the city of peace within ourselves, which means that when our desire is completely subjectified, we have reached the place of accomplishment or fulfillment. We are now at peace (Jerusalem). Our mind is no longer divided. The two (desire and faith) have become one and all is well.

The number *ten* is also a sacred number and bears reference to the line 1, and the circle 0, which produce a cross (X) only when there is a conflict in the mind. This conflict and frustration follows when man is in a double minded state. He has two powers and believes in good and evil. He looks at his environment, circumstances, and conditions and says to himself, "It's hopeless, all is lost, there is no way out of this dilemma, I'm incurable," and many similar statements. He is transferring the power within himself to external conditions, perhaps he is blaming the weather, other people, or a jinx for his trouble.

When desire and fear quarrel, the mind and the body become a battleground resulting in wasteful expenditures of energy, debility of the vital organs, nervous prostration, and exhaustion. Man must learn not to make a created thing or the manifested world a cause. He must not exalt the created thing above the Creator. He must resolve the conflict by going within himself and, like Quimby, placing his case before the Great Tribunal, God, the only Presence and the only Power. In the secret chamber of his own mind, he gives supreme recognition to the Spirit within. He looks at the fearful, negative thoughts and orders them out of his mind, realizing that they are only an illusion of power. There is no principle behind them and there is nothing to sustain them. He reminds himself that there is only one Creative Power and that It is now flowing through his thought-patterns bringing him the good he seeks. He keeps on doing this regularly and systematically until a healing of the situation takes place. He has reached a decision or pronounced judgment in his own mind. He has condemned the guilty cause (the negative thoughts) and has freed his prisoner (desire) into the arms of the Lord (his subjective self), where, through repetition, faith, and expectancy, his desire has sunk deeply into his subconscious mind. This is called depth therapy or as the Bible calls it, *entering Jerusalem* (*uru*—city, *salem*—peace), *i.e.*, reaching the point of conviction.

The cross we have been carrying is now removed because we have reached the place of death. Our desire has been entombed where it dies first; then comes forth as the answer to our prayer. The *word* (thought) has become *flesh* (made manifest in our body and environment).

The *cry of the ten lepers* is the cry of every man. It is the appeal of every troubled, frustrated, and neurotic person to the *Master* or Spiritual Power within, which alone can give peace and health of mind, body, and emotions. *They lifted up their voices.* You lift yourself up mentally when you turn in reverence, allegiance, and adoration to the Spiritual Presence within *who healeth all thy diseases. Master, have mercy on us.* The hundredth Psalm says, *His mercy is everlasting.* How beautiful are these words. They touch the heart strings causing you to go forth with the praise of God forever on your lips.

Go shew yourselves unto the priests. The word *priest* is a symbol of spiritual perception, an intuitive awareness of the great Truths of God. A priest is one who offers up a sacrifice. Every man is a priest of God when he turns away from the false gods and the poisoned feast of the irrational, mass-mind with its fears, superstitions, and terrors in order to give his supreme attention to the one God and His Laws. He *sacrifices* or gives up his negative thoughts, fears, and false beliefs and contemplates love, peace, beauty, and perfection. He must give to receive. He gives up, *i.e.*, fasts from resentment and feasts on love; fasts from the idea of poverty and feasts on the idea of God's abundance; fasts from fear and feasts on faith in

God and all things good; fasts from sadness and secretes the essence of joy, knowing that the joy of the Lord is his strength. The *true priest* fasts from pain and feasts on God's Silent River of Peace. He fasts from self-condemnation, depression, and self-pity, and feasts on amiability, sociability, kindliness, good will, and laughter. He fasts from symptoms and feasts on the mental vision of health and happiness. He fasts from darkness and feasts on the Light of God being reflected on all his problems, knowing the Light (intelligence) of God knows only the answer. He fasts from karma, fate, predestination, and feasts on God, the Eternal Now, knowing the Absolute does not condemn, judge, punish, or send sickness, disease, or death. He knows that though his hands are dripping with the blood of others and though he may have committed das- tardly crimes, he can instantaneously turn to the Presence of God within, lifting himself up to the Heart of God, claiming and feeling that he now is the man God intended him to be, the happy man, the joyous man, the poised man, the peaceful man, the loving man. As this man paints a picture or vision in his mind and his heart, he hungers for an inward change; the Law of God automatically responds to his new mental pat- tern, and the past is forgotten and remembered no more. If man misused the laws of chemistry or electricity for twenty years, the moment he used the principle correctly the under- lying laws of chemistry or electricity would automatically respond. The law cannot possibly hold grudges or try to get even. When we are dealing with our mind, we are also using the principle of mind. It makes no difference if you have been a murderer, a thief, or if you have committed all manner of evil, the moment you decide sincerely to change your life by enthroning a new concept and estimate of yourself in your mind and feel the truth of that which you affirm, the law reverses its former action and responds by corresponding to the new blueprint of your mind.

We must realize that the perfunctory prayer will not suffice. Only when sincerity and a new spiritual view of things takes hold of the mind do you expunge from your deeper mind the former negative patterns which caused all your trouble. You must remember that the law plays no favorites; moreover law is always impersonal. The laws of our mind never punish us. We merely experience the reaction of the law which we set in motion by our thoughts and beliefs. When man understands this, he has no occasion to hate or resent the meanest man who walks the earth. Furthermore, there is no basis for ill will, resentment, envy, or jealousy for all men may turn within for what they want. As they positively assert this claim for the good they seek, the law of mind responds to their mental acceptance. There is no basis for harboring ill feeling toward people who defraud or cheat us. There is nothing lost unless we admit the loss in our mind. All we have to do is to realize that all things exist in Infinite Mind, identify ourselves mentally and emotionally with that which we want, and our exchequer will again be replenished from the Infinite reservoir of God's riches in ways we know not of. There is no loss but the sense of loss. People who rob, defraud, or otherwise deceive us are merely messengers telling us who we have conceived ourselves to be. They testify to our state of consciousness. How could we be angry or hostile to others when they are merely instruments of our own mind, fulfilling the play which we wrote consciously or unconsciously in the book of life, our subconscious mind. It is easy to forgive; all we have to do is to forgive ourselves for having negative, destructive thoughts which hurt us, while those with whom we were angry probably have been fishing, dancing, or having a glorious time.

To heal any situation, *you show yourself to the priest*, for you are the *priest* yourself, forever giving up the lesser for the greater. You may offer your *sacrifice* now, which is your desire for a perfect healing, by directing your attention from the symptoms and the body, and dwelling with the Lord of Life within. Claim that the Infinite Healing Presence is saturating every atom of your body, making you whole, pure, and perfect. Know and feel that the Living Intelligence which made your body is now taking over, causing all the organs of your body to conform to God's eternal pattern of harmony, health, and peace. As you enter into the mental atmosphere of harmony, health, and peace, a rearrangement of your thought-patterns takes place followed automatically by molecular changes in the body structure to conform to the new state of consciousness. You are now transformed because you have had a spiritual transfusion of the Healing Power released by your prayers so that every atom of your being dances to the rhythm of the Eternal God.

Were there not ten cleansed? but where are the nine? The numeral *nine* mentioned refers to the consciousness of possession. Possession is nine points of the law when we enter into the feeling of being what we long to be, or as we continue to claim and feel as true that which we affirm; we add thought to thought, mood to mood, and finally we reach the point of fulfillment in consciousness. The next step is *ten,* or our good made manifest. The cycle of consciousness has been completed; we are back where we started. We began thinking of God (the One), and we ended experiencing God (the One). Everything resolves itself back to ONE, its starting point. You glorify God each time your prayer is answered. Your thought and feeling become one as they are fused together by enthusiasm and love. The *issue* is the son in expression, the idea objectified.

It is said the one who gave thanks was a *stranger*. The *stranger* in your mind might be sickness, fear, worry, or a business difficulty. These negative attitudes are *strangers*, aliens in the house of God. Our mind is supposed to be a house of prayer, not a den of thieves. Fear, worry, and anger are the *strangers* and intruders who rob us of peace of mind. When we starve these states through neglect, by giving all our attention and devotion to God and His Attributes and Qualities, our mind is cleansed. At that moment we are praising and exalting the God in the midst of us.

And one of them, when he saw that he was healed, turned back, and with a loud voice glorified God, And fell down on his face at his feet, giving him thanks. Here is a perfect formula of prayer. You may be expressing yourself in a wonderful way, be happily married, have a very prosperous business, have wonderful friends, yet, you may have a bad heart or have trouble with your eyes.

There was a man in our recent class on the *Book of Job* who wrote me saying that he was leaving the nine harmonious, stable conditions of his life to fill up the one that was lost or missing. He said that he went to work on a quality in which he was sadly lacking, namely, thankfulness. This young man said he rarely praised anybody and that he was not thankful for all his blessings. He was amazed when he began to consider all the wonderful things that happened to him and the many blessings he enjoyed. The *stranger* in his midst was eye trouble. The mood of gratitude and the thankful heart causes us to tune in with the creative forces of the universe and what we send out comes back to us multiplied by the law of action and reaction.

This young man quieted the wheels of his mind and began to imagine he was talking to the King of Kings, the Lord of Lords within himself. He had no mental picture of God, of course. In his mind's eye he sensed that the Divine Presence was there, the very Life of him. He began to say, over and over again, "Thank you Father, Thank you Father." He kept repeating this softly, quietly, gently, and lovingly. He was in a sleepy, drowsy, state each night as he meditated in the manner outlined. He would go to sleep in the mental mood of thankfulness. He had a perfect healing of his eyes. In biblical language *he fell down on his face at his feet*. The word *face* means the Truth and Presence of God; *feet* mean understanding. *To fall down* is to humble yourself and set aside the intellect, knowing that Infinite Wisdom and Power are within and can do all things. He understood that vision is spiritual, eternal, and indestructible, and that all he had to do was to enter into the mood of thankfulness for the gift already received. The grateful heart is the mind which believes and rejoices in the joy of the answered prayer. You have oftentimes thanked the man behind the counter for the coat, wrap, or suit which you paid for, but did not receive. You know that he will send it to you and you trust him implicitly. God's promises never fail and you can also give thanks for the gifts which have already been given you. Rise to the point of acceptance and go forth with a grateful heart for the gift already received.

I have been a stranger in a strange land. Ex. 2:22. All of us are really wanderers, pilgrims, and strangers here. We have left Paradise and do not feel at home here. Our pilgrimage is back to the One. We have loves, urges, ideals, and aspirations; and as we look at the world, it seems to deny the inner whisperings and murmurings of our heart strings which remind us of our origin and urge us back to it.

There is only one thing to do; there is only one thing all men are seeking, and that is the God within, the Creative Presence and Power. Leave the good, sound qualities, aspects, conditions, and circumstances of your life and find the *stranger,* the thing that bothers you, that is at present annoying you. Some desire perhaps is not fulfilled. Turn to God within and still the wheels of your mind; immobilize your attention, focus your mental lens on the fact that the Spirit within you, God, is the Cause and the Source of all your good. Then give thanks by silently repeating, "Thank you," over and over again as a lullaby, until your mind is full of the feeling of thankfulness. Continue to do this until you are filled in consciousness. The moment you qualify or condition your consciousness, the answer will come. The *lepers* are now cleansed. Let your prayer be "O God, give me one more thing, a grateful heart."

EYESIGHT RESTORED

And it came to pass, that as he was come nigh unto Jer-icho, a certain blind man sat by the way side begging: And hearing the multitude pass by, he asked what it meant. And they told him, that Jesus of Nazareth passeth by. And he cried, saying, Jesus, Thou son of David, have mercy on me. And Jesus stood, and commanded him to be brought unto him: and when he was come near, he asked him, Saying, *What wilt thou that I shall do unto thee? And he said, Lord, that I may receive my sight. And Jesus said unto him, Receive thy sight: thy faith hath saved thee. And immediately he received his sight, and followed him, glorifying God: and all the people, when they saw it, gave praise unto God.*

Luke 18:35–43.
Related passages, Mark 10:46–52.

There is the well known, duly authenticated case of Madame Bire. She was blind, the optic nerves were atrophied, useless. She visited Lourdes and had what she termed a miraculous healing. Ruth Cranston, a Protestant young lady who investigated and wrote about healings at Lourdes in *McCall's Magazine*, November, 1955, writes about Madame Bire as follows: "At Lourdes she regained her sight, incredibly, with the optic nerves still lifeless and useless, as several doctors could testify after repeated examinations. A month later, upon reexamination, it was found that the seeing mechanism had been restored to normal. But at first, so far as medical examination could tell, she was seeing with 'dead eyes.'"

I visited Lourdes in 1955 where I, too, witnessed some healings,* and of course there is no doubt but that healings take place at various shrines throughout the world, Christian and Non-Christian.

Madame Bire, to whom we just referred, was not healed by the waters or by the Shrine, but by her belief. The healing principle within herself responded to the nature of her thought. Belief is a thought in the mind. It means to accept something as true. The thought accepted executes itself automatically. Faith means to accept that what you are praying for already is. Undoubtedly Madame Bire went to the Shrine with expectancy and great faith, knowing in her heart she would receive a healing. Her deeper mind responded to her belief and Spiritual forces were released, restoring her vision according to her belief. *According to your belief is it done unto you.* The Healing Presence which created the eyes can certainly bring a dead nerve back to life. What the Creative Principle Created in the first place, It can recreate.

Healings occur sometimes unheralded at various religious services. Some people have told me that they had healings at our healing service on Sunday mornings. They add that they did not expect a healing, that they were skeptical, that

---

* See chapter 1 in my book *Traveling With God.*

they were in no state of exaltation, and were not even thinking of a healing. From what they say one would gather that they lacked faith; therefore the question arises, how could they receive a healing? The answer is rather simple. They are looking for a healing and their minds are open and receptive to receive the prayers of the multitude present. Perhaps they are going to a doctor, osteopath, or chiropractor for treatment, which is highly indicative that they desire to be healed. Desire is prayer; this attitude indicates a very receptive mind for the idea of perfect health to be resurrected, for which the people present are praying. When a group of people, gathered together in prayer, affirm that all those who are present are healed, made whole and perfect, they are establishing a definite psychological and spiritual link among all those present; then even if unbelievers or skeptics are present, it is possible for them to be healed for the simple reason that they desire a healing.

You might ask the question, "What about a person who is full of hatred, ill will, and resentment, would he get a healing at a Shrine or at any church healing service?" If the faucet or a pipeline is full of debris of all sorts, the water will not flow freely; furthermore, the water will be muddy and contaminated. It is necessary to remove the kinks in the hose when watering the garden. Your body is the garden, and when you pray you are watering your garden with the Healing Power of God. The healing waters are love, peace, joy, faith, good will, confidence, and strength. The man full of hate is opposed to the stream of love and joy. He must decide to let go of his grudges and pet peeves, and to let in the sunshine of God's Love. His mental block sets up a resistance to the Healing Principle and a short circuit takes place. When he lets down the bars, the invasion of love and grace can penetrate. A person who refuses to resolve his mental conflicts definitely delays his healing. The consciousness of love is the most potent healing force in the world. The doctor, priest, rabbi, or New Thought minister possessing the greatest measure of God's Love will get the best results.

Jesus said to the blind man, *What wilt thou that I shall do unto thee? And he said, Lord, that I may receive my sight.* The beggar was specific because he knew what he wanted and said so. Life is always asking you, *what wilt thou of me?* What is your desire? Millions of people are blind; *i.e.,* they are psychologically and spiritually blind because they do not know that they become what they think all day long. Man is spiritually blind when he hates, resents, or is envious of others. He does not know that he is actually secreting mental poisons which tend to destroy him.

Thousands of people are constantly saying that there is no way to solve their problems, that the situation is hopeless. Such an attitude is the result of spiritual blindness. Man begins to see spiritually and mentally when he gets a new perception of the mind, knowing that there is an Infinite Intelligence within him that is responsive to his thought which can solve all problems. The cry of the world is, "I want my sight." Men, women, and children should receive their sight. They should be taught in schools, in colleges, and in homes throughout the land, where the Creative Principle of Life is and how to use it. They should be taught the interrelationship of the conscious and subconscious mind.

Emerson said, "A man is what he thinks all day long." The Bible says, *As a man thinketh in his heart so is he.* Men should be taught that the Principle of Life is responsive to their thought and that when they claim that Infinite Intelligence leads and guides them, revealing to them the perfect answer, they find themselves automatically led to do the right thing as the way opens up. They were once *blind* to these truths; they now begin to *see* the vision of health, wealth, and happiness, and peace of mind.

And Jesus said unto him, Receive thy sight: thy faith hath saved thee. Jesus symbolizes the Redeemer or the Healing Principle of Life within all of us which forever responds to our expectancy or faith. Your faith is your feeling, your awareness, your inner conviction that what you are praying for already is. Vision is eternal, spiritual, and indestructible. We do not create vision, we manifest or release it.

Recently a woman came to me with incipient glaucoma, which is hardening of the eyeball. I read some time ago an article which stated that ophthalmologists in one of the larger hospitals discovered that there was a pattern of hatred in about twenty to twenty-five per cent of the cases of glaucoma in the hospital. This is not true in all cases, of course. In others who indulge in negative or destructive thinking, the liver, heart, lungs, or other organs may be affected, depending on the susceptibility of the person. The disease may also be due to fear, or race mind impinging on the consciousness of people who fail to pray. This woman began to pray for a daughter-in-law whom she hated intensely. She did it this way: "I release unto God. I wish for her all of God's happiness, peace, and joy." She repeated this prayer frequently until all the roots were withered in her mind. Actually she began to feel kindly toward the daughter-in-law after a few weeks. This is how true love melts everything unlike itself. We prayed together frequently; we were *en rapport* with each other. All of us are sending and receiving stations. She was open and receptive to the truth, and she prayed frequently using the prayer "Perfect Eyesight" in one of my books of meditations* which is as follows:

---

* See my book *Quiet Moments With God.*

"My eyes are God's eyes, and I see perfectly. The Living Intelligence which made my eyes is now controlling the processes and functioning of my eyes and my entire body. I know and believe that my vision is spiritual, eternal, and indestructible. "If, therefore thine eye be single, thy whole body shall be full of light." This means I see only the Truth; I love the Truth; I know the Truth. I see God in all men and in all things. I see spiritually, mentally, and physically. My eyes reflect the glory, the beauty, and the perfection of God. It is God looking out through my eyes seeing His own ideas of perfection. My eyes are the windows of my soul; they are pure, and are kept single to Love, Truth, and Beauty at all times. The harmonizing, healing, vitalizing, energizing Power of the Holy Spirit permeates every atom, cell, nerve, tissue, and muscle of my eyes making them whole, pure, and perfect. The Divine, perfect pattern is now made manifest in my eyes, and every atom and cell conforms to God's perfect pattern on the Mount. Thank you Father."

She let these truths sink down by a process of spiritual osmosis into her deeper mind and gradually a perfect healing took place. She cooperated perfectly with her doctor, praying for him also. At the end of a few months, she had no longer any occasion for the eye drops. The doctor said all tension had disappeared.

I know many people who have had miraculous results with the following simple prayer. "I see spiritually; I see mentally; I see physically; It is wonderful." They fill their soul (subjective nature) with the sense of wonder, and wonders happen when they pray. Jesus, Moses, Elijah, and Paul could not use any other Healing Principle than the one you are using. It is the same yesterday, today, and forever.

When our thought-patterns are disorganized, we are

sick. Our dark, dismal thoughts hide the vision of our God. When we pray by identifying ourselves with the eternal, spiritual values, a rearrangement of our thought-patterns takes place followed by a molecular change in the body which conforms with the changed mental attitude. The healing follows. Sight is displayed, not created.

If deaf, we hear again the sound of He Who Is. We realize It is God hearing His own sound through His own ears. It is God seeing His own perfect ideas through His own eyes. The woman who was healed of glaucoma had faith and knowledge; she will, of course, have no return of the disease. The healing will be permanent.

A blind faith will bring a healing, but ofttimes it is impermanent and fallible. Keep your mind fixed on God and His Perfection and your healing powers will be more proficient and successful. As you walk the earth in quiet moments with God, you will be practicing His Presence and releasing His Healing Power all the time without even knowing it.

Remember we see *through* the eye, not with it. The cornea of the eye receives vibrations from objects in space; through the optic nerve these vibrations are carried to the brain. When the inner light or intelligence meets the outer light, we see. "We see because the Seer is within." We see because Infinite Intelligence is the light of our consciousness. If your eyes are not functioning perfectly, the Creative Principle which made them hasn't been hurt or injured. He that made your eyes can also recreate, refashion, and heal them. *Behold, I make all things new.* Your eyes symbolize Divine Love, a delight in the ways of God, and a hunger and thirst for God's Truth. You will always have good vision if you tune in to the Love of He Who Is. The *right eye* symbolizes right thought and right action. The *left eye* symbolizes God's Love and His Wisdom. Think right, radiate good will, and you will focus perfectly.

You can receive your sight. Yes, you can perceive the answer to any problem, be it what it may, by recognizing the Source of all good. Give supreme allegiance to the God-Presence within and feel the reality of what you are praying for. You don't go to God with a problem. You come to God giving thanks for the answer which is yours now as you open your mind to receive.

Receive thy sight. And immediately he received his sight, and followed him, glorifying God.

HEARING RESTORED

And one of them smote the servant of the high priest, and cut off his right ear. And Jesus answered and said, Suffer ye thus far. And he touched his ear, and healed him.

Luke 22:50–51.

Many people ask me whether it is right to pray for someone who is sick, troubled, or in some difficulty. Then they usually say, "He didn't ask me to pray for him." As you read the above verses, you are not told that the servant asked Jesus to restore his ear. Jesus apparently didn't wait for the question, but voluntarily restored the ear. It seems like begging the question to ask, "Should I pray for someone in trouble?" Of course you may pray for anyone you wish, and it would be most excellent to pray once a day for all men throughout the world, wishing them harmony, health, peace, and joy. Pray for the President, the Congress, people in your office, your home, and the whole world will be blessed because you have performed such unselfish devotions.

Sometimes I am asked this question, "Should I pray for my mother who does not believe in Divine Healing and is opposed to this teaching about mental and spiritual laws?" The answer is simple. If the mother, father, or relative has no faith in your religious convictions or in your particular technique

or process of prayer, that does not make any difference whatever. When you pray for someone, you must not bother with
the question of whether he believes or disbelieves, whether
he accepts or rejects. Neither do you concern yourself with
his church affiliations or his agnosticism; furthermore you
pay no attention to his symptoms, aberrations, mental conflicts, or blocks of any kind. You simply enter into the silence
of your soul, immobilize your attention, and mentally reject
all sense-evidence. You do this decisively and categorically.
Quietly know that the Infinite Healing Power is timeless and
spaceless and that It embraces the one you are praying for;
then you silently feel or quietly affirm the Truth, just as you
like. You don't have to use any words. You can *feel* the Truth of
what you think, that the Harmony, Health, Power, Peace, Order, and Perfection of God are now being manifested in your
friend's mind and body. Know that there is but one mind, and
in mind there is neither time nor space. You are one with your
friend, because you are thinking of him. In the language of
Troward, you are *en rapport* with him, and in the language
of Quimby, you are one with him, because our minds min-
gle like atmospheres and each has his identity in that atmosphere. What you feel and know as true about your friend
will be resurrected in his experience. You have taken his request, or his desire for health, and made it your own.

As you contemplate the qualities and attributes of God,
knowing that these qualities are now being experienced by
your friend, there is an immediate response in the mental
structure of your friend, and a reordering of his mind takes
place bringing about a perfect healing. Your inner sense of
peace and confidence that the law of health and harmony is
now in operation brings about a sense of faith and trust in
you. As you continue to pray, perhaps two or three times a

day, the time will come when you will lose all desire to pray because your prayer is answered. You can't desire what you have. A doctor does not treat a patient who is healed; the patient requires no further treatment. Prayer operates on the same principle. You pray until you need no longer pray.

We see and hear with the mind. In biblical language *we cut off an ear* when we cease listening to the troubled voice of the world with its false beliefs, terrors, and superstitions. *Jesus touching the ear and healing it* means that we should hear the voice of Truth which says, *I am God and there is no God beside me.* We should hear only that which fills our soul with joy. Hear the good news about the other. To what are you giving attention? If you are listening to gossip, criticism, and condemnation, you are not hearing the Truth. If someone tells you that you are going to fail in your enterprise and if you give him any attention, you are not hearing the gospel or good news about yourself.

Go within yourself, place all your attention on the idea of success. You will immediately begin to enter into a mood or feeling of success. You are now hearing the good news because you are under a good spell. You are now absorbed, engrossed, and fascinated by the idea of success, achievement, and accomplishment. You know that fear and success are simply two ideas in the mind. You know that you were born to succeed, and that you have all the equipment necessary. The fear-thought is false, it's an illusion, it's a shadow of the mind. A shadow has no power or substance. The idea of success is real and your subconscious powers will move on your behalf, compelling you to take all the steps necessary, as you give your attention to the idea of success. You are now hearing the Truth.

It is always right to bless the other. Surely there can't be anything wrong with wishing for the other person health, harmony, joy, peace, and all of God's riches. That is the answer to those who say, "Is it wrong to pray for the other if he didn't ask me?" Of course not. You should wish for everyone what you wish for yourself. Love is the fulfilling of the law. Love is sincerely radiating the sunshine of God's Love, Light, and Truth to all men everywhere. This is the Law which brings fulfillment, happiness, peace, and abundance into your own life. What we withhold from another, we withhold from ourselves. Actually there is no other, all of us are in the One Mind and the One Spirit which is Indivisible. There can be no divisions or quarrels in It. One part can't be antagonistic to another part. If that were so there would be no harmony, only chaos. The Infinite cannot be divided.

For example, if you are praying for prosperity and you are resenting the wealth and riches of another, you are condemning what you are praying for, and your good takes wings and flies away. How can you attract wealth when you resent its manifestation in another. You are thinking and feeling lack instead of abundance, and as you think and feel, so are you. Thinking makes consciousness, and your state of consciousness governs your world. When you see this Truth, you are *Jesus* (illumined reason, awareness of truth) *touching the ear* (hearing the truth which frees you) and *healing it, i.e.,* bringing about a state of wholeness or unity in your mind.

You are told that *he cut off his right ear.* The *right* means the objective world, worldly opinion, sense evidence, and judging according to appearances. *Cut off that right ear now,* once and for all, and give no power to external phenomena. Do not worship or give power to germs, nor bow down in fear before them. Don't get panic-stricken when someone sneezes and say, "Oh, I'll catch a cold." Reject the false belief that a fan will give you a stiff neck, or that the cold night air will give you pneumonia or cause bronchial trouble. The weather has no power over you. We give power to these things because we believe that they affect us; we suffer according to our belief. The fan is harmless, it never said to anyone, "I will give you a cold if you sit near me or under me." The fan is neutral. It is a metallic substance, composed of molecules revolving at a high speed. Bless the fan, bless the weather; God pronounced all things good. When your feet get wet, don't say that the water will give you pneumonia. The water never said that, why do you say it? Man has created countless false gods; and all his trouble arises out of his darkened mind and distorted imagination.

Nicoll of England says that all man's evil is due to misunderstanding. Man sees *through a glass darkly*, due to the twilight in his mind. When the shadows fall in the evening, sometimes man mistakes a stump of a tree with some branches for an enemy with a gun aimed at his heart. He becomes frozen with fear. This is the twilight in his mind. He has not heard, he has not seen. Become Jesus; *i.e.*, become awakened to the Truth and know that there is but one Primal Cause which is your own Consciousness; cease making secondary Causes. To know that your I AM is the only Power, the only Cause, the only Substance, is to free you from all the false gods of the world, enabling you to go forth with the song of God in your heart.

Your *ears* are symbolic of understanding. Many people who complained of their inability to hear the writer at his public lectures on Sunday now sit at the rear of the lecture hall and hear perfectly. Their interest in Truth was aroused; their attention was quickened; and there was a normal, healthy response from the deeper mind. The following is a simple prayer which I give to people suffering from ear troubles of any kind:*

---

* See my book *Quiet Moments With God*.

"I hear the Truth; I love the Truth; I know the Truth. My ears are God's perfect ideas functioning perfectly at all times. My ears are the perfect instruments which reveal God's harmony to me. The Love, Beauty, and Harmony of God flow through my ears; I am in tune with the Infinite. I hear the Still, Small, Voice of God within me. The Healing Presence quickens my hearing and my ears are open and free."

My experiences with people have convinced me that a great number of people become deaf, or partially so, because they don't want to hear the voice of someone. They are trying to shut out certain things. If a man has a nagging wife, he may not want to hear her, and gradually he loses his hearing capacity. These negative auto-suggestions sink into his subconscious mind, and the latter proceeds to follow out the suggestion given. You can place man in a trance state and suggest to him that he can't hear until you tell him he can. The subconscious, being amenable to suggestion, accepts the suggestion of the operator and he can't hear; this shows us how our mind works. We must, therefore, be exceedingly careful of the thoughts we entertain and give attention to in our mind.

There are many people who deliberately shut out the Truth. They say, "I don't want to hear a word of that. Shut that man off, I don't want to hear his voice. I hate that voice. I don't want to hear it. I won't hear it," etc. These and similar statements are expressed with such emphasis and feeling that they become highly destructive. Our subconscious mind accepts these statements as requests, and proceeds to bring them to pass in our experience. You have heard the old maxim which contains a great Truth, "There are none so deaf as those that will not hear."

Dr. Flanders Dunbar, famous authority on psychosomatic medicine, cites many cases where deafness was due to mental and emotional disturbances. In her book *Emotions and Bodily Changes*, she cites a case of a man of forty-five who had been married for twenty years and had to use a hearing aid. He ascribed his deafness to swimming. He thought that one advantage of being deaf was that he didn't have to listen to his wife. The doctor asked to examine the hearing aid, but went right on talking. They became engaged in such an animated conversation that it was not until half an hour later that he discovered the doctor was still holding his hearing aid. By now, of course, you have deduced what was wrong with his hearing. His subconscious mind responded to his desire not to listen to his wife. There are people who have a form of deafness due to the fact that their mind is closed to all ideas but their own. They are unyielding, inflexible, dogmatic, and full of pride.

Hearing is a mental and spiritual process. Trust the Divine Intelligence which made your ears and all their parts. *I will restore health unto thee and heal thee of thy wounds saith the Lord.*

PRAYER WIPES OUT
ALL KARMA

We have finished with the miracles of healing reported in the book of *Luke*, which have parallel accounts in *Mark* and *Matthew*. The book of *John* is the most mystical book in the Bible. In the ninth chapter of *John*, a story is told of a man *which was blind from his birth*.

And as Jesus passed by, he saw a man which was blind from his birth. And his disciples asked him, saying, Master, who did sin, this man, or his parents, that he was born blind? Jesus answered, Neither hath this man sinned, nor his parents: but that the works of God should be made manifest in him. I must work the works of him that sent me, while it is day: the night cometh, when no man can work. As long as I am in the world I am the light of the world. When he had thus spoken, he spat on the ground, and made clay of the spittle, and he anointed the eyes of the blind man with the clay, And said unto him, Go, wash in the pool of Siloam (which is by interpretation, Sent.) He went his way therefore, and washed, and came seeing. The neighbours therefore, and they which before had seen him that he was blind, said, Is not this he that sat and begged? Some said, This is he: others said, He is like him: but he said, I am he.

John 9:1–9.
Related passages, Matt. 9:27–30, 12:22, 20:30–34;
Mark 10:46–52.

You can read a more extensive account in my books, *The Meaning Of Reincarnation*, and *Peace Within Yourself* which gives the psychological meaning of the book of *John*.

In ancient times it was believed that if a man were born blind, it was due to past *karma*, and that he was here to expiate for his sins. The people of that day also believed that the sins of the parents were communicated to the children. For example, if the parents were insane, all their children would be insane.

The *sin* spoken of in the Bible refers to the mental attitude, the mood, the feeling of the parents. All sin refers to movements of the mind rather than that of the body. Parents transmit their habitual thinking, fears, tensions, and false beliefs through the mind, not the body. Our feelings and moods create. What tone do you strike during the marital, creative act?*

There are blind and deaf states of consciousness from which blind and deaf children come forth. Whatever tone is struck by the parents, a corresponding expression comes forth by the laws of reciprocal relationship.

There is no instance in the Bible in which anyone was ever refused a healing. The Absolute cannot and does not

---

* See chapter 4 in my book *The Meaning of Reincarnation*.

judge or condemn. All judgment is given to the son, *i.e.*, all judgment is pronounced in our own mind. Each man arrives at his own decision or conclusion, and there is an automatic response of the law. If man thinks negatively, the response is negative. If he thinks positively and constructively, the reaction of the law of his mind is good and very good.

The laws of nature and our mind cannot hold a grudge against us. There is not one law for a child and another for a man of ninety. The moment man goes within himself, claims his good, and presses his claim with faith and confidence, there is the automatic response of the law which honors the mental acceptance of his good. The past is forgotten and remembered no more.

Reason rejects the popular, superstitious belief of the people that man's blindness is due to his *karma*, that he may have blinded people in a former life and is now back on this plane to suffer and atone for his crime. Another very popular, superstitious belief was, and still is, that a child may be born blind because his parents were blind, or because they had sinned or had some physical disease. A man and wife though congenitally blind or blinded by accident may give birth to children with perfectly normal vision.

A mother through prayer, may change the mental and physical nature of her child while he is still in the womb, and bring about a perfect healing. In God's eyes there are no blind, deaf, halt, or lame people. God sees everyone perfect, and His Creation as Infinite Perfection.

I must work the works of him that sent me, while it is day. This means while the Light of Truth is shining, we consciously direct the law.

To make clay of the spittle represents a drooling state, like a boy hungers for candy and drools at the mouth. It represents a joyful, bubbling up state. You have seen geysers bubbling up which make clay look very much alive. The *clay* in the natural state represents the average man who is dead and unaware of the Healing Principle within him. He is, in other words, dead to his inner potentialities. As he awakens and becomes enthusiastic about the discovery of the powers within, he becomes alive to God; this is the meaning of *he spat on the ground and made clay of the spittle*. This latter phrase is an oriental, idiomatic, figurative expression meaning a deep, inner conviction that we now have the consciousness of what we want, and that we reject blindness or the old state of limitation.

We are not here to suffer or expiate for sins or errors. We are here to awaken to the Truth about ourselves and realize that *Beloved, now are we the sons of God*, that *Now is the day of salvation, and the Kingdom of Heaven is at hand*. Like Paul you can be changed in the twinkling of an eye.

Remember what is true of God is true of man. God can't possibly be blind, deaf, dumb, or sick. The Truth about man is that the Living Spirit Almighty is within him. God is all Bliss, Wholeness, Joy, Perfection, Harmony, and Peace. God is all the wonderful things you have ever heard of. There cannot possibly be any quarrel or division in this Boundless Wisdom. As you anchor your mind on these Eternal Verities about God, identify yourself with them mentally and a rearrangement of the thought-patterns will take place in your mind and the Wholeness and Perfection of God will be made manifest.

The *clay* spoken of is a hard, dry, false belief. It is a muddy, confused mind which must be cleansed; then we *spit* (bring forth) our conviction of Truth.

Go wash in the pool of Siloam means give up and send away. Detach your consciousness from the old state which washes away the false idea and feel and affirm the spirituality of all substance. The blind state also represents our inability to see the state that would bless us. When man does not know that his savior is the realization of his heart's desire, he is truly blind.

We might also mention in this chapter dealing with the man born blind that all men are born blind. We are born into all that our environment represents. We have to learn how to choose and differentiate so that gradually we awaken to the Presence and Power of God within us.

There is a tendency among people to take everything literally. In your daily newspaper you may see a cartoon depicting some extravagance or waste in Government. You understand it as an allegorical picture of things, that is, visual allegory. We must remember that the Bible is an allegory in words. When people read of the blind, the halt, and the lame in the Bible they usually think of it only from the physical side.

We must see that there is also an internal deafness and an inner blindness though the eyes and ears may not be impaired or diseased in any way. A man can be psychologically lame when he is afraid to take on a new project. In some instances men refuse promotion because they are afraid they might fail. This is lameness even though the physical legs are perfect.

Dr. Nicoll of England stresses the fact that the transformation of meaning from the sensual or sensory level to the emotional and mental level is an act of faith.

For we walk by faith, not by sight: 2 Cor. 5:7. Most people "walk by sight," that is, the literal meaning of everything dominates their consciousness. The blind man is the one who is blind inside.

In *Matthew* we read:

And, behold, two blind men sitting by the way side, when they heard that Jesus passed by, cried out, saying, Have mercy on us, O Lord, thou son of David. And the multitude rebuked them, because they should hold their peace: but they cried the more, saying, Have mercy on us, O Lord, thou son of David. And Jesus stood still, and called them, and said, What will ye that I shall do unto you? They say unto him, Lord, that our eyes may be opened. So Jesus had compassion on them, and touched their eyes: and immediately their eyes received sight, and they followed him.

Matt. 20:30–34.

The two blind men refers to the average man who walks the earth because he is intellectually and emotionally blind. We have a conscious and subconscious mind, *i.e.,* two phases or functions of the One Mind in all. If we do not consciously choose good thoughts and meditate on the lovely and beautiful, our intellect is blind. If we fail to realize and draw forth the wisdom, intelligence, and power of the subjective self, we are blind to the Kingdom of Heaven within.

A *blind man* thinks that hard work will make him wealthy. He fusses, frets, and fumes because he doesn't know that wealth is simply a state of consciousness. The feeling of wealth produces wealth; the feeling of health produces health. Confidence in the One Eternal Source and aligning ourselves mentally with it will take the form of wealth, health, peace, and all the blessed things of life.

I just spoke with a young actress who receives a thousand dollars a week for a few hours work each week. She said there

were other actresses far prettier, more attractive, better educated than she, getting a hundred or a hundred and fifty dollars a week in small parts. Her explanation was that they had a
low estimate of themselves and lacked confidence. They were
blind and did not know that if we make a bargain with life for
a penny a day, that is what we will receive. If they would overcome their estimate of themselves and claim their good in consciousness, there would be an automatic response, for *according
to your belief is it done unto you.*

A few hours ago I chatted with a man who is leaving this
city to take a sales manager job in San Francisco. Last month
he was getting meager wages according to some union scale.
His eyes were opened in our recent class on the inner meaning
of the book of *Job.* He began to picture himself receiving con-
gratulations from his wife on his marvelous promotion. He
kept running the picture in his mind until it was fully developed in the subconscious, and much to his delight the promotion was confirmed objectively. The two blind states in him
began to see because he brought about a harmonious union
of his conscious and subconscious mind. These two phases
synchronized and agreed on promotion, and what he subjectively felt as true became an objective manifestation.

The cry of the world is *Lord, that our eyes may be opened.*
Jesus is your awareness of the Spiritual Power within you and
your capacity to use it so that you can rise above any predicament or limitation.

The Bible says, *Jesus touched their eyes.* When you touch
something you become aware of it as a sensation, a feeling.
You have made contact, so to speak. You touch the Spiritual
Power or the Presence of God with your thought, your mental
picture.

And immediately their eyes received sight. This means that you will get an immediate response from the Spirit within you whose nature is responsiveness. You now receive your sight because you mentally perceive and lay hold of the Spiritual Power within you. You comprehend its nature and give it your sole allegiance and loyalty. The Maker of your eyes can heal your eyes.

Jesus is always *passing by* for the simple reason that your desire is your Jesus. Every problem has its solution or savior in the form of a desire. The desire is walking down the streets of your mind now. There is a *multitude* of fears, doubts, and anxious thoughts which challenges your desire and divides your allegiance. This is the *multitude* which, according to the parable, tries to restrain the blind men. *But they cried the more,* meaning that you must dynamically and decisively break through that motley crew of negative thoughts in your mind. You must push them all aside and have eyes only for your savior, *i.e.,* your desire.

Set your desire on high; love it; be loyal to it; kiss it affectionately; let it captivate you. You are now being loyal and you will succeed in touching the Healing Presence. At the moment you touch It, the Infinite Healing Power flows through the channel you created and your prayer is answered.

We should not ask for more Light. Rather, our prayer should be, "O God, give me eyes to see the Light." The Light of God always was, now is, and ever shall be. It is wonderful.

WALK WITH THE POWER
OF GOD

After this there was a feast of the Jews; and Jesus went up to Jerusalem. Now there is at Jerusalem by the sheep market a pool, which is called in the Hebrew tongue Bethesda, having five porches. In these lay a great multitude of impotent folk, of blind, halt, withered, waiting for the moving of the water. For an angel went down at a certain season into the pool, and troubled the water: whosoever then first after the troubling of the water stepped in was made whole of whatsoever disease he had. And a certain man was there, which had an infirmity thirty and eight years. When Jesus saw him lie, and knew that he had been now a long time in that case, he saith unto him, Wilt thou be made whole? The impotent man answered him, Sir, I have no man, when the water is troubled, to put me into the pool: but while I am coming, another steppeth down before me. Jesus saith unto him, Rise, take up thy bed, and walk.

John 5:1–8.

Related passages, Luke 13:11–12.

Mankind is at the *pool*. The *pool* is consciousness, and all of us are living with our thoughts, feelings, beliefs, opinions, and mental images. Some of these states are *blind, halt, withered,* and *lame.* Furthermore, man is full of dreams, hopes, and aspirations which have never seen the light of day. Thousands are frustrated, unhappy, and sick because they have failed to realize their dreams, ideals, plans, and purposes. These dead hopes and dreams symbolize the *impotent folk, blind, halt, withered, waiting for the moving of the water.*

Are you waiting for something to happen? Don't sit around waiting for God to do something. You must begin, and when you begin Omnipotence begins to move on your behalf. God has provided you with everything. He has given you Himself; therefore, all His powers, qualities, and attributes are within you, waiting for you to call them forth and use them to grow.

Expand, unfold, and multiply your good a thousand-fold. The initiative is with you. The God-Presence within is now governing all your vital organs, regulating your heart beat and general circulation. The earth, the stars, the sun, and moon, and the whole world is here for you to enjoy, but if you want to transcend your present concept of yourself, you must take the necessary steps.

Begin now to think constructively and heal the *blind, deaf,* and *withered* states within you. In this drama of healing, prayer is called a *feast.* When you meditate on your good, you are *feasting, i.e.,* you are consciously uniting with it; then you make it a living part of you in the same manner that a piece of bread becomes hair on your face or flesh of your body.

The pool has five porches which means we have five senses. Our senses usually deny what we pray for; furthermore, our five senses impregnate us with all kinds of rumors, false beliefs, and limitations.

Now you can put into application the teaching of this drama. You are *Jesus* when you recognize the Spiritual Power within as Omnipotent, and you enter *Jerusalem* (city of peace) when you still the mind and focus on the Living Spirit Almighty within you. You are now back at your Divine Center where you become perfectly quiet in God. You can enter into a deep peace, the Peace of God. You have exchanged the mood of worry and fear for the mood of faith, confidence, and an inner peace. This is why the Bible refers to a *sheep market*. All of us are in the market place every moment of our lives. You are constantly exchanging or giving up one idea for another. You must give up fear and buy faith in God and His Laws. Give up ill will and buy radiant good will. Give up the *blind states* in your belief and buy the idea that there is a way out of any problem. Contemplate the Truth that God has the answer, and therefore you know the answer.

The angel disturbs the pool. The *angel* spoken of is your desire, your wish. A man in our class on the "Miracles of Healing," on which this book is based, told me of a wrong done to him. He was very bitter. He had a desire for a Divine adjustment, but didn't know how to bring it about, and he was very disturbed. He learned how to resolve the conflict. *Whosoever stepped in first was made whole.* No one could get in before him. He was always in the Holy Omnipresence and he perceived the Truth that actually no one could really rob him or defraud him. When he learned of his Oneness with God and the fact that nothing can be lost, he realized his unity with the Infinite. He prayed that through the action of God his relationship with the other man was now transformed into order, harmony, goodness, and love. He began to see as God sees, and God sees everything in Infinite Perfection.

In other words, this young man ceased to gaze at the outward chaos and confusion, but he went within himself and claimed interior harmony and a Divine adjustment. The blurred, confused, outer picture was transformed into Divine order and peace between them. There was a remarkable solution. Trust the God-Wisdom which knows all and knows the way. "There's a Divinity that shapes our ends, Rough-hew them how we will."

In one of the class-lessons on the book of *Job*, which I have just finished, I told the students that if they had a problem, and could not see any way out, to sit still that night and quietly recognize the Presence of God within themselves, in the situation itself, and within all those concerned. After a few minutes of silent contemplation on that Truth, they were to turn the matter over completely to the subjective self, knowing it will order everything aright. This procedure kindles a fire in the heart which brings about an inner glow and warmth; and while this fire of love is burning in the heart, go off to sleep. Many received remarkable answers the next morning.

No one really can *get in before you*. No one can prevent you from realizing your goal or objective. The only power you are aware of is your own thought. When you think, that process is really Omnipotence in action. One with God is a majority. Your own thought causes the Omnipotent Power of God to move in your behalf. There is nothing to oppose, challenge, or thwart the action of the Infinite One. There can't be two omnipotent powers; if there were, one would cancel and neutralize the action of the other and there would be no order anywhere. There can't be two Infinites, that is unthinkable and mathematically impossible.

The Infinite moves, Troward tells you, as unity, as oneness, as wholeness, and as harmony. Your mind must also move as a unity, a sense of oneness with your ideal. If you are divided in your mind by acknowledging some other power, you are like a soldier marking time, you get nowhere and reach an impasse. Your mind is divided, two ideas or thoughts are quarreling. You must be the referee and come to a decision by realizing that there is but One Power; and that being so, you are free from fear. Desire without fear is realization.

Recall to mind that the suggestions of others, the race mind and its fears have no power over you. External conditions and suggestions of others are not causative. Your thought is in control. If you say that the other hurt you or made you angry, it means you permitted yourself to move in thought negatively. It was your fault and not the other person's. The other person is certainly not responsible for the way you think about him or the way you think in general. When you think of God, you are one with Omnipotence. The Source is Love; It knows no fear.

While I am coming, another steppeth down before me. Have you ever said that? Perhaps not, but you have heard people say, "It was John's fault," "Except for Mary or Johnny I would have been promoted." If you say anything of that nature, your allegiance is divided and you are disloyal to the One Power which knows no other. *I am God and there is no God beside me.*

I am sure that you are very familiar with the fact that no one can say *I AM* for you. That statement is in the first person, present tense. It means you are announcing the Presence of God within as Cause and Creator. Notice when you speak to your sister or son you say, "You are." When you speak in the third person you say, "They are."

One of our students in the Bible class on the book of *John** said to herself, "I possess the power to say "I AM." No one can say it for me. I now believe I AM what I wish to be. I live, move, and have my being in that mental atmosphere and no person, place, or thing can get in before me or prevent me from being what I long to be; for, *according to my belief, is it done unto me*." She had a remarkable demonstration using the above prayer.

The *impotent man* is the man who does not know where the power is and believes it is outside himself. The *thirty and eight years* in the numerical symbology or science of the Bible means the conviction of God's Presence and coming of age spiritually. The number *thirty* refers to the Trinity or the creative working of our own mind; the *eight* means the octave or man's capacity to rise higher through knowledge of mental and spiritual laws. The Trinity is your thought and feeling and from the fusion of these comes the third step which is the conviction of your good, or God. When your idea is mothered by feeling or emotion and the two become one, you are at peace, and God is Peace. You are constantly putting the Trinity into operation. Ouspensky used to call the third element which entered in the neutral element. We call it God.

The idea of perfect health can be resurrected by you as you now claim, feel, and believe that the Healing Principle is instantly transforming your whole being into God's Perfect Pattern of harmony, health, and peace.

I read a remarkable article which appeared in the magazine *Nautilus* some years ago. It was written by Fred-

---

* See chapter 5 in my book *Peace Within Yourself.*

erick Elias Andrews of Indianapolis. He said that as a boy he was pronounced incurable. He began to pray and from a crooked, twisted, cripple going about on hands and knees, he became a strong, straight, well-formed man. This young man decided what he wanted and that was a perfect healing. He created his own affirmation, mentally absorbing the qualities he needed. He affirmed over and over again: "I am whole, perfect, strong, powerful, loving, harmonious, and happy." He persevered and said that this prayer was the last thing on his lips at night and the first thing in the morning. He prayed for others also by sending out thoughts of love and health. This attitude of mind and way of prayer returned to him multiplied. Like Job of old who prayed for his friends, God gave him twice as much as he had before. His faith and perseverance paid off big dividends. Negative thoughts came to him but he did not entertain them. When thoughts of anger, jealousy, fear, or worry came into his mind, he would start his affirmation going in his mind. The answer to all fearful thoughts is to turn on the lamp of love forever burning in your heart.

The man in the Bible had the infirmity *thirty and eight years*. We have already discussed the Trinity. The number *eight* is added when healing takes place. *Eight* is composed of two circles representing the synchronous or harmonious interaction of your conscious and subconscious mind, or idea and feeling. When your desire and your emotional nature agree, there is no longer any quarrel between the two, and a healing follows.

The command by Jesus, or your own illumined reason, *Rise, take up thy bed and walk*, is your voice of authority, based on your inner conviction telling you that you are healed. We can actually hear the inner sound of our belief. It is veritably a command on the inside. You have *taken up your bed* (truth) and walk the earth a free man. All this happens on the *sabbath*.

The *sabbath* is an inner certitude or inner stillness which follows true prayer. It is really a state of mind in which you are unconcerned, unmoved, and undisturbed, because you know that just as surely as the sun rises in the morning there will be a resurrection of your desire. When you have reached the point of complete mental acceptance, you are *resting in the sabbath* or in the conviction "It is done." *And it was on the sabbath day he was healed.*

THE IMPOSSIBLE MADE POSSIBLE

I shall give the highlights of the wonderful healing technique in the raising of Lazarus mentioned in Chapter Eleven of *John*. For a complete, detailed interpretation of this wonderful chapter, I recommend my book *Peace Within Yourself*, which is an interpretation, chapter by chapter, of the book of *John*.

Lazarus represents any dead state, the desire, plan, enterprise, or goal which is frozen within and has not been made alive and resurrected in your world of experience. It may also represent your desire for health which has failed to materialize.

Jesus at the grave of Lazarus represents you and your awareness of the Power which can resurrect your ideal which has been covered with the *grave clothes* of fear, doubt, and anxiety for a long time, and has been *suppressed in the tomb* of the subconscious.

Jesus said, Take ye away the stone. The *stone* of superstition, fear, and ignorance must be removed. *Martha*, representing the worldly viewpoint says to you, *"By this time he stinketh: for he hath been dead four days."* *Four* represents the completed state, the termination, the manifestation. According to sense-evidence the situation seems absolutely hopeless, or the condition may seem to be incurable. Regardless of the external circumstances, even though the whole world would deny what you pray for, *if thou wouldest believe, thou shouldest see the glory of God.*

In other words, if you will turn away from sense-evidence and go within and contemplate the reality of what you pray for, and sing the song of triumph, you will see the Glory of God— you will see the answer to your prayer. *To believe* is to live in the state of being or having what you pray for. Your thought is your belief, and whatever you think, you become. Live with the thought and reality of the answered prayer, and there will be an atomic and molecular change in the diseased body to conform to the new mental pattern.

The stone is lifted as you positively refuse to give power to sickness, disease, or fear. As you give all power to God, *the stone is removed* and you are no longer weighted down with the burdens of the world. Your new mental attitude is *the angel who rolls away the stone* of fear and false belief.

You are now *Jesus, lifting up your eyes saying, Father, I thank thee that thou hast heard me. And I knew that thou hearest me always. He cried with a loud voice, Lazarus, come forth.* John 11:41–43. These latter verses give a magnificent formula for prayer. The thankful attitude works miracles.

Many years ago, a friend of mine who had tuberculosis took these wonderful words of the Bible, *I thank thee Father that thou hast heard me, and I knew that thou hearest me always.* He reasoned it out this way. His human father always gave him whatever he promised him. At one time his father promised him a trip to France (he lived in Ireland). The trip was to take place in August, but the promise was made in May. He remembered how joyous and enthusiastic he was. He recalled bubbling over with expectancy and being thrilled beyond words. This happened even though the trip had not taken place. All he had was the promise; he knew it was certain because his father never failed him.

He said to himself, "Why shouldn't I be thankful and grateful to my Heavenly Father for the promise of perfect health, for 'I know that he heareth me always,' 'I will restore health unto thee and I will heal thee of thy wounds saith the Lord.'" Two or three times a day he would still his mind, relax, and let go. Then he would imagine he was talking to the Invisible Healing Presence within, and he began to whisper, "Thank you," over and over again. He did this until his mind was saturated with the feeling of thankfulness. At the end of three weeks the sputum test and all the others were completely negative. He cast God's Spell over himself. He became magnetized as he contemplated the harmony and perfection of God which he knew would be experienced by him, as it was already given to him by God. When he contemplated the Peace, Order, and Healing Power of God within him, there was a complete rearrangement of the atoms of his body. He became like a magnetized piece of steel which draws to itself other steel, and not nickel and other metals. In the diseased state he was demagnetized, the atoms were still present, but he ceased to vibrate harmony, health, and peace. His feeling of thankfulness and sense of confidence in the One Healing Power drew like a magnet the conviction that made him healthy, vital, harmonious, and whole.

Like the man mentioned above, give up the false belief that other powers can make you ill without your consent. Contemplate yourself the way you want to be, happy, healthy, radiant, and strong. Identify yourself with these qualities, and accept nothing else. Give up completely all fear in any other so-called causes or powers. Reject categorically and dynamically all false beliefs. Turn in confidence to the Supreme Power within which moves as your feeling, your faith, and trust. When you do this, you are becoming a marvelous mental and spiritual magnet and you will inevitably attract harmony, health, peace, and joy.

The three steps in *raising Lazarus from the dead are:*

1. Recognition of your consciousness as supreme cause.

2. Accept the idea of perfect health and live with it in your mind. To believe is to live with the idea, *i.e.,* make it alive.

3. The inevitable conviction which follows the previous two steps. You are now filled with the feeling of being what you want to be.

Your mood is now one of authority and you say inwardly, *Lazarus, come forth.*

This is the command from the inside of the one who knows that *I and my Father are one.*

A PRAYER FOR HEALING

A personal healing will ever be the most convincing evidence of the power of prayer. About thirty-five years ago I resolved a malignancy by using a prayer based on the 139th Psalm. I had just heard an interpretation of the Psalm and was meditating intensely on its profundity.

For thou hast possessed my reins: thou hast covered me in my mother's womb. I will praise thee; for I am fearfully and wonderfully made: marvellous are thy works; and that my soul knoweth right well. My substance was not hid from thee, when I was made in secret, and curiously wrought in the lowest parts of the earth. Thine eyes did see my substance, yet being imperfect; and in thy book all my members were written, which in continuance were fashioned, when as yet there was none of them.

This magnificent, inspired Psalm teaches that the body and its organs are formed in idea before it is made manifest, just as surely as we can observe that a watchmaker has the idea first in mind before the watch becomes an objective reality. Creative Intelligence fashions and molds the entire body. The Intelligence that creates the body must know how to heal it; furthermore, the Psalm states that *in thy book all my members were written*. The *book* is the Life Principle where the arche-type of all organs are inscribed.

Using this Psalm as a basis for my prayer, I prayed in a very simple way as follows:

"My body was made in secret by God. His Wisdom fash-ioned all my organs, tissues, muscles, and bones. His Heal-ing Power saturates my mind and body, making me whole and perfect. I will give thanks unto thee. Wonderful are thy works."

I prayed aloud for about five minutes two or three times a day, repeating this simple prayer. In about three months my skin was whole and perfect.

Wonderful are thy works; and that my soul knoweth right well.

THE HEALING POWER
OF LOVE
(1958)

THE HEALING POWER OF LOVE

One of the most beautiful, soul-stirring stories in the Bible is the loving, moving account of Ruth and Boaz. *Ruth* means that which lovingly clings. *Boaz* means God's Truth. These are the two pillars which lead to the Holy of Holies within you.

You love God when you steadfastly refuse to give power to error and false beliefs, giving at the same time, all your allegiance and devotion to the Spiritual Principle within you, insisting that the Principle of Harmony be manifested in your life. When you mentally reject the power of the phenomenalistic world and give all your allegiance to the Spirit within as Omnipotent, knowing It is responsive to your thought, you have the Lord of Life as your shepherd and you are loving God because you are being loyal to the One Power.

Ruth said to her mother-in-law, Naomi, *"Intreat me not to leave thee, or to return from following after thee: for whither thou goest, I will go: and where thou lodgest, I will lodge: thy people shall be my people, and thy God my God."* Ruth 1:16.

Naomi is the emotional self. The Bible says her two sons are dead, which means that the body and environment are expressing lack and limitation. When you are not manifesting or expressing the desires of your heart, you become frustrated and disappointed. This is a story about all of us. A woman's husband is dead, Biblically speaking, when the action of God has ceased to be expressed through her. She is no longer being impregnated by Divine Ideas such as Goodness, Truth, and Beauty. To put this in simple, psychological language, the emotions of defeat and despair are governing the consciousness. When a person lacks faith and confidence, and when initiative and the forward push are absent, truly the husband is dead. The woman in all of us is our emotional or subjective nature. Thought is the husband, and feeling is the woman.

"Thy maker is thy husband." The male quality of the mind is your husband which means thought, action, desire, or the image-making faculty. When you are functioning spiritually, you desire to grow, expand, and move forward. Life is a progression. When the mind is sick and confused, the emotions are disturbed; in such a case the tendency is to withdraw within yourself and brood; then your ideas, dreams, and aspirations die within you, and you feel frustrated. Your present state of consciousness and your desire are your two sons. If you are healthy, happy, joyous, and prosperous, your two sons are alive. If you are full of fear and foreboding, and wallowing in the mire of despair and despondency, your two sons are dead. Naomi (mother-in-law, the emotional nature) may be full of despair; yet the spiritual urge within all of us pushes us to move on, to press on up higher. It is the Voice of God crying in the wilderness, saying to all men, "Make straight in the desert a highway for our God."
Isaiah 40:2.

Ruth represents that which lovingly clings to us. It is the Cosmic Urge, the Divine Impulse in all of us. It clings to us, haunts our minds, and is a persistent voice insisting upon our attention. Life is always seeking to express itself.

"Whither shall I go from thy spirit? or whither shall I flee from thy presence"? Psalms 139:7. The Presence of God is in the sick man, in the man whose body is racked with pain. "Behold, I am there." There is something within man which reminds him of his origin and urges him back to it. It is his mission and purpose to cherish, enlarge, and liberate this memory so that it grows from a spark to a flame, and floods his whole being.

Ruth is called the female companion. She represents the unconscious desire of life to express itself and preserve itself at all costs. This inner female companion, or God in you, acts as a stimulus to your depressed state causing you to think and reason a way out of your dilemma. She could be called the mother in you, or the intuitive sense in you. All men want to be good, do good, and express good because their nature is divine. God is in all men seeking to express Himself through them. Every man is an incarnation of God, and when you have a desire to be greater than you are, it is God seeking to express that concept or urge through you. Relax, let go, adopt the mood of receptivity, and let God's fullness flow through you. "There is a Divinity Which shapes our ends, rough hew them how we will."

Note carefully what Ruth in you says, "Whither thou goest, I will go; and where thou lodgest, I will lodge: thy people shall be my people, and thy God my God." For tender beauty, this statement is unsurpassed. Here is portrayed love, faith, and devotion to the end. "Where thou diest, I will die, and there will I be buried." Your faith in your ideal or goal must be maintained unto the end; then the old state dies and the new state (answered prayer) is resurrected. Ruth is really Life's urge seeking expression and progression through you. The journey is ever onward in consciousness. Ruth's urge in you is your love for God and all things spiritual. Fall in love with Wisdom, Truth, and Beauty, and wonders will take place in your life.

Boaz is the goal, the ideal you seek in life. You must have a goal in life, an aim, a purpose. You must be going somewhere, otherwise you simply drift aimlessly. Listen to Ruth, the inner promptings and murmurings of your heart strings. If you do not know what your true place in life is, pray for guidance, and you will get a lead such as a strong, persistent feeling or tendency in a certain direction. An idea may suddenly come to your mind like toast pops out of a toaster. The desire that lingers week in and week out is the true desire of your heart.

A boy of sixteen who recently prayed for guidance, for true expression in life, found himself joining religious groups, studying religious books, being interested in the Bible, etc. He plans to go to divinity school, and is very happy about it. Later on he will teach the laws of life and the way of the Spirit to all men. He prayed for guidance, so the deeper mind responded accordingly. If a certain premise is enthroned in the mind, the response must be the correlate of the premise. The premise and conclusion are one; the beginning and the end are the same; the seed and the plant are one. He had invoked the spirit of guidance, and having once invoked it and believed in it, he came under the spell of right action.

I talked to a man who was offered a position overseas. He could not accept because of his intense fear of water and airplanes. He became panic-stricken at the thought of getting on a boat. Undoubtedly there was a subconscious pattern behind this, a terrifying childhood experience, perhaps at the hands of some bully in the neighborhood pool. He had prayed for true expression, his prayer had been answered, but he said he could not accept.

There is a way to overcome such fear. Ruth is the predominant part of the soul in man telling him there is always a way out, a solution. The mere fact that he came to see me regarding help for his problem showed that he knew instinctively there was a way to overcome this fear. He was recognizing a Higher Power than his intellect.

He began to use his imagination constructively. He imagined and felt himself swimming in a pool, he felt the chill of the water, he made it vivid, real, and dramatic. He heard friends congratulate him on his progress. He became thoroughly immersed in the water mentally; it was a victorious, loving, interested movement of the mind.

He entered the water mentally until he was compelled to enter it physically. With the help of an instructor, he learned to swim and mastered the water. This was the working of the Spiritual Power Which he invoked. The Spiritual Power responded according to the nature of his invocation or prayer, and compelled him to respond; such is the law.

What we do on the inside, we experience on the outside. The Bible says, "Acquaint now thyself with Him, and be at peace, therefore good shall come to thee." Acquaint yourself with the mental and emotional operations of your own mind. Apply the principle of mind, realize your desire, and peace shall come unto thee.

Boaz means the Power and Wisdom of God. Boaz is that which blesses, heals, and makes you happy; Ruth (inner guidance) will lead you to it. It might be an invention you wish accepted, a desire to achieve in some field such as that of a singer, composer, great artist, or musician. Boaz is that which you wish to unite with in consciousness. You must marry Boaz. How do you marry or become one with your ideal (Boaz)? *"Wash thyself therefore, and anoint thee, and put thy raiment upon thee."* Ruth 3:3.

Your good is your God. *Wash thyself* means to cleanse your mind by refusing to give power to anything but your own consciousness, and the reigning power of your thought. Refuse positively and definitely to let your mind dwell on any negative state. To lift up your ideal, is the meaning of *anoint thyself*. Look to your ideal, let the light shine on it, honor it, count it worthy, praise it, exalt it, tell yourself how wonderful your ideal is, and mentally accept it. Let your ideal captivate and enthrall you (wearing the garment). You will find a deific response within you. The Power or Principle within responds to your dominant thought and mood. It is called in modern science the law of action and reaction. You must fulfill certain conditions. There is something you must do before there is a divine response. Isaiah says, "Ask me of things to come concerning my sons, and concerning the works of my hand, command ye me."

God works through you; *i.e.*, through your own thought and belief. In order for you to advance and grow spiritually, you must begin; then God begins. God will do nothing for you except through you. God works, of course, on a cosmic, universal scale in the control of all your vital functions and other body processes; beyond that you must initiate further growth and spiritual unfoldment. You must individualize and personalize the spirit in you.

The greatest study of man is man. This seems to be forgotten in our world today where we are feverishly engaged in building new hydrogen bombs. We must go back to God from whence we came. *"So Boaz took Ruth, and she was his wife; and when he went in unto her, the Lord gave her conception, and she bare a son."* Ruth 4:13. That son was to be the father of Jesse and the grandfather of David. When you come to God, to Truth, and to the Eternal Source, realizing the Source is Love, there is no fear, only peace.

Begin now to meditate, to eat of the nourishing Truths of God Which have stood the test of time. Feast on God's Love, Peace, Joy, Bliss, Beauty, and Perfection. Your mind will be nourished. Your soul will be fortified. God and His Peace will move on the waters of your mind. You will then be Ruth marrying Boaz, and you will give birth to a mental and spiritual child. He will be the father of the line of Jesse and David, meaning that you will experience the joy of the answered prayer—peace, health, and happiness.

Jesse means I AM or God, and *David* means Love. Your sense of union with God will be the progenitor or father of all things good in your world. Jesse (I AM), the awareness of the Presence of God, is born in your mind, and David, which is God's Love, rules your heart. You will have found your savior, your companion, your guide, your loving friend who will remain with you always. You will have arrived at the state of consciousness called Ruth when your human love is raised to Divine Love by detaching yourself from the false beliefs of the world, and by giving all your devotion and attention to the real spiritual values of life. In other words, you will be functioning as Ruth and Boaz by following always where Divine Love leads, and remaining steadfast in your belief and loyalty to the One Power.

Love in the highest and best degree, and acknowledge the God of Love as Lord of your life. Such loyalty and devotion is always rewarded, and you will find yourself a ruler of your world full of joy, happiness, and peace. You will go from glory to glory, ever onward, upward, and Godward.

ABOUT THE AUTHOR

Dr. Joseph Murphy was a major figure in the human potential movement—a spiritual heir to writers like James Allen, Dale Carnegie, Napoleon Hill, and Norman Vincent Peale. He was a precursor of and inspiration to contemporary motivational writers and speakers like Tony Robbins, Zig Ziglar, and Earl Nightingale. He was one of the bestselling authors of the mid-twentieth century, and his book *The Power of the Subconscious Mind* has sold millions of copies and has been translated into seventeen languages.

Continue the journey and harness the power
of your subconscious mind with more from

JOSEPH MURPHY.

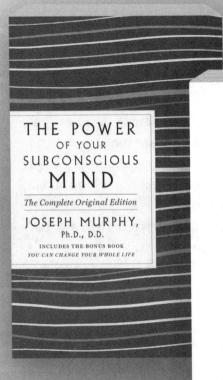

THE POWER
OF YOUR
SUBCONSCIOUS
MIND

The Complete Original Edition

JOSEPH MURPHY,
Ph.D., D.D.

INCLUDES THE BONUS BOOK
YOU CAN CHANGE YOUR WHOLE LIFE

The
Prosperous
Power of Your
Subconcious
Mind

JOSEPH MURPHY

**COMING IN
SPRING 2025**

Explore the full GPS Guides to Life series at
us.macmillan.com/series/gpsguidestolife.

ST. MARTIN'S
ESSENTIALS